THE REALITY OF OTHERS

THE REALITY OF OTHERS

Is Hell Other People?

GARY COX

ROWMAN & LITTLEFIELD
Lanham • Boulder • New York • London

Published by Rowman & Littlefield

An imprint of The Rowman & Littlefield Publishing Group, Inc.

4501 Forbes Boulevard, Suite 200, Lanham, Maryland 20706

www.rowman.com

86-90 Paul Street, London EC2A 4NE

Copyright © 2024 by The Rowman & Littlefield Publishing Group, Inc.

British Library Cataloguing in Publication Information Available

Library of Congress Cataloging-in-Publication Data on File

ISBN 978-1-5381-9348-8 (cloth)
ISBN 978-1-5381-9349-5 (pbk.)
ISBN 978-1-5381-9350-1 (electronic)

Contents

Preface

The French existentialist philosopher, novelist, playwright, biographer, journalist and all-round literary genius Jean-Paul Sartre once wrote, 'There's no need for red-hot pokers. Hell is . . . other people!'.

Of all the thousands of fascinating things that Sartre wrote and said, 'Hell is other people!' has become by far the most famous. People quote it hourly on X alongside #Sartre, #Existentialism and #NoExit, as though it were an unquestionable truth set in stone for all time. T-shirts, mugs, stationary, badges, and bumper stickers emblazon the motto, making 'Hell is other people!' merchandise-heaven for the manufacturers of such tack. It is a handy, soothing, philosophical *bon mot* to utter when other people irritate, misunderstand, insult, or otherwise upset us, or when we embarrass or mortify ourselves before them, which for most of us, sadly, is quite often.

But what does 'Hell is other people!' really mean on a deeper level? Sartre was a deep thinker so he must have had more in mind than simply dramatically and hyperbolically summing up the seemingly obvious truth that other people are quite often, in a wide variety of ways, a pain in one's ass. Who, indeed, was Jean-Paul Sartre? What, exactly, is the philosophy of life and death known as existentialism that Sartre and his associates so relentlessly advocated? What circumstances, ideas, and influences led Sartre to make the bold and pessimistic claim that 'Hell is other people!'? Where did he say it? In what broader context did he say it? Did he even really mean it? To what extent is it true?

You've only got to look at the world, at 'Man's inhumanity to man' (Robert Burns, *Man was made to Mourn*), to see that 'Hell is other people!' has a certain ring of truth to it. But, is 'Hell is other people!' entirely true? For all the evil and corruption in the world, it is surely a sweeping statement, a massive even grotesque generalisation. As good philosophers we should always be wary of sweeping statements that do not distinguish between 'always' and 'sometimes', between 'all' and 'some'. Is 'Hell is other people!' a statement that at the very least needs qualifying and moderating? It is certainly a statement that is well worth examining more closely, a statement well worth questioning, for a lot can be learnt from doing so.

The investigation, the interrogation, the grilling of this infamous statement is an interesting and highly rewarding exercise. It takes us on a fascinating philosophical journey. So, if you can abide my company, Sartre's company, and the company of various other people besides, real and imagined, climb aboard this existential, sexistential express. In due course it will roll us on to a consideration of how the excess and damaging heat that undoubtedly often characterises human relations might be realistically and practically reduced by you or anyone else. Like all the finest philosophies, existentialism is not just about understanding the world, ourselves, and others; it is about changing the world for the better, for the good of everyone.

CHAPTER I

No Need for Red-Hot Pokers

THE ROAD TO 'HELL IS OTHER PEOPLE!'
To begin with, to pick up whatever valuable clues may lie along the way,
let us trace Sartre's fascinating life journey from his birth to his writing
of the immortal line 'Hell is other people!'.

Jean-Paul Charles Aymard Sartre was very much alive, mostly in
his beloved Paris, from 21 June 1905 to 15 April 1980. He, therefore,
survived both world wars that this planet has so far hosted. Here, surely,
must lie some of the motivation for his declaring that 'Hell is other
people!'.

The Great War began the month after Sartre's ninth birthday, and
although Paris was shelled by long-range German guns and bombed
by Zeppelins, he does not appear to have been impacted by this war in
any major way. It did little to disturb the comfortable, Parisian cocoon
of familial love in which he dwelt, a spoilt, precocious, only child — pet
name 'Poulou' — cosseted by his mother Anne-Marie and his grandfather Charles. Sartre's father Jean-Baptiste had died when Sartre was less
than fifteen months old, sparing Sartre, as he later noted, from at least
one familiar form of oppression.

It was not the Great War that shattered the cocoon in which Sartre's
being-for-others was an almost exclusively positive affair characterised by
adoration. As he says in his autobiography, *Words*, 'I respected grown-ups
provided they idolized me' (*Words*, p. 23). It was not even starting formal
education in 1915 at the age of ten by becoming a pupil of the nearby

Lycée Henri IV. It was Anne-Marie's marriage to Joseph Mancy in 1917 that destroyed forever her son's Shangri-La. The marriage meant competition for his beloved mother's affections, subordination to a sensible man with little patience for the boy's antics, a move to La Rochelle, a port on the Bay of Biscay troubled by the shadows of war, and worst of all, a daunting new school.

Young Sartre's suffering was not that of the young David Copperfield. Mancy was no tyrannical Mr Murdstone and the school in La Rochelle — despite 'Rochelle' containing the word 'hell' — was no Salem House. For David Copperfield, of course, things became far worse than Salem House before they improved, positively Dickensian indeed. Sartre never descended to bottle washing for twelve hours a day for a pittance of coin in a damp, rat-infested, riverside warehouse. But like David Copperfield, like so many children, Sartre was suddenly and unceremoniously cast out of an all too soft maternal love nest that had done nothing to instil in him an attitude of realism. He was forced to grow up fast.

Sartre was bullied, perhaps no more than many a child who survives the company of other children, but he was certainly bullied. Does anyone, including the bully, entirely escape being bullied? Sartre's know-all ways and miniaturised Parisian pretentiousness made him an obvious target for provincial boys full of anger that the Great War had claimed their fathers. To be harsh, the bullying did him some good, providing a long overdue cure for his preening narcissism.

Sartre learnt that he was not the centre of the world, that nobody is, that the world is full of conflict because it contains the dreaded *Other*, a creature often not inclined to be kind or even cooperative, an alien consciousness that repeatedly judges and belittles our grand self-image and thwarts our aspirations, an ever-present and threatening obstacle that must be constantly and carefully negotiated.

In the autumn of 1920 Sartre's exile finally ended when he was allowed to return to his spiritual home of Paris to take up his rightful place among France's young intellectual elite as a boarder at his former school. He returned more self-reliant and less self-obsessed, equipped with early insights into a troubled wider world. Though hardly an outsider, he had experienced a little of what it is to be an outsider. He understood the meaning of injustice, that it is always meted out by others.

Far from finding other people to be hell back in Paris, however, Sartre took to the lively, cheerful social scene of school then college like a gregarious debutante to a coming out ball. He renewed old friendships and established new ones, especially with those who shared his particularly intellectual bent. Among his peers he became something of a legend in his own lunchtime, a witty mainstay of am-dram and satirical reviews.

He read widely, devouring every avant-garde book he could, among them the works of Marcel Proust and Henri Bergson. He had long been a lover of literature and had written novels since his childhood. Bergson added a love of philosophy to Sartre's literary passions, and Sartre decided there and then to excel at both. He went on to write philosophical works that at times read like literary fiction, and plays, stories, and novels that are genuinely philosophical.

Alongside his paper-and-ink passions Sartre pursued flesh-and-blood passions too. By the late 1920s, despite his relative physical ugliness and his famous, much caricatured squint resulting from an eye infection at the age of four, he had already had several affairs with women. The first was a childhood, largely summer vacation romance with his first cousin, Annie Lannes. Sartre's double in looks, brains, and confidence, Annie died of tuberculosis in 1925 aged nineteen. At Annie's funeral Sartre began another affair with a distant in-law, Simone Jollivet. Tall, blonde, blue eyed, stylish, an immodest Toulouse socialite who became an actress, Jollivet flirted with Sartre and little else for several years.

Now a student of the prestigious École Normale Supérieure (ENS), Sartre was proud to have Jollivet as his daringly dressed date at the college dance. Generally, however, judging by his extensive correspondence at that time, the relationship gave him more grief than joy. Indeed, it was a minor hell of frustration for not delivering the heavenly intimacy he craved. As Dante notes in *The Divine Comedy*, hell is a complex inferno with many circles, lust not the worst of them.

In 1929, Sartre met Simone de Beauvoir, Castor (the Beaver), his great lover, companion, confidante, defender, carer, travelling partner, mentor, editor, and unrivalled intellectual sparring partner. Their first proper meeting was at Sartre's grubby, book-strewn and cigarette-soiled digs after a mutual friend invited her along to help them revise the German rationalist philosopher Leibniz, most famous for arguing that far from being hell this is 'the best of all possible worlds' (*Theodicy*, Part 2, 168, p. 99). Sartre and de Beauvoir's relationship had its highs and lows over the years, but it endured until death parted them. It was as near to a match made in heaven, as near to being the best of all possible relationships, as any relationship in history.

They took their finals together, coming first and second out of seventy-six candidates. Exams over, they relaxed for a while, roving around Paris revelling in each other's company, often engrossed in conversation. Their heady student days over, however, adult responsibilities loomed. Sartre faced a period of compulsory military service, after which they both faced taking up miserable teaching posts in the French provinces. De Beauvoir remained in Paris while the army trained Sartre to use meteorological equipment. He grumbled about wasting eighteen months on the stupidity of army life but coped well with the discipline and routine. His only serious complaint was of boredom, which he overcame by writing.

On 1 March 1931, Sartre became a schoolteacher in Le Havre on the northwest coast of France, covering for a colleague who had suffered the all too familiar teacher's nervous breakdown. Hell is a classroom heaving with naughty children, at least for the teacher. For most of the children it is riotous fun. The golden boy of the ENS, who in his youth had expected to be a great writer long before the age of twenty-five, found himself once again in provincial exile.

Fortunately, he enjoyed teaching and was good at it, his friendly, laid-back manner making him more popular with his students than with his superiors. The long summer holidays soon rolled around, which he spent touring Spain with de Beauvoir. In October she took up her own teaching post in Marseilles, which she writes about in *The Prime of Life*, volume two of her superb autobiography. They were now in opposite corners of a huge country.

As they would often be apart, they came to a very avant-garde relationship arrangement. They would see each other as often as possible and their attachment would constitute 'necessary love'. but they would also indulge in 'contingent love': affairs with other people. Anything other than polyamory would disrespect their highly valued personal freedom. They eventually made personal freedom (and responsibility) the cornerstone of their existentialist philosophy. Even though Sartre always loved to see himself as a scholarly Don Juan with a silver tongue, he later confessed that his insistence on his right to have affairs with a variety of women was somewhat ludicrous as women were not exactly swooning over him at the time.

Le Havre was an atmospheric place with its wide expanses, sea breezes, and sharp coastal light. In Sartre's imagination, it became Bouville, the setting for his brilliant, brooding, nihilistic first novel *Nausea*, which he worked on for years alongside his teaching commitments. At the core of the novel is *the nausea*, the anxious, terrifying, loathsome realisation that reality is inexorable and overwhelming, yet elusive, unnecessary, and superfluous.

Sartre got the idea of the nausea, at least partly, from a heavy, hallucinogenic mescaline trip he took in 1935 that left him thinking he was being pursued through the streets of Le Havre by a giant lobster that never quite appeared. Sartre had a crustacean phobia. The feeling and revelation of the nausea is suffered by the novel's main character, Antoine Roquentin, a misanthropic loner who wonders around Bouville thinking far too deeply about reality and repeatedly freaking out about the naked, pointless existence of trees, trams, himself and, of course, other people.

Roquentin mostly despises other people, holding the middle-class townsfolk of Bouville in especial contempt for their shallowness and desperate desire to be acknowledged and approved of by one another. He hates their deluded faith in themselves as necessary beings with God- and society-given rights. They do not see they are mere cosmic accidents, and flee any such apprehension through busyness, promenading, chit-chat, lack of imagination. and idiotic hat-raising rituals. As deluded as the townsfolk are in thinking that their existence has a purpose, they are apparently a lot happier than Roquentin — not that happiness is allowed to count for much in the existentialist worldview.

Roquentin avoids friendships like the plague but is nevertheless befriended during his frequent visits to the library by a man he dubs the Autodidact. 'I for my part live alone, entirely alone. I never speak to anybody, I receive nothing, I give nothing. The Autodidact doesn't count' (*Nausea*, p. 16). The Autodidact is a socialist and a humanist, an unattractive, lonely, unloved man who ecstatically proclaims his love for everyone while respectfully labelling Roquentin a misanthrope. His vacuous, universal love for people is a desperate attempt to establish a connection with them, a wretched compensation for the fact that nobody, including Roquentin, cares about him.

Roquentin finds the Autodidact physically and intellectually abhorrent and flees a meal with him in disgust, overwhelmed by an attack of the nausea. 'I glance round the room and a feeling of violent disgust comes over me. What am I doing here? Why did I get mixed up in a discussion about humanism?' (*Nausea*, p. 175). This attack is primarily a response to the Autodidact's celebration of his humanism, which is both ridiculous and creepy:

> One of the first times they locked us in that shed [two hundred prisoners of war] the crush was so great that at first I thought I was going to suffocate, then suddenly a tremendous feeling of joy came over me, and I almost fainted: at that moment I felt I loved those men like brothers, I would have liked to kiss them all. (*Nausea*, p. 165)

The Autodidact is eventually exposed as a paedophile when he is caught stroking a boy's hand in the library. It emerges that he has fondled little boys in the library before but hitherto has not been confronted with his wrongdoing. He was vaguely aware of his habit, was even dimly resigned to the fact that it would one day land him in trouble, but he only becomes *ashamed* of it, is forced to become ashamed of it, when it becomes an undeniable and defining feature of his being-for-others. He does not feel *guilty* about it even when he is caught. From his own deluded point of view, his sad habit of groping little boys is not sordid paedophilia but rather refined aesthetic appreciation or subtle humanism.

The Corsican, an ill-tempered library attendant whose job is to keep order, ejects the Autodidact from the library after punching him in the nose. Roquentin, who has watched the whole scene with fascinated horror, takes rare pity on the Autodidact and pursues him outside after challenging the Corsican for his unnecessary violence. Roquentin awkwardly offers to take the Autodidact to a chemist, but he begs to be left alone and walks away.

Exposed and shamed, the Autodidact's alienation from other people is complete. His dreams of socialism and humanism and completing his education from A to Z are destroyed:

> He must be walking about at random, filled with shame and horror, that poor humanist, whom men don't want any more . . . He was guilty in so small a degree: his humble, contemplative love for little boys is scarcely sensuality — rather a form of humanism. But it was inevitable that one day he should find himself alone again. (*Nausea*, p. 228)

The Autodidact is a ruined man who will be haunted for the rest of his life by this shameful event. 'He walks, he doesn't want to go home: the Corsican is still waiting for him in his room and the woman and the two boys: "Don't try and deny it, I saw you". And the scene would begin again' (*Nausea*, p. 242).

Other people are hellish at times because shame is painful and dreadful. Shame is what Ziyad Marar, in his excellent book *Judged: The Value of Being Misunderstood*, repeatedly refers to as a 'social pain'.

> And in some ways this pain is even worse than physical pain. Contrary to the dismissive shrug expressed in the line 'sticks and stones may break my bones, but words will never hurt me', how often, when asked to remember the most painful experiences in their lives, do people turn first to memories of physical pain? (*Judged*, p. 24)

William Shakespeare's Coriolanus, a courageous soldier who totally disregards his war wounds and the hurt they cause him, nonetheless finds it deeply painful to deal with other people, especially if he has to humble himself before them in order to be diplomatic. He would rather be butchered in battle than be subjected to the expressed opinions and judgements of others. 'When blows have made me stay I fled from words' (*Coriolanus*, Act 2, Scene 2).

It is other people who cause us to feel the social pain of shame when they look at us in certain contexts, when they judge us negatively and attach derogatory labels to us that it is difficult or impossible for us to shake off. We cannot ultimately dictate what labels are attached to us by other people, though we spend a great deal of time and effort trying to do so. As Marar notes, echoing the social psychologist Nick Elmer, 'reputation management is one of the primary goals of communication' (*Judged*, p. 68).

We want to be free to define ourselves, to evade all simple categorisation, to control our destiny as far as the opinion of others is concerned, but others easily clip our wings by pigeonholing us as foolish, mean, arrogant, despicable, depraved, perverted, and so on. Much more of this as we go forward.

In 1933, Sartre took a sabbatical from his teaching job in Le Havre to study the philosophy of Edmund Husserl in Berlin. He was so cocooned in the bookish student life that he scarcely noticed the rise of the Nazis. He returned to Le Havre after a few months and remained there until 1936 when he took another teaching post closer to Paris.

This was a difficult time for Sartre. The mescaline trip of 1935 and the elusive giant lobster it spawned had not helped his mental health. *Nausea* — working title *Melancholia* — was still not finished and he and de Beauvoir began to worry that they were never going to amount to anything, that their youth had gone and life was passing them by.

As a desperate remedy for their malaise, they both fell in love with Olga Kosakiewicz, one of de Beauvoir's students, the beautiful, haughty, impetuous daughter of a Russian nobleman. Olga became their shared obsession. They pursued, charmed, and discussed her, quarrelled over her, and tried to sort out her chaotic life as though she was their daughter.

As Sartre's passion for Olga intensified, he became increasingly possessive of her. Besotted, he was happy only when he had her undivided attention and tried every trick of his charm and intelligence in a vain effort to keep the fickle, erratic, flirtatious girl, more than a decade younger than himself, focused solely on him. From 1935 to 1937, as he struggled relentlessly to win her, her refusal to reject or accept him drove him repeatedly from the heights of rapture to the depths of despair, from Olga heaven to Olga hell.

Sartre claimed later that the only time he ever experienced jealousy was during his infatuation with Olga. His frustrated relationship with her was a life-defining episode which haunted his writings for many years. He often explored the theme of our frustrated efforts to determine the affections and desires of others, to take possession of their freedom yet have them still free. As Sartre and others recognise, love is not love that is not freely given, an idea we shall explore further in due course.

In April 1937, the major Parisian publisher Gallimard finally accepted *Nausea*, and the novel was published the following year. It was soon a significant commercial and critical success. Alongside it, Gallimard began publishing short stories by Sartre in their magazine *La Nouvelle Revue Française*. The stories were collected into a book in 1939 under the title *The Wall*. Sartre's early philosophical works also saw publication around this time. As a consequence of his success, Sartre was given a teaching job in Paris and the lurking lobster went away. Even his frustrated passion for Olga had cooled, thanks partly to a more gratifying affair with her similarly capricious and engaging sister, Wanda.

Sartre was reinvigorated with self-belief and positivity. He began attracting the very welcome attentions of numerous young women who seemed to find his newfound celebrity improved his looks. Some of them positively threw themselves at him. His work received critical acclaim, not least from an as yet unknown Albert Camus, a French-Algerian philosopher and novelist who became one of the most famous of the French existentialists. Camus won the 1957 Nobel Prize for Literature seven years before Sartre won it himself. So, Sartre was finally on the road to the fame and glory he had always modestly imagined for himself. No path in life is ever entirely straightforward of course, and Sartre's journey soon took him down into the shadows of war.

On 1 September 1939, Hitler invaded Poland. Every French reservist was immediately mobilised. The following chill morning saw Sartre and de Beauvoir at the Gare de L'Est as he and his kitbag awaited a train that would take him close to the German border. On 3 September 1939, France and Britain declared war on Germany.

With the French and Germans at a standoff, Sartre spent the next few months in the eye of a storm, at the centre of a phoney war, launching weather balloons from various small towns around Strasbourg to establish wind speed. Away from the charms and distractions of Paris with only light military duties to attend to, living as he had long done in a series of seedy hotel rooms, Sartre found himself on the ideal writer's retreat. It is estimated that he wrote a million words during the Phoney War. Copious letters to his mother and his lovers, an extensive war diary, what would become his second published novel *The Age of Reason*, and the beginnings of his vast philosophical magnum opus *Being and Nothingness*.

The Age of Reason somewhat reflects Sartre's life at the time. A story about a bohemian, Parisian, Philosophy professor, Mathieu Delarue, who is called to fight in World War II. Weary of his unrequited obsession with the young, capricious Ivich Serguine (a character based on Olga Kosakiewicz) and tired of his passive mistress Marcelle Duffet, Mathieu, in true existentialist style, welcomes the opportunity to do something heroic, to assert his freedom through decisive action that affirms the stark reality of his situation. Before taking on valiant military responsibilities, however, Mathieu must evade other more mundane, bourgeois responsibilities by obtaining funds for Marcelle to have an abortion.

The novel contains many existentialist themes that Sartre was also developing in other works, particularly *Being and Nothingness*. Not least, the idea that the opinion and judgement of others *enslaves* our freedom and reduces us to a mere object in their world by undermining our highly valued sense of our own predominance, mastery, self-creation, self-actualisation, ascendency, and transcendence. Most of the central characters in the novel suffer this unpleasant, relatively hellish sense of enslavement to the opinion and judgement of others to a lesser or greater extent.

Mathieu, for example, feels enslaved by Marcelle when he leaves her house after she has told him she is pregnant and he has shown no enthusiasm for keeping their child. Though physically alone, Mathieu is haunted by Marcelle and her negative, reproachful estimation of him.

He cannot find *genuine* solitude and the peace of mind that goes with it, because he cannot free himself of the uncomfortable, all-consuming social pain of knowing that Marcelle disapproves of him. A guilty, ashamed, embarrassed, or mortified person is never alone:

> He stopped, transfixed: it wasn't true, he wasn't alone. Marcelle had not let him go: she was thinking of him, and this is what she thought: "The dirty dog, he's let me down." It was no use striding along the dark, deserted street, anonymous, enveloped in his garments — he could not escape her. (*The Age of Reason*, p. 19)

The Phoney War ended on 10 May 1940 with the invasion of the Low Countries. Paris fell on 14 June, and a week later, on Satre's thirty-fifth birthday, with the French Army in disarray, he was swept up by the German advance. He was locked in a police barracks for several days, where he witnessed the undignified behaviour of grown men fighting over scraps of bread, an incident echoed in his 1949 novel *Iron in the Soul*.

His captivity then became a form of camping. He lived in a tent subjected to cold nights and meagre, disgusting rations. His biggest grumble, however, was the uncouth behaviour of his fellow prisoners. He was not particularly fond of his unsophisticated comrades, ordinary Frenchmen whose main occupation in life seemed to be to sweat, belch, and fart, and he wrote in his diary that his situation had cured him of socialism.

Sartre became a champion of socialism, but like most educated socialists, he preferred the more refined company of bourgeois intellectuals to that of the common man. To escape the common man, he allowed himself to become absorbed in the eternal and elevating truths of philosophy, churning out seventy-six pages of *Being and Nothingness* in just a few weeks before being moved to a prisoner of war camp inside Germany.

Kicked in the backside by a guard for breaching the night curfew, he valued his solidarity with the other French prisoners. He succeeded in becoming one of the camp artists responsible for maintaining prisoner morale. The artists had their own hut with musical instruments and were even paid a small wage for their entertainment services. He made more intellectual, less uncouth friends than at any time since his mobilisation, helped put on plays as he had done at college, and even taught the philosophy of Martin Heidegger. It was a good setup, considering, and no doubt he rather enjoyed himself.

Escape was on his mind, however, and in March 1941 he was either released on medical grounds with the help of a forged medical certificate that said his eyesight made him unfit for military service, or he walked out of the camp disguised as a German farmer. Either way, his captivity ended, and he was reunited with de Beauvoir in a Paris café at the end of March 1941.

He returned to his old teaching job, dispensing with his former friendly and laid-back manner in favour of standoffishness. Formal and efficient in a smart suit, he dictated dry summaries and told his students nothing of his war adventures. It was all about keeping a low profile, rather than foolishly attracting the attentions of a dangerous occupying authority by playing the unconventional, opinionated teacher.

He founded his own resistance movement, 'Socialism and Freedom'. It took some genuine risks producing and disseminating subversive literature, but there was no real place for it between the far larger Gaullists on the right and the Communists on the left and, in the autumn of 1941, it was dissolved.

Resistance generally gathered pace as the United States entered the war and German defeat seemed possible. Relations between Germans and Parisians deteriorated as assassinations were met with reprisals and the harsh conditions of occupation — militarisation of public spaces, loss of tourist revenue, rationing, and deportations — bit ever deeper.

When he was not teaching, Sartre wrote in the Café de Flore on the Boulevard Saint-Germain, not least to keep warm. Customers enjoyed the benefit of their pooled coal rations. Sartre wrote and smoked in one corner while Picasso sipped fake coffee in another. As the hazardous yet dreary occupation dragged on and Paris gradually starved, the only solace was philosophy, literature, art, and sex, interspersed with news of the all too slow demise of the Third Reich.

The Age of Reason was complete, but with its references to abortion, homosexuality, and personal freedom it was far too scandalous to be published until after the war (it was published in September 1945). By the spring of 1943, *Being and Nothingness* was approaching completion, and rehearsals began for Sartre's play, *The Flies*. June 1943 saw both the opening of the play and the publication of the 650-page philosophical magnum opus. I will return to *Being and Nothingness* later. It has so much to say that is relevant to the main aims of this book that it is best explored independently of this largely biographical account and build-up.

The Flies is based on the Greek legend of Orestes. Fly-infested Argos, where the play is set, represents occupied Paris. Orestes returns to Argos having been sent away as a child when Aegisthus murdered his father King Agamemnon and married his mother Clytemnestra. The flies infesting the town epitomise the corruption of the people of Argos and the remorse they suffer for failing to defend Agamemnon or avenge his murder. Against the will of Zeus, Orestes avenges the murder of his father by killing his mother and stepfather. Orestes refuses to feel remorse for his deed and takes full responsibility for it. Rather than take the throne as the rightful king, Orestes leaves Argos taking the flies with him.

The Flies explores key existentialist themes that are examined more formally in *Being and Nothingness*. For example, *The Flies* considers freedom and responsibility through the radical conversion of Orestes from peace-loving intellectual to warrior. Orestes resists the bad faith of choosing not to choose and achieves authenticity by bravely rising to the demands of his grim circumstances. He fully realises his *being-in-situation* by taking full responsibility for his circumstances without regret or complaint.

Orestes is free to choose not to choose in the situation in which he finds himself, to flee Argos and its troubles, but instead he chooses to act positively, to avenge his father's death and to live with the consequences of killing his mother. Unlike his unfortunate sister Electra, who falls into the bad faith of regretting her past deeds and praying for absolution, Orestes triumphs over God and guilt to become a true existentialist hero.

Sartre and de Beauvoir spent the late summer of 1943 near Angers, at the comfortable home of their eccentric friend Madame Morel, where they always enjoyed much needed rest and recuperation and a healthier diet than in occupied Paris. While there, they heard that Italy had surrendered and that the Soviet Red Army was regaining swathes of lost territory. The Nazis would not surrender easily, but their eventual defeat now seemed inevitable.

Back in Paris, Sartre was once again bitten by the theatre bug and decided to write another play. There was good, quick cash in plays. It took him just two weeks of frantic effort to draft *Huis Clos*, probably his best play and certainly his best known and most iconic. The literal English translation of this title is *In Camera* or *Behind Closed Doors*, although the play is now often titled *No Exit*. It is also sometimes called *No Way Out*, *Vicious Circle* or *Dead End*. These days it might be called *Eternal Lockdown* perhaps, or *The Bad Place*. Hell is a play with too many alternative titles.

Sartre invited his new friend Albert Camus to direct the play and take the lead male role of Joseph Garcin. Camus accepted and rehearsals began, though he later withdrew. The job of director finally went to Raymond Rouleau and the role of Garcin to Michel Vitold.

In Camera premiered at the Théâtre du Vieux-Colombier on 27 May 1944. Unlike *The Flies*, *In Camera* is not an implicit commentary on the contemporary political situation, but in focusing on confinement and conflict generally it certainly considers themes that were highly relevant to Parisian audiences enduring Nazi occupation.

So, at last, we arrive at that point in Sartre's life, at that particular work, in which the immortal line is uttered: 'Hell is . . . other people!' (*In Camera*, p. 223). To be precise, it is not Sartre who asserts that 'Hell is other people!'. It is not Sartre who makes the radical claim. It is his lead male character Joseph Garcin. So perhaps 'Hell is other people!' is what Garcin thinks, rather than what Sartre thinks. Perhaps it is an assertion that applies in the peculiar, unworldly context of the play, rather than in *this* world, our *real* world, a world pitched somewhere between heaven and hell. Arguably, for reasons that will be revealed in the next section focusing entirely on *In Camera*, hell is other people *in the play* and *only in the play*.

It certainly seems to be the case, having chronicled Sartre's life to the point where he dashed off *In Camera*, that although he had good reason to think, like most of us, that other people are a torment at times, his *personal* experiences gave him little or no grounds for asserting that others are hell incarnate. As we have seen, Sartre was a people person. He greatly enjoyed the company of others, and others greatly enjoyed his. He had many good, interesting, loyal, and loving friends who, apart from writing perhaps, constituted the greatest pleasure and fulfilment of his life and continued to do so until the day he died.

The hell of other people is far more in Sartre's writing than in his own life. Writing that correctly recognises that some people's lives are made hell on Earth by the despicable actions of others. Sartre was, after all, a man who lived through the time of the Holocaust, a man who saw Jewish friends deported, a man who soon discovered, not as history but as *news*, the full horror of their fate, the full horror of Auschwitz-Birkenau and other concentration camps.

Sartre would have sympathised with the German philosopher Theodor W. Adorno, who later wrote, 'To write poetry after Auschwitz is barbaric' ('Cultural Criticism and Society', *Prisms*, p. 34) — certainly poetry that is at all cheerful or optimistic or expresses any faith in humankind.

Utterly horrific though Auschwitz was, however, is it unfair to reduce the whole of humankind entirely to the level of those responsible for its worst atrocity, to equate all of us, to the exclusion of all else that is human, with the perpetrators of the many holocausts and genocides there have been and will be? The capacity for these horrors is clearly in some of us, perhaps in all of us under extreme conditions, but is that capacity *all* we are in the sense that it *eclipses* all else we are? Hopefully, light will be shed on such difficult questions, even their answers, as we go forward.

Meanwhile, it is important to note, as Auschwitz survivor and poet Primo Levi does in his memoir *If This Is a Man*, that there were great acts of kindness and sacrifice in the hellhole of Auschwitz that shone all the brighter because of the darkness of their setting.

Sartre's drafts of *The Age of Reason* were typed by Simone de Beauvoir's sister, Hélène. He sent them to her in Paris at regular intervals from his various military postings in Northern France during the Phoney War of 1939–40. As he tells us in his *War Diaries: Notebooks from a Phoney War*, Hélène wrote to her sister commenting on her experience of being immersed in Sartre's work:

Typing Sartre's works always makes me gloomy. Talking to him is a tonic. Reading his works, then thinking about something else — that might still be all right. But living up to one's neck in them is dreadful. I hope that, within himself, he isn't like the people he portrays in his books, for his life would be scarcely endurable. (*War Diaries*, p. 338)

There is more wit, irony, and dark humour in Sartre's writing than he is often credited with — not least in *In Camera* — but the fact remains that he is not exactly a laugh a minute and nobody in their right mind reads him for the fun of it. Sartre does not undertake, as some writers do — Dickens, for example — to give his readers a warm glow during or after the experience of reading him, unless such a glow can be derived from the satisfaction of having learnt something, of having gained some profound insight into human existence.

Of course, in this respect Sartre is like many or most great authors. Nobody reads Kafka, Dostoevsky, or Conrad for the fun of it either, although in the end it depends on your idea of fun. I can only speak for myself, but I certainly find reading Sartre more enjoyable and certainly more rewarding than watching Australian soap operas or reality TV competitions. Living up to my neck in countless episodes of *Neighbours* or *Love Island* really would be hell. I am surely not alone in thinking that there is little in life more dreadful than that which is mindless and inane. Sartre, to give him his due, is always the very antithesis of mindless and inane.

Incidentally, *In Camera*, in being about the interminable confinement and minutely scrutinised interactions of nasty, self-centred, narcissists, is not unlike *Love Island*, *Big Brother* and *I'm a Celebrity . . . Get Me Out of Here!* The main difference is that *In Camera* features intelligent conversation.

Sartre is personally committed to considering weighty subject matter — insanity, anxiety, shame, guilt, hatred, war, death, and so on — in order to deliver hard, uncompromising lessons on the human condition, the human predicament. He pushes his readers out of any comfort zone they might be hiding in, forcing them to confront unpleasant truths, not least about themselves. The reader is obliged to recognise his own flaws in Sartre's all-too-human characters; he is obliged to ask himself, 'How would I cope in that terrible situation? What choices would I make?'

So, Sartre does not write simply to tell stories and to entertain. As he argues in his 1948 work *What Is Literature?*, the purpose of literature is not to entertain but to challenge and provoke. If a work, a passage, or a maxim does not shake a reader up and goad him into new attitudes and actions, then it is failing to do its job, it is simply not literature but some other lesser art form; a mere diversion. Whatever we conclude about 'Hell is other people!', for example, it is certainly a maxim designed to provoke endless debate and inspire entire books in response to it.

Sartre was intrigued rather than offended by Hélène's remarks and spent most of his diary entry for 14 March 1940 reflecting on them. Indeed, he continued to ponder the whole issue of so-called gloomy literature for many years, finally stating in *What Is Literature?*, that 'there is no gloomy literature' (*What Is Literature?*, p. 47). True literature is never gloomy, he argues, for it always aims to liberate people by making them aware of their freedom.

In his diary entry he identifies himself closely with his two most significant character creations, his alter-egos, Antoine Roquentin and Mathieu Delarue, acknowledging the undeniable fact that they are both, as we have seen, extremely gloomy. They are him, he insists, but he adds that he is never so gloomy and that life for him is not all that bad. He writes: 'In reality, they are *me, stripped of the living principle*' (*War Diaries*, p. 338).

What has been stripped from them, Sartre insists, or denied them in the first place in order that they may better serve Sartre's philosophical and literary purposes, is his own passion, pride, faith, and optimism. This is true not only of Roquentin and Mathieu, but also of other central characters, such as Garcin, that Sartre created later. 'I stripped my characters of my obsessive passion for writing, my pride, my faith in my destiny, my metaphysical optimism — and thereby provoked in them a gloomy pullulation. They are myself beheaded' (*War Diaries*, p. 339).

Sartre appears to consider 'the living principle', the hope, pride, passion, and faith that springs eternal in the hearts of men and women despite the stark, inescapable truths of the human condition, to be philosophically unjustifiable if not inexplicable — the reason why he refers to his optimism as 'metaphysical'. Nonetheless, he recognises that as a living man rather than a fictional character he, too, possesses an abundance of 'the living principle'. He is not his characters, and it is far easier to create a character that serves certain literary objectives by being consistently negative than it is to be so consistently negative oneself. 'The essential difference between Antoine Roquentin and me is that, for my part, I write the story of Antoine Roquentin' (*War Diaries*, p. 338).

Sartre seems to have found it far easier to create gloomy angst-ridden characters than positive, happy ones. Characters who are full of the joys of life are, it seems fair to say, totally lacking from his pantheon. Was he unable to create them, or would such characters fail to serve his serious literary and philosophical purposes? Considering his books, his characters and what he expects the overall effect of the *ensemble* of his works to be, he writes:

> My novels [etc] are experiments, and they're possible only through disintegration. It seems to me that the ensemble of my books will be optimistic, because through that ensemble the *whole* will be reconstituted. But each of my characters is a cripple. To tell the truth, Mathieu is to become a totality in my last volume — but he'll die immediately afterwards. That's the reason, I think, why I write gloomy books without myself being either sad or a charlatan, and believe in what I write. (*War Diaries*, p. 339)

And so to the gloom, misery and torment of *In Camera* itself.

IN HELL: ESTELLE, GARCIN, INEZ

Simple in structure — one act, one scene — and accessible intellectually, *In Camera* typifies the anxiety, absurdity and despondency associated with existentialism in popular culture. Existentialism is, in reality, a far more optimistic philosophy than it is usually given credit for, but in so far as it has a reputation for being thoroughly wretched, miserable, and bleak, that reputation is even more the doing of *In Camera* than it is the doing of *Nausea*, which has at least moments of beauty and respite.

The central theme of *In Camera* is *conflict*; the internecine conflict that in Sartre's view lies at the heart of all personal interactions between human consciousnesses. It is this damning conclusion, made the year before in *Being and Nothingness*, that Sartre sought to reinforce and further publicise in his forceful 1944 play.

In Camera begins with a valet showing Joseph Garcin into a Second Empire–style drawing room with three sofas. On the mantelpiece are large bronze ornaments and a paper knife. The room has no windows or mirrors. The room surprises Garcin; he had expected to find something different. He asks where the instruments of torture are, 'The racks and red-hot pincers and all the other paraphernalia' (*In Camera*, p. 182). The valet assumes Garcin is joking. There is no conventional torture paraphernalia, and no need for any.

It soon emerges that Garcin is dead and that the room is in hell. The valet says there is nothing beyond the room but passages and more rooms, that there is no outside. Garcin learns that sleep is impossible in the room. It is never dark there, and he cannot blink let alone shut his eyes. Without windows, mirrors, darkness, sleep, dreams, books, or anywhere to escape to, there is no respite, none of the distractions that made Garcin's life on earth bearable, distractions that made Garcin bearable to himself.

> No eyelids, no sleep; it follows, doesn't it? I shall never sleep again. But then — how shall I endure my own company?' . . . Down there I had my nights. I slept. I always had good nights. By way of compensation, I suppose. And happy little dreams. (*In Camera*, p. 184)

The valet exits, closing the only door behind him. Garcin explores the room before trying to ring a bell by the door that does not work. He tries the door without success. He beats it with his fists and calls the valet. Nothing happens. He gives up and sits down just as the valet enters with Inez Serrano.

Inez has no questions for the valet, who exits once again. Inez briefly inspects the room then asks abruptly where Florence is. Garcin doesn't know where or who Florence is. He introduces himself politely to an unfriendly Inez, who asks, 'Must you be here all the time, or do you take a stroll outside now and then?' (*In Camera*, p. 187). Garcin would like to be alone, too, to ponder his life and set it in order, but the door is locked, trapping them in each other's company.

As he sits in silence Garcin's mouth twitches with fear, which soon irritates Inez. Garcin asks, 'How about you? Aren't you afraid?' (*In Camera*, p. 187). Inez argues that as she has no hope she has no fear. They wait for something to happen, Garcin hiding his twitching mouth behind his hands.

The valet enters with Estelle Rigault, an attractive young woman who immediately mistakes Garcin for someone she knows whose face has been shot away. She realises her mistake when Garcin removes his hands. Revealing herself as vain and superficial, Estelle laughingly complains that the unoccupied sofa will clash with her blue dress. Garcin politely offers his sofa. Estelle introduces herself to Inez and Garcin, who vie for her attention. The valet exits for the last time. No one else is coming, ever.

Each tells how they died. Estelle died of pneumonia the day before. She can picture her funeral and her sister trying to cry. Inez died of gas inhalation last week. Garcin took twelve bullets in the chest a month ago. He can picture his wife waiting outside the barracks where he was shot, not knowing he is dead. He says she got on his nerves.

They consider their lives, how quickly time passes on earth now they are dead, all the while irritating each other. Though it is hot, Estelle forbids Garcin to remove his coat as she loathes men in shirtsleeves. Inez admits to not caring much for men at all. They wonder why they have been put together as they have nothing in common.

Estelle had expected to meet old friends and relatives. She wonders if she knew Inez in life but rejects this possibility snobbishly when Inez tells her she was only a postal clerk. Garcin puts their being together down to chance. Inez thinks there is method in it. They wonder if they have been put together deliberately, if anything is expected of them. They grow increasingly suspicious of the situation and of each other.

The question of why they are in hell inevitably arises. Estelle claims not to know, snobbishly accusing 'understrappers' (*In Camera*, p. 193) of making a mistake. Garcin is equally evasive. He claims he was a man of principle shot for being a pacifist. Inez tells them they are play-acting. People are not sent to hell by mistake. 'Yes, we are criminals — murderers — all three of us. We're in hell, my pets, they never make mistakes, and people aren't damned for nothing' (*In Camera*, p. 194). In confronting the other two, Inez realises why there is no torturer in *their* hell: they will torture each other. Attempting to avoid this, they agree to ignore each other, to work out their own salvation in silence, but the silence is brief.

Inez begins to sing about beheadings while Estelle tries to put on make-up without a mirror. It makes her feel strange. She feels nonexistent when she cannot see herself. Inez offers to be her mirror. The tiny reflection Estelle sees in Inez's eyes is not useful. Inez guides Estelle's hand as she applies her lipstick, telling her she looks lovely. Estelle is embarrassed by this intimacy and distrustful of Inez's words. How can she know, without a real mirror, that Inez is telling the truth? Inez realises she can torture Estelle by being a false mirror and lying to her about how she looks.

Estelle wants Garcin to notice her looks. A man, she thinks, will confirm her beauty with his desire. Inez is annoyed that Estelle is more interested in Garcin, who is trying to ignore her, than in Inez, who is attentive.

Garcin insists it is better if they try to forget each other's presence. Inez retorts that it is impossible to do so. 'To forget about the others? How utterly absurd! I *feel* you there, down to my marrow. Your silence clamours in my ears' (*In Camera*, p. 200). She says she would prefer to fight it out with them, so they return to the question of why they are in hell.

Garcin admits that he treated his wife badly. 'Night after night I came home blind drunk; stinking of wine and women' (*In Camera*, p. 202). He took a live-in lover and allowed his wife to serve them.

Inez broke up a relationship between her cousin and Florence by turning Florence against him. The women began an affair, giving him hell until he was run over by a tram. Inez cruelly teased Florence that they had killed him until one night Florence crept out of bed, turned on the gas and killed them both.

Inez's story echoes to some extent the story told in Simone de Beauvoir's 1943 novel *She Came to Stay*. Sartre and de Beauvoir were intrigued by the theme of the *ménage à trois* and had been since their own emotionally charged ménage à trois with Olga Kosakiewicz. Like Ivich Serguine in *The Age of Reason*, Inez has some of Olga's impish qualities.

Estelle is less forthcoming, but eventually her story is prised from her. She had an affair with Roger, a poor man of lower social class. A baby was born in Switzerland, in secret. Roger was delighted; Estelle was not. She drowned the baby in a lake and returned to her rich husband in Paris. Roger shot himself. Estelle tries to cry, but the distraction of tears is not possible in hell.

As each pictures life on earth moving rapidly on, as they are dismissed or forgotten by the living, they turn increasingly to each other for attention and confirmation. Inez wants Estelle to turn to her, while Estelle, who wants to exist only as an attractive object, turns to Garcin to be loved. She hopes to see herself as a lover sees her, as an object of value, even though in truth she is a worthless murderer.

Garcin is not interested in Estelle for her own sake. Neither is he sorry about his treatment of his wife. His main concern in hell is for his reputation. Did he refuse to fight because he was a pacifist or a coward? In constantly asking himself this question he is similar to Philippe, a character that appears in Sartre's novels *The Reprieve* (1945) and *Iron in the Soul*. Like Philippe, Garcin is plagued by the suspicion that he is a coward. He meant to die well at his execution but failed to do so. He pictures friends on earth dismissing him as a coward and is tortured by the fact that, being dead, he can no longer act to change their opinion:

> What else is there to do now? I was a man of action once . . . Oh, if only I could be with them again, for just one day — I'd fling their lie in their teeth. But I'm locked out; they're passing judgment on my life without troubling about me, and they're right, because I'm dead. Dead and done with. A back number. (*In Camera*, p. 216)

Sartre's wartime experiences meant that he and people he knew were regularly confronted with a choice between courage and cowardice. It is not surprising then that it is a recurrent theme in both his factual and fictional writing. He has characters who act in a cowardly way but evade acknowledging that cowardice is the meaning of their conduct. And he has characters who act courageously yet still fear deep down that they are a coward.

Sartre's philosophical conclusion is that because of the indeterminate, unfixed nature of the self there is no such *thing* as a coward or a hero. As he argues in his 1946 book *Existentialism and Humanism*, based on a famous lecture he gave the year before, nobody is born a coward or a hero with a cowardly or heroic temperament. There are only cowardly or heroic deeds:

> A coward is defined by the deed that he has done . . . the existentialist says that the coward makes himself cowardly, the hero makes himself heroic; and that there is always a possibility for the coward to give up cowardice and for the hero to stop being a hero. (*Existentialism and Humanism*, p. 43)

Garcin turns to Estelle for confirmation that he is not a coward, but she is so superficial he cannot take her opinion seriously. To her, a coward is only someone who looks cowardly. She does not care if Garcin is a coward or not; she just wants a man, any man, to love her and confirm her existence as a desirable object. Estelle is grateful for any attention she gets from Garcin, whatever his motive.

Garcin is so disgusted that Estelle would have him even as a coward, and moreover that she can do nothing to confirm that he is not a coward, that he says he would rather endure physical torture. 'Open the door! Open, blast you! I'll endure anything, your red-hot tongs and molten lead . . . Anything, anything would be better than this agony of mind' (*In Camera*, p. 219). The door flies open but Garcin will not exit, which surely raises the question of whether the eternal agony of being thought a coward and thinking oneself a coward is actually worse than the eternal agony of physical torture.

It is a stark choice, no doubt, but which would you choose if you had to? Perhaps choosing the physical torture would at least allow you to conclude that you are not a coward, but such peace of mind seems insignificant when set against the agony of, say, burning forever! Of course, such reasoning may well take *In Camera* too literally. Arguably, *In Camera* should be taken, above all, as an allegorical tale illustrating a philosophical theory as to why relations with others are often so difficult and unpleasant.

Estelle tries to push Inez out the door. Inez begs to stay; she fears going and responds in a cowardly manner. Estelle releases Inez in surprise when Garcin announces that he has decided to stay because of Inez. Inez is surprised, too. Garcin shuts the door. He has recognised that, unlike Estelle, Inez knows what it is to be cowardly. It is *her* he must convince that he is not a coward in order to be released from the hell of other people considering him a coward: 'She — she doesn't count. It's you who matter; you who hate me. If you'll have faith in me I'm saved' (*In Camera*, p. 220).

Garcin offers Inez arguments: He chose the hard path of pacifism. Had he lived longer he would have done brave deeds. He died too soon. Inez is not impressed. She tells him, 'One always dies too soon — or too late. And yet one's whole life is complete at that moment, with a line drawn neatly under it, ready for the summing up. You are — your life, and nothing else' (*In Camera*, p. 221).

This all fits with one of the central claims of existentialism that to be is to do, that we are nothing beyond the sum total of our actions. Just as there is no bravery apart from the deeds of bravery, so 'there is no love apart from the deeds of love . . . no genius other than that which is expressed in works of art' (*Existentialism and Humanism*, p. 41).

Inez is able to make Garcin a coward simply by thinking him one, by wishing it. Garcin is at her mercy, but she is also at his mercy because he can exclude her by giving Estelle his attention, attention that Estelle is very willing to receive, not least because it upsets Inez. In turning to Estelle to spite Inez, however, Garcin is plagued by the thought that Inez sees him as a coward. He turns back to Inez to convince her he is not a coward.

In realising that Inez will always see him and judge him and that he cannot control her opinion of him, Garcin understands he is in hell. He can never escape the searing, deprecating, belittling look of the Other.

GARCIN: Will night never come?

INEZ: Never.

GARCIN: You will always see me?

INEZ: Always.

GARCIN: This bronze. Yes, now's the moment; I'm looking at this thing on the mantelpiece, and I understand that I'm in hell. I tell you, everything's been thought out beforehand. They knew I'd stand at the fireplace stroking this thing of bronze, with all those eyes intent on me. Devouring me. What? Only two of you? I thought there were more; many more. So this is hell. I'd never have believed it. You remember all we were told about the torture-chambers, the fire and brimstone, the 'burning marl.' Old wives' tales! There's no need for red-hot pokers. Hell is . . . other people! (*In Camera*, pp. 222–23)

Garcin tells Estelle that he cannot love her while Inez is between them, watching. Estelle stabs Inez with the paper knife. Inez just laughs and stabs herself to show Estelle the futility of it. All three laugh at their eternal damnation to this intolerable situation before slumping dejectedly on their respective sofas. Before the final curtain comes down, Garcin says, 'For ever, and ever, and ever. [*A long silence.*] Well, well, let's get on with it . . .' (*In Camera*, p. 223).

It is worth considering at this point an alternative reading of the play offered by Jonathan Webber in his book *Rethinking Existentialism*. Webber argues that Inez is not like Garcin and Estelle:

She [Inez] does not face the predicament that Garcin and Estelle face. Their inability to establish their preferred image in the eyes of the other two threatens their view of themselves as being tough or feminine. Inez, by contrast, is in no doubt about her cruelty and neither is anybody else. (*Rethinking Existentialism*, p. 97)

As we shall discover in more detail in due course, Sartre does not think people have a fixed nature; they always have to *aim* at what they want to be, *play* at it, without ever being able to become it once and for all. Yet Inez appears to have a fixed nature. She is a cruel-*thing* and accepts herself as such. 'When I say I'm cruel, I mean I can't get on without making people suffer. Like a live coal. A live coal in others' hearts. When I'm alone I flicker out' (*In Camera*, pp. 203–4). Webber argues that Inez can be seen as 'metaphysically different from the other two characters, as genuinely having the fixed nature that she claims to have' (*Rethinking Existentialism*, p. 98).

This means that Inez cannot be human. Indeed, there is evidence in the play to suggest that she is a demon, there to torture Garcin and Estelle with what troubles them most: their inability to control what other people think of them. Inez is literally *their* demon, rather like the demon Michael in the philosophical fantasy comedy TV series *The Good Place*. For her part, Inez is remarkably unconcerned by the whole nightmare situation and does not care what opinion others hold of her. Even her name in French, Inès, as has been pointed out by various commentators, is the last two letters of Garcin and the first two letters of Estelle. This emphasises the profound extent to which Inez comes between them.

Inez, Webber argues, is not only there to torture the others but to draw them out. To induce them, through the tension she generates between them, to confess more about their lives and their misdeeds than they otherwise would, so that the audience can pass judgement on them as though presiding over a trial taking place *huis clos*: behind the closed doors of a courtroom.

Inez tells Garcin and Estelle they are in hell, and they assume they are in hell, but on this reading they can be seen as facing the *last judgement*. It is important, argues Webber, that Garcin and Estelle do not know they are being judged, that they think they have already been judged and damned: 'If the characters knew that their lives were being judged, their words and actions would be calibrated to present themselves in the best light. Each of us wants other people to affirm our positive self-image, as the play dramatizes' (*Rethinking Existentialism*, p. 100).

The standard reading, that the characters are in hell, is not necessarily wrong. The play can be read quite reasonably as saying the characters are in hell, and there is certainly evidence for this view. Webber's persuasive arguments, however, show that the play is ambiguous, that it can be viewed in different ways, that different readings and interpretations are possible, each emphasising different, if related, philosophical themes. Webber also forces us to acknowledge that Sartre is a more cunning and subtle playwright than he is sometimes given credit for. That his plays, at least some of them, are more than clunky dramatisations of his current philosophical concerns.

Webber's reading certainly reveals new possibilities within the play, an even deeper level of meaning. It gives a new significance to the role of the audience, demystifies the character of Inez and even identifies a glimmer of hope in this apparently bleakest of bleak dramas. If Garcin is not yet in hell but still at the last judgement or in purgatory, perhaps there is still a chance for him to come to terms with his past actions and stop regretting them. A chance to achieve the authenticity of no longer worrying what others think of him, the authenticity of no longer struggling to determine how others view him. In short, a chance to escape his conclusion that 'Hell is . . . other people!' (*In Camera*, pp. 223).

Inez has some of Olga's Kosakiewicz personality traits, as does Ivich Serguine in Sartre's novel *The Age of Reason*. Sartre and de Beauvoir were infatuated with Olga, certainly because she was young, pretty, and vivacious, which always gives a person a head start when it comes to infatuating others, but also because in her haughtiness and impetuosity she was more or less unconcerned what other people thought of her, or at least did not try to influence what other people thought of her. Other people also found it impossible to really influence what she thought of them. Despite all his wit, charm, and powers of persuasion, this included Sartre.

Sartre was addicted to Olga's little devil, 'force of nature' personality and, like any drug, it gave him a good deal of pleasure and a good deal of grief. Her personality drove him to distraction not least because he so admired it, felt it to be so superior and authentic. He wanted, against his better judgement, to be more like her, to emulate her spontaneity, to evade routine, to act on emotion rather than reason, to cease feeling he was stuck in the tedious role of older, prudent, rational, pensive teacher and philosopher.

If he could be more like her, she might love him. He certainly wanted her to determine herself to love him, wanted to tame her in that respect, yet for her to remain very much the free, untamed spirit that so captivated him. More on this final point regarding romantic love and freedom when we come to examine concrete relations with others in Chapter 3.

What Sartre really wants to examine in *In Camera* is not some impossible, supernatural, nightmare scenario but a key aspect of our being on Earth. Namely, the existence of other people and the profound and often disturbing impact that their existence has on the nature and value of our own personal existence. In short, he wants to examine the phenomenon of what, in *Being and Nothingness*, he calls *being-for-others*.

Every person exists for others as well as for himself or herself. A person is his being-for-others, but he is it over there for the Other. The Other only has to look at me to take possession of at least a part of what I am. Indeed, they don't even have to look at me. I only have to believe they are looking at me from behind that twitching curtain or through that CCTV camera lens. In fact, I only have to believe they are thinking about me. Recall Mathieu's inability to escape Marcelle, to escape her negative judgement of him, even though he is 'alone' in the street.

Under the gaze of the Other you are made to be responsible for what the Other sees. You are subject to the Other's judgement of you, and although you can try to influence this judgement you can never gain complete control over it or even know for sure what it is.

Consider the scene in which Inez offers to be Estelle's mirror (*In Camera*, pp. 197–99). As there are no real mirrors in the room, Inez offers to tell Estelle what she looks like, but Estelle cannot trust this pseudo-mirror. If Estelle wants to know how she looks, how others see her, then it would help her to look in a mirror, but it is not at all helpful for her to take feedback from Inez on how she looks. Nobody can be just a mirror. A real mirror can distort, but it cannot lie as Inez does when she tells Estelle she has a pimple on her cheek.

Even when Inez tells the truth, Estelle cannot know it is the truth, and whatever honest view Inez expresses is subject to change, subject to her freedom. Inez makes an unreliable and uncomfortable mirror for Estelle. Estelle wants to see herself as a familiar object, as a face in a mirror; she does not want to see the Other seeing her and forming unknowable evaluations of her. Inez suggests that she is nicer than Estelle's mirror, to which Estelle replies:

> Oh, I don't know. You scare me rather. My reflection in the glass never did that; of course I knew it so well. Like something I had tamed . . . I'm going to smile and my smile will sink down into your pupils, and heaven knows what it will become. (*In Camera*, p. 198)

In being subject to the judgement of the Other, a person is at the mercy of the freedom of the Other. He is, as Sartre puts it, 'enslaved' (*Being and Nothingness*, p. 291) by the freedom of the Other. The freedom of the Other reduces him to what he is for the Other.

This situation is clearly illustrated in the relationship — as it is by the end of the play — between Garcin and Inez. Garcin cannot convince himself that he is not a coward. Hence, he desperately needs Inez to assure him he is not a coward. But Inez is a free being, possibly a demon. Either way, he cannot determine her opinion. Even if he could determine her opinion, he would not be satisfied with it because he needs her opinion to be freely given for it to have any power to persuade him.

Furthermore, because Garcin is not directly conscious of Inez's consciousness, not a mind reader, he can never know, even if she eventually expresses the desired opinion, that she is saying what she really thinks. Hence, he would not be satisfied even if she told him she had decided he was not a coward. He would endlessly seek further assurances. Not least, even if she genuinely decided he was not a coward, she is free to change her mind again.

Have you ever tried hard to persuade someone of something then felt dissatisfied with their display of agreement? This is because you cannot be sure they are not simply *pretending* to agree with you, perhaps because they cannot be bothered to openly disagree with you anymore, perhaps because they have decided you are not worth disagreeing with. Other people are ultimately unreachable because we can never know, despite what they might say, that we have reached them, that we have shaped their thoughts to ours and so on, especially in any kind of enduring way.

Garcin suffers the agony of being subject to Inez's freedom. She can make him the coward he loathes to be simply by thinking him a coward. Being dead, he cannot *act* as a hero in order to influence her opinion, but even if he could act the hero there is no guarantee she would adopt the view of him he wants her to adopt. She might simply dismiss him as rash or foolish, as a coward nonetheless. Even if Inez were not cruel and inclined to think the worst of him, there would still be no guarantee.

Garcin is obliged to exist, to suffer, Inez's negative opinion of him. He cannot stop thinking about it; it prevents him from making love to Estelle. If he were alive, he could act to try and convince himself, or others besides Inez, that he is not a coward. He could flee Inez's presence and, in time, dismiss her as an insignificant Other, as people tend to do with those who have formed very low opinions of them. But in Sartre's nightmare scenario, Garcin can no longer act; he can no longer transcend himself towards the heroic being he would like to be. He can no longer flee his present, unsatisfactory being towards a brighter, more self-satisfied future, or flee the one who judges him so negatively.

Estelle is too superficial to count as a genuine Other, and all other beings have faded, so Garcin is stuck, pinned down as the vile, cowardly thing Inez's cruel freedom wishes him to be. As the only remaining Other, Inez is to him all others. She is his supreme and only judge on an apparently everlasting judgement day.

Philosophically, Sartre rejects the possibility of any form of afterlife, arguing that death is not a possibility one can experience for oneself. Death is the end of all possibility; it is complete annihilation. *In Camera*, therefore, is not a prediction of a possible afterlife. The play is simply claiming that *if* there were an eternal afterlife, it would be hell to spend it in the company of other people. Indeed, it would be so bad that annihilation is infinitely preferable.

The play progresses inexorably through mounting conflict towards Sartre's damning conclusion, his famous sweeping statement — but is it really true that hell is other people? Does the play actually allow this damning conclusion to be drawn? There is so much else in that miserable room besides the people present that makes it hellish. In that place, hell is not only other people, hell is no windows, no mirrors, no darkness, no sleep, no books, no tears, no exit.

An eternity in one miserable room with a handful of people and no distractions would be hell, but would it not be the circumstances rather than the company that made it so? Maybe it depends on the company. The characters in the play are particularly unpleasant, selfish, and pathetic — the reason why they are in hell — but what about an eternity with Buddha or Mandela or other decent people, or even indecent people, but of *your* choice? Presumably not so bad as an eternity with Garcin the drunken, cowardly adulterer; Inez the self-confessed 'damned bitch' (*In Camera*, p. 202); and Estelle the baby killer.

Arguably, the play does not allow the universal conclusion to be drawn that hell is other people but simply the conclusion that an eternity trapped in a single miserable room with Garcin, Inez, and Estelle, or people like them, would be hell. Either that or, under the aspect of eternity, everything becomes hell: other people whoever they may be, solitude, oneself, pleasure, consciousness — anything. It would all become unbearable, yet a person would have to bear it, wouldn't they?

Before we can properly tackle the question that forms the subtitle of this book, we need to examine far more closely what has really only been touched upon and alluded to so far, namely the phenomenon of *being-for-others*, as detailed in Sartre's major philosophical work, *Being and Nothingness*.

Being-for-others is one of the central pillars of Sartre's grand theory of the relationship between human consciousness and the world, a world that invariably includes the existence of other people. Understanding clearly what being-for-others is and where it fits into Sartre's remarkably holistic and coherent philosophy of the human condition, as one of the inalienable existential truths of that condition, is to understand why he draws such stark conclusions about our personal relationships and interactions.

It might be that we will go on to disagree with Sartre's claim that 'Conflict is the original meaning of being-for-others' (*Being and Nothingness*, p. 386), or at least find grounds for seriously qualifying it, but in order to do that convincingly we need to appreciate precisely where Sartre is coming from *philosophically*.

CHAPTER 2

Being and Nothingness

THE IDEA OF BEING-FOR-OTHERS IS A KEY PART OF SARTRE'S GRAND theory of the relationship between human consciousness and the world. To properly understand being-for-others, we first need to understand Sartre's view of human consciousness, what he thinks consciousness is and is not, and how consciousness interacts with the world in which it finds itself. In other words, before we can go forward, we need to take several steps back to see exactly where being-for-others fits into the broader picture of Sartre's comprehensive view of the human condition.

BEING-IN-ITSELF AND BEING-FOR-ITSELF

Sartre did not just name his major work *Being and Nothingness* because it is a cool, mystical, recherché-sounding title. Being and nothingness, the relationship between being and nothingness, the dialectical dance between being and nothingness (non-being), is what Sartre's philosophy, his existentialism — as most thoroughly expressed in that weighty tome — is all about. It is its backbone, its mainspring, its driving force.

It is not surprising then that grasping the logic of the being-nothingness relationship is the key to simplifying Sartre's complexities and to understanding his many paradoxical and apparently peculiar formulations. Indeed, it is the best and perhaps only reliable guiding thread through his magnificent, labyrinthine system. Keeping that in mind and Ariadne's thread in hand, it is time to put on your thinking cap and your head torch of reason, time to head into the phenomenological maze to slay the mythical Minotaur of Sartrean complexity.

At the very heart of Sartre's entire philosophical theory are two related terms: *being-in-itself* and *being-for-itself*. These related terms underpin virtually everything Sartre says about everything else, so much so that if a newcomer to Sartre can acquire even a basic grasp of the meaning of these two terms, he or she will have already made significant progress towards understanding Sartre's existentialism. For reasons that will become clear, it is best to begin unfolding an account of Sartre's philosophy from the starting point of being-in-itself.

Most philosophers have a view about what exists in the most general or fundamental sense. René Descartes, for example, thinks that there is mind, matter, and God. Sartre thinks that fundamentally there is being-in-itself. All that can really be said about being-in-itself is that it *is*. It is its own foundation. That is, it is founded upon itself and not upon anything else. It is that which exists fundamentally, exists *in itself*, exists in its own right, rather than being that which does not exist in itself and is dependent upon something else for its existence. It is self-sufficient, uncreated, and unchanging.

It is tempting to suppose that being-in-itself has always been and will always be, but it is eternal only in the sense of being timeless. There is no past or future for being-in-itself. It is also tempting to suppose that the existence of being-in-itself is necessary, but to describe it as necessary is to characterise it as that which cannot not be, when it has no characteristics whatsoever other than *being*. Being-in-itself exists utterly, yet its existence is not necessary as in compulsory or inevitable. It *is*, yet it need not be. This is the contingency, superfluity, or even absurdity of being-in-itself. Thinking about it too hard can freak you out, as it does Roquentin in Sartre's novel *Nausea*, which we considered earlier. Being-in-itself exists without reason or justification. The fact that being-in-itself has no characteristics leads Sartre to describe it as *undifferentiated being*.

Not only is being-in-itself timeless and unnecessary, it is non-spatial. It should not be thought of as an infinite block of stuff, although Sartre does sometimes refer to physical objects as 'in-itself', in contrast to persons who are 'for-itself'. If being-in-itself were spatial, it would be differentiated in the sense of having different areas, here and there and so on, but being-in-itself has no zones or parts just as it has no past or future. It contains no differences or contrasts; it has no distinguishing features. It just *is*.

To think accurately of this featureless existence seems to be to think of nothing at all. If I try to imagine being-in-itself, I end up giving it some attribute like dimension or colour that it does not have. I end up thinking of some infinite, grey, monobloc of stuff.

Interestingly, the German philosopher Georg Hegel argues in his *Science of Logic* that being (he does not use the term *being-in-itself*) is so undifferentiated and featureless that it is in fact indistinguishable from non-being or nothingness. For Hegel, being and non-being are only abstract concepts produced by philosophical reasoning. In reality, there is neither being nor non-being but only *becoming*. Sartre disagrees with Hegel, insisting that being-in-itself *is* while non-being or nothingness *is not*. For Sartre, being in itself is logically primary. All else — non-being — is logically subsequent to it, dependent upon it, and derived from it.

Non-being, nothingness, or what Sartre calls *being-for-itself* or *the for-itself*, does not exist fundamentally; it does not exist in its own right. Only being-in-itself exists in that way. Being-for-itself exists only as a denial or negation of being-in-itself, only as a *relationship* to being-in-itself. It borrows all its being from being-in-itself, existing as a lack or absence of being-in-itself. Sartre refers to being-for-itself as a *borrowed being*. 'Nothingness *is not*. If we can speak of it, it is only because it possesses an appearance of being, a borrowed being' (*Being and Nothingness*, p. 46). Like a shadow, a reflection, or an echo, its borrowed being is entirely dependent on something other than itself.

Although Sartre says that being-in-itself *is* and non-being *is not*, the phenomenon of non-being or being-for-itself is crucially important in his philosophy. Indeed, his entire philosophy is essentially an exhaustive investigation and description of the phenomenon of being-for-itself.

It is vital to note that being-for-itself refers to the essential nature or way of being of *consciousness* or *personhood*. Every consciousness or person is essentially a being-for-itself. So, in many contexts, the terms *consciousness*, *person*, and *being-for-itself* can be used interchangeably. Sartre's investigation into the nature of being-for-itself amounts to an investigation into the essential, existential features of human consciousness and reality.

It is tempting to suppose that being-in-itself intentionally gave rise to being-for-itself, as though giving rise to its negation was a project that being-in-itself undertook at some point in time. Being-in-itself, however, because it is what it is and can never be other than what it is, cannot have projects or conceive of possibilities.

Sartre argues that it is impossible to answer the question of why being-for-itself came about. In his view, any attempt to account for what he describes as the *upsurge* of being-for-itself from being-in-itself produces only metaphysical hypotheses than cannot be validated or invalidated (*Being and Nothingness*, p. 641). For Sartre, the emergence or upsurge of being-for-itself is an unfathomable mystery, just as the existence of being-in-itself is an unfathomable mystery.

> Ontology will therefore limit itself to declaring that *everything takes place as if* the in-itself in a project to found itself gave itself the modification of the for-itself. (*Being and Nothingness*, p. 641)

As said, being-for-itself is not a non-being in itself, its own non-being; it is the non-being or negation of being-in-itself. In not being its own non-being, being-for-itself always has to strive to be its own non-being without ever being able to become it. Being-for-itself always has to be both the project of negating being-in-itself in order to realise itself as the negation of being-in-itself, and the project of negating itself in order to avoid a coincidence with itself that would be its own annihilation.

Being-for-itself is a paradoxical, ambiguous, indeterminate being that always lacks identity both with being-in-itself and with itself. It is perpetually not what it is (being) and what it is not (non-being) and can only exist in this perpetually self-eluding way, as a flight or escape from any kind of self-identity. 'Yet the for-itself *is*. It is, we may say, even if it is a being which is not what it is and which is what it is not' (*Being and Nothingness*, p. 103).

The easiest way to understand the paradoxical, ambiguous, and indeterminate nature of being-for-itself is in terms of time or *temporality*, as a temporal view of it brings to mind ideas we are all familiar with from our own experience. Given that each of us is a being-for-itself on a lifelong temporal journey, its key features should not be too difficult to recognise.

TEMPORALITY

Being-for-itself, human consciousness, exists as a flight or *transcendence* that continually moves forward in time away from its past towards its future. It is a *temporal* flight or transcendence. Being-for-itself is always both its past which is no longer and its future which is not yet. Paradoxically, being-for-itself is always not what it is (past) and what it is not (future). Being-for-itself is never 'in the present' as the present is commonly understood. If the temporal motion of being-for-itself could ever be stopped, could ever be frozen in the present, it would immediately cease to exist. But then, as is explained below, the present does not really exist anymore than being-for-itself can be frozen in the present.

These ideas can certainly seem complicated at first sight, but actually you already know what they mean if you think about them a little because you live the paradox of *temporality* every day; we all do. Yesterday has always gone, tomorrow never comes, today is fleeting. Although your past has gone, is now past, it continues to make you who you are in many ways. For instance, the memories that make you who you are today are all, by definition, directed towards the past and comprised of past impressions and proceedings. Your character is shaped by your past experiences. The projects you are currently involved in, your goals and hopes for the future, were all conceived in the past, and so on. In short, you are your past which is no longer, and all your actions in a world that is the result of the past aim at your future which is not yet.

As for the present, there is no such *moment* as the present, for when being-for-itself reaches the future at which it aims, that future does not become the present but rather immediately becomes the past. It is a fluid situation. The present, argues Sartre, is actually the *presence* of being-for-itself to being-in-itself as a temporal flight from being-in-itself towards the future. The present is not a moment but rather like what people mean when they answer 'present' in response to a roll call.

Past, present, and future are not three distinct and substantial elements but three unified dimensions, each of which, being nothing in itself, is outside of itself in the other two and has meaning only in terms of the other two. Sartre refers to this structure as 'ekstatic', and to each of the three dimensions of time as an 'ekstasis' (*Being and Nothingness*, p. 160). 'Ekstatic' is derived from the Greek 'ekstasis', meaning 'standing out from'.

Viewing time as an ekstatic structure reveals the future as *future-past*, the past as *past-future*, and the present as the presence of being-for-itself to being-in-itself rather than a discrete moment that can be considered as *now*. There is, strictly speaking, no such thing as now. Say 'Now!' as quickly as you can. Time passed even as you said it, such that there really was no now. You can't hit the target of now, because really there is no target to hit. As to what is ordinarily described as 'the here and now', it is the situation to which being-for-itself is presence; the situation that being-for-itself realises by perpetually surpassing it towards the future.

> It would be absurd to say that it is nine o'clock for the for-itself, but the for-itself can be present to a hand pointed at nine o'clock. What we falsely call the Present is the being to which the present is presence. It is impossible to grasp the Present in the form of an instant, for the instant would be the moment when the present *is*. But the present is not; it makes itself present in the form of flight. (*Being and Nothingness*, p. 146)

Being-for-itself is a flight towards the future. It is a flight that realises the past and the future as its past and future. It is a flight by which the future is constituted as a future-past and the past as a past-future. It is a flight by which the future becomes the past.

Being-for-itself is not in the world as objects are. Being-for-itself transcends the world and it does so by constantly escaping every situation towards future situations. It is what Sartre calls a *temporal transcendence*. Why? Because it transcends temporally. Being-for-itself, however, because it is only the ongoing negation of being-in-itself, is an escaping that continues to require, as the foundation of its borrowed being, the being-in-itself it seeks to escape. It is an ongoing escaping that cannot finally escape. If it escaped entirely, it would no longer be the escaping it must to be in order to exist and would immediately cease to exist. Being-for-itself is a transcendence that is constantly recaptured by the physical world, precisely because the physical world is and must always be the ground, the launch pad, of the transcendence of being-for-itself.

To be a transcendence towards the future being-for-itself must have something to transcend. What being-for-itself transcends is the human body, what Sartre calls the *embodiment* of being-for-itself, and the wider situation and circumstances of the body. Much more on the body in the final section of this chapter. Sartre refers to all this — embodiment and the wider situation of the body — as the *situatedness* or *facticity* of being-for-itself.

What being-for-itself transcends is facticity. That is, the indifference, resistance, inconvenience, toughness, fragility, complexity, and so on of the world — what Sartre describes as, 'The coefficient of adversity of things' (*Being and Nothingness*, p. 503). In short, being-for-itself is not a transcendence-in-itself, a pure transcendence, but the transcendence *of* its facticity. Being-for-itself *is* the transcendence of facticity and nothing beyond that. Transcendence requires facticity, just as to fly an aircraft requires air resistance.

In everyday terms, it is human projects that constitute the transcendence of being-for-itself. A person's projects always aim at a future in which she will have overcome something presently lacking or absent, a future in which she hopes and desires to be more satisfied, fulfilled, and at one with herself. Sartre argues that ultimately being-for-itself always aims at coinciding with itself, at being its own foundation, at being what he calls *in-itself-for-itself*.

In so far as God is conceived as in-itself-for-itself, as a consciousness that is nonetheless identical with itself, as a consciousness that is its own foundation, Sartre argues that the fundamental project of every being-for-itself is to be God.

> The possible is projected in general as what the for-itself lacks in order to become in-itself-for-itself. The fundamental value which presides

over this project is exactly the in-itself-for-itself; that is, the ideal of a consciousness which would be the foundation of its own being-in-itself by the pure consciousness which it would have of itself. It is this ideal which can be called God. Thus the best way to conceive of the fundamental project of human reality is to say that man is the being whose project is to be God. (*Being and Nothingness*, p. 587)

God, certainly as conceived in the Abrahamic religions, is essentially a for-itself, a conscious, knowing being. Yet his consciousness is held to exist fundamentally rather than as a relation or a negation. In short, God's existence and essence are assumed to be one. The ontological argument for the existence of God — first formulated by the medieval philosopher Anselm in his *Proslogion* — assumes this unity of existence and essence. For Anselm, the most perfect conceivable entity must have the attribute of existence. So, for Anselm, God's essence implies his existence. God is the ultimate in-itself-for-itself.

Being-for-itself, however, can never achieve this godlike state of self-supporting self-identity because it exists only as the negation of being-in-itself and as such is grounded upon it rather than upon itself. It is destined always to be grounded upon a being that it is not, upon the world, upon its situations and circumstances, and as such can never be its own foundation.

It is largely because he holds that being-in-itself-for-itself is an impossible state of being for any consciousness whatsoever that Sartre is an atheist. He denies the existence of God, a divine consciousness, on logical grounds. This has been described as Sartre's anti-ontological argument.

Sartre's examination of the impossibility of being-for-itself becoming in-itself-for-itself provides an explanation of why complete satisfaction and self-fulfilment are unachievable, why, in Sartre's view, 'Man is a useless passion' (*Being and Nothingness*, p. 636). Our inability to become in-itself-for-itself manifests itself not as an inability to satisfy particular desires but as an inability to satisfy desire as such, as an inability to overcome the evanescence of satisfaction. 'Hence the constant disappointment which accompanies repletion, the famous: "Is it only this?" which is not directed at the concrete pleasure which satisfaction gives but at the evanescence of the coincidence with self' (*Being and Nothingness*, p. 126). More on desire and lack shortly.

Being-for-itself is nothing in itself; therefore, it must constantly make itself be something, or rather, it must constantly aim at being something without ever being able to become it once and for all. A person can 'become' a lawyer, for example, but this does not mean that he has become a lawyer-*thing* in the way that a table is a table. He has to constantly choose to play the role of a lawyer and can always choose to do otherwise.

Being-for-itself aims at being something through choice and action. This is what Sartre has in mind when he argues along the lines that *to be is to do*. By doing, however, a person does not become her being absolutely; her being is rather a constant becoming. Being-for-itself is burdened with always having to choose itself, with always having to choose its responses to its situation. It has to constantly choose its way of being. It cannot not do so because not to choose is still a choice — a *choice* not to choose.

That being-for-itself always has to choose its responses, the path it takes, or choose to allow other people and circumstances to dictate the path, leads Sartre to insist that we are radically free, indeed, that we are 'condemned to be free' (*Being and Nothingness*, p. 462). We are each of us condemned to freedom because we cannot not choose and are responsible for the choices we make. Existentialism is well known as a philosophy of radical personal freedom and choice. It is somewhat less well known that this implies that it is also a philosophy of radical personal responsibility.

CONSCIOUSNESS

As we have seen, consciousness is or exists as being-for-itself. Each conscious human being is essentially a being-for-itself in relation to being-in-itself. To focus in a rather abstract way on the logic of the relationship between being-for-itself and being-in-itself, as we have done so far, produces what is called an *ontological* description of the relationship. To focus in a less abstract way on the concrete, existential relationship between consciousness and the world produces what is called a *phenomenological* description of the relationship. It is basically the same relationship that is being described; what is different is the level or focus of the description. If an ontological description reveals or comprises the bones of Sartre's philosophy — his *phenomenological ontology* — a phenomenological description puts flesh on those bones.

At the heart of Sartre's phenomenological description of the relationship between consciousness and the world is the notion of *intentionality* or *aboutness*. Consciousness does not exist as a thing; it is not any kind of object. It is not, as the philosopher Descartes supposes in his *Meditations*, a mental substance that exists in its own right and, thereafter, entertains thoughts. In fact, it is nothing in itself. It exists only in relation to what it *intends* or is *about*; only in relation to what it is consciousness *of*. If it were not conscious *of* anything, it would not exist. Sartre sums this view up with the maxim: consciousness *is* consciousness *of*_____.

> To say that consciousness is consciousness of something means that for consciousness there is no being outside of that precise obligation to be a revealing intuition of something. (*Being and Nothingness*, p. 17)

Sartre did not invent the theory of intentionality— the theory that consciousness exists only in so far as it intends something or is about something. Recall Sartre's 1933 sabbatical in Berlin to study the work of German philosopher Edmund Husserl. Husserl, in turn, inherited the theory from another German, the philosopher and psychologist Franz Brentano, who introduced the theory in his book *Philosophy from an Empirical Standpoint*. Brentano writes:

> Every mental phenomenon includes something as object within itself, although they do not all do so in the same way. In presentation something is presented, in judgement something is affirmed or denied, in love loved, in hate hated, in desire desired and so on. This intentional inexistence is characteristic exclusively of mental phenomena. No physical phenomena exhibit anything like it. We can, therefore, define mental phenomena by saying that they are those phenomena which contain an object intentionally within themselves. (*Philosophy from an Empirical Standpoint*, pp. 88–89)

The theory of intentionality implies that because consciousness is always *about* something and nothing beyond that, any attempt to investigate consciousness must always lead immediately to an investigation of whatever consciousness is about. The philosophy of Brentano, Husserl, Sartre, and others, formally known as *phenomenology*, seeks to understand consciousness by investigating the way in which different *phenomena*, different *intentional objects*, appear to consciousness.

An intentional object is whatever consciousness is *about*, be it perceived, imagined, believed, or felt. Hatred, for example, is an intentional object, a collection of appearances to consciousness. Bill's hatred of Ben does not exist as such; it is an intentional object. In this case, an intentional *psychic object* composed of Bill's anger when he sees Ben, his feelings of aversion when he thinks of Ben, the negative things he says about Ben, his wish or intention to harm Ben, and so on. These appearances are not manifestations of an underlying hatred; they are the hatred. There is no hatred in itself beyond the various appearances that we collectively describe as Bill's hatred for Ben.

A physical object is also an intentional object, a collection of appearances to consciousness. Far away, a book, for example, appears small. Close up it appears large. When turned, different sides appear and disappear. Its shape appears differently as its orientation changes; its colour alters with the light. It makes a thud as it is thrown back on the table. The same things can be said of the book as was said for hatred: There is no book in itself beyond the various shifting appearances that we collectively describe as this book.

Phenomenologists talk of reducing things to their appearances, or of there being nothing beyond appearances. They want to get away from a distinction that has often been drawn in philosophy between appearance and reality. The view that what is real is somehow hidden behind appearances, that objects in themselves lie beneath their appearances and support them like an obscured pin cushion supporting pins. Phenomenology does not equate the being of physical objects with a supposed underlying ground or substratum that never appears but rather with appearances themselves, with sets of appearances, actual and possible.

Actual appearances, Sartre argues, do not indicate an underlying *noumenal being*, a thing-in-itself, but rather an infinite series of possible appearances that could appear. He describes these possible appearances as *transphenomenal*. Transphenomenality is the mark of the real. An object is real not because there is a hidden thing-in-itself underlying what appears but because it has an infinite series of transphenomenal aspects which are not presently appearing but which could appear.

> We must understand that this being is no other than the transphenomenal being of phenomena and not a noumenal being which is hidden behind them. It is the being of this table, of this package of tobacco, of the lamp, more generally the being of the world which is implied by consciousness. (*Being and Nothingness*, p. 18)

The notion of transphenomenality allows Sartre to distinguish between a real, perceived object and an unreal, imagined object. An imagined object does not have transphenomenal aspects. An imaginary rotating cube, for example, does not reveal, as it rotates, sides that were transphenomenal. The sides that appear were not unrevealed before they appeared; they simply did not exist. What appears to emerge is only what is added by the consciousness concerned, that which *is* the intending of the imaginary rotating cube.

In *The Imaginary*, an exploration of the imagination and mental images published in 1940, Sartre argues that understanding a perceived object is like serving an 'apprenticeship' (*The Imaginary*, p. 9). We learn more about the object the longer we perceive it and the more aspects we explore. A mental image, on the other hand, has no hidden appearances, no transphenomenal aspects. It discloses nothing because it has only the appearances a person's intentions give it as he gives them. A mental image is known all at once; there is no apprenticeship to be served.

> In perception, knowledge is formed slowly; in the image, knowledge is immediate . . . An image is not learned: it is organised exactly as the objects that are learned, but, in fact, it is given whole, for what it is, in its appearance . . . I can keep an image in view as long as I want: I will never find anything there but what I put there. (*The Imaginary*, p. 9)

When Sartre argues as he does above about transphenomenality, there seems no doubt that he is a realist about appearances. Appearances are not distinct from reality; they are reality. They appear to us, but they exist as they appear to us independently of us. At other times, and this is arguably an inconsistency in his philosophy, he is less of a realist about appearances, insisting that appearances must appear to someone in order to have any reality *as appearances*: 'Relative the phenomenon remains, for "to appear" supposes in essence somebody to whom to appear' (*Being and Nothingness*, p. 2).

When Sartre argues like this, he presents himself less as a realist and more as a *transcendental idealist*, somewhat in the style of the great German philosopher Immanuel Kant. Sartre is certainly more Kantian than Berkeleyan. George Berkeley, in his *Principles of Human Knowledge*, argues that *to be is to be perceived (esse est percipi)*. The so-called external world for Berkeley is composed of collections of ideas that exist only in so far as they are thought by a mind.

Berkeley's philosophy seems to imply that there is no external world. It seems to imply *solipsism*. Solipsism is the view that only one's own mind exists and that there is nothing beyond it. Berkeley gets around the problem of solipsism by arguing that the external world exists independently of my mind because God's mind perceives the entire universe all the time. For Berkeley, God makes those collections of ideas I call 'things' *objective* by perceiving them even when I am not perceiving them.

Unlike Berkeley, Sartre at least thinks that there is something independent of any mind, namely being-in-itself. Indeed, being-in-itself is the foundation of the nothingness or negation that is consciousness. It can be said that whereas for Berkeley being depends on consciousness, for Sartre consciousness depends on being. Importantly though, the appearances that arise through the negation of being-in-itself, the appearances that arise *for* consciousness, are not how being-in-itself appears when consciousness is not present. Indeed, being-in-itself has no appearances, no characteristics. As said, being-in-itself has no distinguishing features. It just *is*.

In leaning towards transcendental idealism Sartre holds that being-in-itself is undifferentiated. All that can be said of it is that it is.

45

'Being is. Being is in-itself. Being is what it is' (*Being and Nothingness*, p. 22). Being-in-itself is disclosed and differentiated only from the point of view of non-being; only from the point of view of being-for-itself. That is, it is only by virtue of consciousness that being is transformed into phenomena or phenomenalised. So, Sartre undoubtedly draws a distinction of some kind between being-in-itself and phenomena, between being-in-itself and that which appears, between the phenomenon of being and the being of phenomena.

In drawing this distinction, does Sartre assert the existence of a noumenal being or thing-in-itself that underlies phenomena, having elsewhere clearly denied the existence of an underlying noumenal being? It might be argued that there is some confusion or inconsistency in what Sartre says about appearances in *Being and Nothingness* or, at least, that he does not quite manage to say what he wants to say about them. Be that as it may, the solution to the confusion seems to lie in considering Sartre's position in light of Kant's key distinction between noumena and phenomena as detailed in his *Critique of Pure Reason*.

Some commentators have identified Sartre's distinction between being-in-itself and phenomena with Kant's *two worlds* view of noumena and phenomena, in which a world of noumena is said to lie concealed behind the world of phenomena. This two-worlds view is a somewhat traditional reading of Kant, a view that has been subjected to reappraisal by recent commentators who argue that Kant does not in fact hold that noumena and phenomena denote two distinct realms of being.

These recent commentators argue that for Kant there is in fact only a *single* realm of being that can be encountered from two distinct standpoints. A divine mind capable of non-sensory perception — Sartre denies the possibility of such an entity — could encounter being *noumenally*, as it is in itself. Ordinary minds like ours, on the other hand, capable only of sensory perception, must encounter being *phenomenally*, as *phenomena*, as those collections of appearances we call objects. What the English philosopher, J. L. Austin, in his book, *Sense and Sensibilia*, wittily refers to as 'familiar objects — moderate-sized specimens of dry goods' (*Sense and Sensibilia*, p. 8).

This more recent and subtle interpretation of Kant is surely closer to what Sartre proposes. Indeed, Sartre explicitly rejects the traditional two worlds view of Kantian noumena, arguing that being-in-itself does not lurk behind appearances as a noumenal foundation that underlies phenomena (*Being and Nothingness*, p. 4). There is nothing beyond appearances because noumenal being and appearances are, so to speak, different modes of the same being, the former the mode when consciousness is not present, the latter the mode when consciousness is present.

It is worth repeating that, for Sartre, phenomena are not in fact directly founded upon being but upon non-being. It is the negation of being that is consciousness that gives rise to phenomena. Being is not directly the foundation of phenomena; being is the foundation of the non-being of the for-itself that phenomenalises being by negating it. Sartre's view of being-for-itself as a *double negation* can help us here.

Being-for-itself is the negation of being. Sartre calls this logically prior dimension of the double negation the *radical negation*. The radical negation is so called because it is the negation of the whole of being. As the negation of being, however, the for-itself also negates being, not in the form of a radical negation of the very being of being but in the form of particular concrete negations of being. Sartre calls this dimension of the double negation the *concrete negation*.

The concrete negation is so called because it is that by which particular concrete phenomena appear: this as distinct from that, this as not that, this as external to that, and so on. Phenomena are for the for-itself in the sense that indeterminate and undifferentiated being is determined and differentiated into distinct phenomena by the negations (the negativities or négatités) that the for-itself places into being. The negation negates in the form of particular negations of being.

The German existentialist philosopher Martin Heidegger, who greatly influenced Sartre, put it well in his 1929 lecture, 'What is Metaphysics?', when he said, 'The nothing itself nihilates (The nothing nothings)' (*Basic Writings*, p. 105). In aiming at but not achieving the negation of being as a whole, these particular negations realise phenomena as entities that are not grounded directly upon being but upon particular privations or lacks of being.

So, consciousness is a negation that places particular negations or negativities into being that, so to speak, carve up being into particular phenomena. Phenomena can only arise through the negation of being-in-itself that is being-for-itself; they can exist only from the point of view of being-for-itself. As said, phenomena are not grounded upon being but upon particular privations or lacks of being. Particular privations or lacks of being occur when, for example, being is *questioned*. Here we begin to see in more down-to-earth terms how negation, non-being, nothingness, privation, lack, and absence give rise to the world of phenomena we all inhabit.

The relationship of consciousness to the world is primarily characterised by a *questioning attitude*. This attitude is not just the capacity to judge that something is lacking but the constant expectation of a disclosure of non-being.

> If I expect a disclosure of being, I am prepared at the same time for the eventuality of a disclosure of a non-being. If I question the carburetor, it is because I consider it possible that 'there is nothing there' in the carburetor. Thus, my question by its nature envelops a certain pre-judicative comprehension of non-being. (*Being and Nothingness*, pp. 31–32)

To take another example, if I check to see if my cake is baked, it is because I consider it possible that it is *not* baked. Even supposing there are cakes apart from consciousness of them, apart from consciousness organising appearances into those intentional objects we call cakes, a cake can only be 'not baked' for a consciousness that experiences the cake in the mode of not yet being what it will be in future. The cake does not lack being baked for itself, it lacks being baked for a consciousness that has desires and expectations with regards to it.

Consciousness constantly introduces non-being, negation, negativities, lack, and absence into the world in order to make sense of it and to act purposefully within it. A situation is always encountered and comprehended not in terms of what it is but in terms of what it lacks for the consciousness encountering it, what it lacks for the person whose situation it is. In itself, a situation is a fullness of being; it lacks nothing.

In itself, however, it is precisely not a situation because to be a situation it must be a situation *for* someone, the situation *of* someone. The lacks that make it a situation, that give it future possibilities and so on, are given to it by the consciousness, by the desires and intentions, of the person for whom it is a situation.

Not least, a situation cannot be its own situation, a situation for itself, because there would be no point of view from which it was orientated as a situation *with possibilities* — the possibilities of the situation being the possibilities of the conscious, active person who renders the situation a situation by taking a point of view on it and acting within it. As a biscuit advert encouraging children to venture outdoors more weirdly put it, those puddles won't jump in themselves, those trees won't climb themselves.

As to trees falling over in forests when there is no one around, it seems clear by our present line of reasoning that they do not make a sound. Even if we suppose that there are trees and vibrations in the air apart from our consciousness of them, vibrations in the air by themselves are not sound. Sound requires the presence of an ear to detect these vibrations and a consciousness to experience them, to hear them, as sound. Sound is primarily consciousness of sound.

In Sartre's view, a person interprets every situation according to her desires, hopes, fears, expectations, and intentions. Every situation a person encounters is understood as presently lacking something desired, expected, intended, or anticipated. If the glass is half full, it lacks being full. If the glass is half empty, it lacks being empty. As said, the situation in itself does not lack anything; it lacks something for the person whose situation it is. For Sartre, consciousness is always predisposed to find something lacking. Indeed, he maintains that lack is intrinsic to the very meaning of every situation for any particular consciousness.

Every situation, he argues, is a situation for consciousness. Consciousness, as that which exists by negating the situation, must be situated in order to be. Consciousness, for which the situation is a situation, is not part of the situation but the negation of the situation. Consciousness is always *not* what it is consciousness *of.* The first condition of all consciousness is: *I am not this, I am consciousness of this.*

Consciousness transcends the situation in order to realise the situation. Every situation is understood not in terms of what it is but in terms of what it lacks, and what every situation lacks is precisely consciousness or being-for-itself. Being-for-itself is those particular lacks that make the situation a situation, those lacks that give the situation the potential to become something as yet unrealised. Sartre explores the phenomenon of lack with the example of judging that the moon is not full (*Being and Nothingness*, pp. 110–11).

In itself, a crescent moon is neither complete nor incomplete; it is simply what it is. In order to understand it as a partial appearance of the full moon, it must be judged in terms of the full moon that is presently lacking. The meaning of the crescent moon is founded upon the non-being of the full moon as that which the crescent moon lacks.

The crescent moon itself does not lack the full moon. The crescent moon lacks the full moon for a consciousness that is the temporal surpassing of the being of the crescent moon towards the non-being of the full moon. It is the non-being of the full moon that gives the crescent moon its meaning for consciousness. For consciousness the crescent moon exists in the mode of being the non-being of the full moon. As that which is given the crescent moon is what it is. As a *meaningful* phenomenon, the crescent moon is understood as what it is by virtue of what it lacks.

As consciousness is those particular lacks that determine the situation, it is itself a lack. Recall that being-for-itself, unlike being-in-itself, is that which can never achieve identity with itself. Being-for-itself is that which lacks identity with itself, or, to put it simply, being-for-itself is that which lacks itself.

This is not to say that being-for-itself is a lack in itself. If it were a lack in itself it would be identical with itself as lack, whereas it is that which cannot achieve identity with itself either as being or as non-being. Its being is to be what it is not and not to be what it is. Being-for-itself has rather *to be* its own lack. As the negation of being, being-for-itself is a lack of being, but as the negation of itself as a lack of being it is that which strives in vain to lack itself as nothing in order to be being, in order to be a being-in-itself-for-itself.

As said, this godlike state of self-identity and self-fulfilment is impossible to achieve. In short, complete satisfaction is impossible. In Sartre's view 'Man is a useless passion' (*Being and Nothingness*, p. 636), because being-for-itself is always constituted as a lack. 'If I could just win her hand in marriage', sighs the lover, 'I would never want anything again', fooling himself that by winning her hand he would achieve the impossible and become a permanently fulfilled lack. Constituted as a lack that it has to be, being-for-itself cannot be completely fulfilled. As the negation of being, it must surpass any particular obtained object of desire towards a further un-obtained object of desire.

Closely linked to the phenomenon of existential lack is the phenomenon of existential absence. Sartre outlines existential absence by describing the experience of discovering that his friend Pierre is absent from a café where he has arranged to meet him (*Being and Nothingness*, pp. 33–35). 'When I enter this café to search for Pierre, there is formed a synthetic organisation of all the objects in the café, on the ground of which Pierre is given as about to appear' (*Being and Nothingness*, p. 33). Pierre, as the person Sartre expects to find, is existentially absent.

This *existential absence* is distinct from an abstract and purely *formal absence* that is merely thought. 'Wellington is not in this café, Paul Valéry is no longer here, *etc.*' (*Being and Nothingness*, p. 34). The distinction between existential and formal absence emphasises that non-being does not arise through judgements made by consciousness after encountering the world, but that non-being belongs to the very nature of the world as it is for consciousness. Pierre's absence from the café is not merely thought. His absence is an actual event at the café that characterises the café as the place from which Pierre is absent.

Sartre was struck at an early age by what he later termed *existential absence*. In his autobiography *Words*, he tells of a gathering of the Institute of Modern Languages where his grandfather Charles pronounced, 'Someone's lacking here: it's Simonnot' (*Words*, p. 58). This pronouncement caused Sartre to almost see Simonnot's absence like a pillar in the centre of the crowd. He also recounts his thoughts when, as a child, he read about the huge anticipation generated in New York by Charles Dickens' imminent arrival. New York was 'lonely, widowed, orphaned, and depopulated simply by the absence of the man it was expecting. I murmured: "There's someone lacking: it's Dickens!" (*Words*, p. 106).

A person's entire world can exist in the mode of the negative; in the mode of not being the presence of whatever is desired. The misery of missing something or someone is rooted in this negating of the entire world.

For a withdrawing nicotine addict, for example, physical withdrawal lasts only a few weeks. The misery of psychological withdrawal, however, can last much longer and arises from the withdrawing smoker's experience of her entire world as the flat, monotonous, depressing, distressing absence of a cigarette. Nothing really interests or inspires a withdrawing smoker except that absent cigarette. The withdrawing smoker's entire world can be reduced to not being cigarettes.

Even things that have no direct association with cigarettes can refer the withdrawing smoker to cigarettes simply because they are not cigarettes. In being nowhere, cigarettes seem to be everywhere, which is why some people argue that it is better to have a packet of cigarettes to hand when trying to give them up, so that there is something tangible to resist, rather than the whole world to resist in the form of a vast signifier of absent cigarettes. It is the difficulty of finding value in a cigarette free world, the difficulty of achieving a life in which cigarettes are no longer existentially absent, that is the biggest challenge for any person trying to become a genuine ex-smoker.

As to missing *someone*, the misery of romantic rejection, for example, lies in the loss of the diverse pleasures the beloved gave the lover, and in the hurt the lover feels at no longer being wanted by the beloved. But it also lies very much in the reduction of the whole world to a dull background that has no significance or value other than to be the perpetual affirmation of the beloved's absence. Not only has the beloved gone, taking the lover's self-esteem with them, the beloved has also stolen the *value* of everything that remains. Such is the triple whammy of rejection.

BEING-FOR-OTHERS

So, every person is a being-for-itself. According to Sartre and his followers, however, this is not all they are. There is a further aspect of human subjectivity that accounts for certain distinct modes of consciousness, certain ways of experiencing one's own existence, that cannot be accounted for simply in term of being-for-itself. This further aspect of human subjectivity is *being-for-others*. Every person has a *being-for-others*, an essential aspect of themselves that exists for them by existing for other people.

Every person exists for others and is subject to the scrutiny, opinion, and judgement of others. Being-for-others is manifested as shame, guilt, embarrassment, jealousy, gratitude, pride, love, and all those other emotions and dispositions that are essentially other-related and without which a person would be incomplete. Sartre says, 'I need the Other in order to realise fully all the structures of my being. The For-itself refers to the For-others' (*Being and Nothingness*, p. 246).

Sartre favours exploring the phenomenon of being-for-others by exploring the mode of consciousness that is *shame*. We have already seen the central role that the phenomenon of shame plays in *In Camera*, and anyone who has ever experienced shame — and that is surely most of us — will understand how acutely and uncomfortably shame reveals our being-for-others to us, the extent to which the negative judgement of others obliges us to evaluate ourselves from their point of view.

Shame is the stark realisation that I have lost control of the positive image I like to project, the realisation that it is now the disapproval of other people that controls my image and shapes who I am. Above all, shame is my acceptance, despite possible protestations, that their negative evaluations of me are justified. Not surprisingly, shame plays as much of a starring role in *Being and Nothingness* as it does in *In Camera*, so let's explore what Sartre says about it there.

Shame is *for* consciousness, and a person is ashamed in so far as he is conscious of shame. However, although shame is a structure of the self, a person does not realise shame for himself and by himself. Shame requires a direct apprehension of another person as one who *sees* me and evaluates me as a person I am not proud of, as a person I would rather disown.

Shame is not originally a phenomenon of reflection . . . it is in its primary structure shame *before somebody*. I have just made an awkward or vulgar gesture. This gesture clings to me; I neither judge it nor blame it. I simply live it. I realise it in the mode of for-itself. But now suddenly I raise my head. Somebody was there and has seen me. Suddenly I realise the vulgarity of my gesture, and I am ashamed. . . . The Other is the indispensible mediator between myself and me. I am ashamed of myself *as I appear* to the Other. (*Being and Nothingness*, pp. 245–46)

Sartre recognises that there are some forms of shame that in a certain sense a person can realise for himself, shame before God or ancestors, for example. Some people imagine spirits are staring down at them with their unsleeping, all-seeing eyes, gawping and judging. Such forms of shame, however, are derivatives of the primary structure. Sartre describes shame before God as 'the religious *practice* of shame' (*Being and Nothingness*, p. 245).

To fully understand what is involved in *being seen*, or involved in simply suspecting that one is seen, or realising with horror later on that one was seen, filmed, photographed, and so on, as an experience that is not merely comprehended but lived and suffered, is to understand the meaning and significance of being-for-others.

Human beings are objects. They have bodies, objects that are externally related to other objects and which are affected by the same physical determinants that affect all objects. However, although human beings are objects and the Other is a human being, it is not as an object that the Other is originally revealed to me. Sartre develops his view of the way in which the Other is revealed to me by exploring the phenomenon of *encounter* through a range of concrete examples.

Sartre's first concrete example is not one in which the Other encounters me but one in which I simply see another person who does not see me (*Being and Nothingness*, pp. 277–79). The purpose of this example is to outline certain structures that will help elucidate the central case Sartre is interested in: that of being encountered.

I see a man in an otherwise empty park. Immediately, my awareness of the man's presence in the park affects my situation. The man's appearance constitutes the start of the disintegration of the world from my own point of view. Suddenly, the situation, which was mine to evaluate as I pleased, contains a new source of values which are not mine and which escape me.

> The appearance of the Other in the world corresponds to a fixed sliding of the whole universe, to a decentralisation of the world which undermines the centralisation which I am simultaneously effecting. (*Being and Nothingness*, p. 279)

The reorientation of the world towards the man, the fact that meanings unknown to me flow in his direction, constitutes him as a 'drain hole' into which my own world flows. 'It appears that the world has a kind of drain hole in the middle of its being and that it is perpetually flowing off through this hole' (*Being and Nothingness*, p. 279). This is why a person seeking the joys of solitude in the wilds might well feel irritated when she sees another person, even if that other person does not see her. The very appearance of another person prevents her from playing God. She ceases to be the centre, sole judge and unchallenged boss of all she surveys because a source of re-evaluation has appeared on the scene to steal the world away from her and with it her glorious godlike supremacy. A desert in which a person enjoying solitude sees a stranger in the distance can feel more crowded than a busy street in town.

Many people have told me they identify with this feeling of irritation at the sight of the Other, as I do myself. They do not mind a crowded street in town as they expect streets in town to be crowded, but when they head for the hills they want it all to themselves. No small ask these days given the massive increase in world population. This feeling of irritation, however, does not appear to be universal. Some people have told me they feel no irritation whatsoever when they are walking alone in the hills and they see someone in the distance walking towards them who will soon inevitably see them, draw close to them, pass by them, and evaluate them as they pass.

Perhaps we who are irritated are greedy and egocentric, wanting vast spaces to ourselves so that we can play God. Perhaps we are oversensitive to the presence of the Other, certainly on our grand solo expeditions. Perhaps those who are not irritated place no value on solitude, or always consider themselves to be on display, always with others mentally even when they happen to be alone physically. Some people, of course, contrive always to be in company. Or perhaps their sense of the existence of the Other is so obtuse, so mild, that the mundane materialisation of the Other in their world leaves them largely unaffected.

This is not to say they would remain unaffected if the Other caught them in some seriously shameful act, although of course some people have very little capacity for shame, and some people have no capacity for shame at all. I do not know how to resolve all this here. My aim is only to suggest that here at least Sartre may not have identified a *universal* human attitude or disposition, even if he has surely identified a common one.

At the stage when I see the Other but he does not see me, he is still only a special kind of object. Although he is a drain hole in my world and a threat to the centralisation I effect, he remains an object in my world. However, that he is recognised as a threat to my centralisation suggests that there are occasions when this threat is realised; occasions when he brings about a radical reorientation of my being, a radical shift in my sense of myself.

In describing this radical reorientation, Sartre offers the following famous example: He invites us to imagine that he is a jealous, curious, or corrupt person who, finding himself alone, listens at a door and spies through the keyhole (*Being and Nothingness*, pp. 282–84). He is completely absorbed in his voyeuristic activities. 'I am a pure consciousness of things. . . . My consciousness sticks to my acts, it *is* my acts, and my acts are commanded only by the ends to be attained' (*Being and Nothingness*, p. 283). While absorbed in his actions, he does not judge them. He does not know his actions; he is them.

> But all of a sudden I hear footsteps in the hall. Someone is looking at me! What does this mean? It means that I am suddenly affected in my being and that essential modifications appear in my structure. (*Being and Nothingness*, p. 284)

Before considering the essential modifications that being looked at (*the look*) brings about, it is important to stress that in order to experience himself as seen, a person need not be directly aware of another person's eyes turned in his direction. Consider the above example again. Simply hearing footsteps in the hall can be enough for a person to experience himself as seen.

> The look will be given just as well on occasion when there is a rustling of branches, or the sound of a footstep followed by silence, or the slight opening of a shutter, or a light movement of a curtain. (*Being and Nothingness*, p. 281)

Occurrences of the look have greatly increased in the modern world. We are frequently if not almost constantly stared at by devices that we cannot stare down. There are now so many gadgets that see us — CCTV, webcams, smartphones, drones, satellites — that it is probably wise always to assume that one is being looked at and never do anything compromising. This has profound implications for our sense of ourselves and what we allow ourselves to do.

On the upside, it has to be acknowledged that this almost ubiquitous surveillance reduces crime. Many people already resist breaking the law in visible ways believing they would certainly be caught in the act by CCTV. Indeed, there are so many cameras about these days that even going in disguise to commit a burglary or a stabbing is of no use, as a succession of cameras can often track a culprit back to his lair.

On the downside, however, people are less likely to indulge in spontaneous behaviour, such as acting the giddy goat at a party, if they believe it will be all over social media the next day, the next minute. Many young people enjoy performing to camera when all set and ready to project a controlled image of themselves but more generally young people are often very restrained in their behaviour these days, not just because they are forever transfixed by their smartphone but because they are terrified of appearing on that smartphone making a fool of themselves, images posted on Facebook, Instagram, and X courtesy of so-called friends. These days, for every person who loses their temper in the street or embarrasses themselves in some other way, ten people will whip out their phone and film the incident, condemning that person to the shame of losing their temper in the street ad infinitum on You Tube. Privacy ain't what is used to be.

In the mode of for-itself, the self is precisely not an object. It is a surpassing negation of being that is founded upon a being that it is not. It is not in the world as objects are but as a transcendence. Borrowing the terminology of Heidegger, as employed in his major work *Being and Time*, Sartre refers to this mode of being as *being-in-the-world*. Being-in-the-world refers to a person's being for himself as 'the being which causes there to be a world by projecting itself beyond the world towards its own possibilities' (*Being and Nothingness*, p. 81).

For himself, a person is not a thing alongside other things. He is not *in* being. Rather, he is that which freely transcends being towards the future. Being-in-the-world refers to the transcendent aspect of his being. The transcendent or transcending person is the person who is not currently pinned down by the look of the Other or his belief that he is being looked at by the Other.

The self, however, has another mode of being that Sartre, again following Heidegger, refers to as *being-in-the-midst-of-the-world*. Being-in-the-midst-of-the-world refers to a person's presence in the world as an object among other objects. Here, his free transcendence is transcended by the Other and he becomes a thing alongside other things.

He is still his possibilities, but these possibilities are now a given fact for the Other. They belong also to the Other and are subject to the Other's judgements. This mode of being corresponds to a person's being-for-others and is realised when he experiences himself as looked at and seen by the Other, or when he regards himself from the point of view of the Other.

Sartre argues that when a person experiences himself as seen by the Other, he immediately ceases to be a transcendent *subject*, a pure point of view upon the world, and becomes instead an *object* in the midst of the world seen from the point of view of the Other. To experience himself as an object for the Other is to experience the Other as a subject. It is this direct and unmediated experience of himself as an object for the Other's subjectivity that reveals the Other to him as Other.

He experiences the Other through the immediate negation of his own transcendent subjectivity by the transcendent subjectivity of the Other. To experience the Other is for a person to exist his own being as a *transcendence transcended*. 'The Other as a look is only that — my transcendence transcended' (*Being and Nothingness*, p. 287).

Returning to the example of the spy at the keyhole. So long as the spy is not caught in the act, he remains a transcendence. That is, he perpetually transcends the meaning of his act. 'Since I am what I am not and since I am not what I am — I cannot even define myself as truly *being* in the process of listening at doors. I escape this provisional definition of myself by means of all my transcendence' (*Being and Nothingness*, pp. 283–84).

Even later on when he reflects upon his deed, he is not forced to identify himself with it. 'I am not really a voyeur,' he might say to himself. 'What I did was simply an aberration. Besides, the me that I am now cannot be held responsible for past conduct. Already, I am no longer the person I was.'

Such reasoning, however, such bad faith, is far more difficult to indulge in, though not impossible, if he is caught in the act. If he is caught in the act, he is no longer entirely free to determine the meaning or lack of meaning of his act, for in a very real sense he is no longer in possession of its meaning. As a transcendence, he escapes the meaning of his act. As a transcendence transcended, the meaning of his act escapes him and is lost to him. Suddenly, it belongs to the Other. The Other's possession of the meaning of his act is the negation of his capacity to freely interpret himself. Like Garcin beneath the stern appraisal of Inez, or the Autodidact confronted by the disgust of the people at the library, or Mathieu before the disappointment of Marcelle, his freedom is enslaved by the freedom of the Other.

A judgement is the transcendental act of a free being. Thus being-seen constitutes me as a defenceless being for a freedom which is not my freedom. It is in this sense that we can consider ourselves as 'slaves' in so far as we appear to the Other. . . . I am a slave to the degree that my being is dependent at the centre of a freedom which is not mine and which is the very condition of my being. In so far as I am the object of values which come to qualify me without my being able to act on this qualification or even to know it, I am enslaved. (*Being and Nothingness*, p. 291)

A person's being-for-others is very much a being that he is, but he is it over there, for the Other, in so far as the Other is free to interpret and evaluate his actions as he sees fit. A person's being-for-others constitutes a whole range of 'his' possibilities, but they are alienated possibilities. They are not possibilities that he maintains and controls through his own transcendence but possibilities fixed by the transcendence of the Other.

I grasp the Other's look at the very centre of my *act* as the solidification and alienation of my own possibilities. In fear or in anxious or prudent anticipation, I perceive that these possibilities which I *am* and which are the condition of my transcendence are given also to another, given as about to be transcended in turn by his own possibilities. (*Being and Nothingness*, pp. 286–87)

To be transcended by the transcendence of the Other is to be *in danger*, in so far as I am reduced to the instrument of a will which is not my own, in so far as I am subject to possibilities which are not mine, and in so far as I am constituted as a means to ends of which I am ignorant. 'This danger is not an accident but the permanent structure of my being-for-others' (*Being and Nothingness*, p. 291). Sartre could not be clearer; being-for-others is *danger*. The Other is always dangerous. Keep in mind, however, that a little danger is not always a bad thing and certainly a thrill.

Shame is one way in which being-for-others is revealed existentially. Alongside shame can be listed such related phenomena as guilt, embarrassment, and paranoia. However, being-for-others is not limited to these unpleasant states of being. Being-for-others also accounts for pleasant states such as being proud or feeling flattered. Pleasure is gained here precisely because a person makes himself an object for the Other. In making himself an object for the Other, he enjoys relinquishing responsibility for his free transcendence, a responsibility that may well be a source of anguish. He may well also take pleasure in reflecting on the pleasing object that he is for the Other, a pleasing physical object or the locus of pleasing achievements and virtues.

Sartre even argues (*Being and Nothingness*, Pt. 3, Ch. 3) that the basis of the masochist's pleasure is that he or she is a sex object for the Other. As will be seen in our next chapter, 'Concrete Relations With Others', being-for-others is an integral aspect of sexual relationships and sexual arousal.

In describing being-for-others, it is important to note that the look does not permanently render a person an object for the Other. It is not the case that when the Other has transcended her transcendence she remains a transcendence permanently transcended. A person can also become Other for the Other by recovering her transcendence, thereby reducing the Other to an object. This is certainly the case in genuine interpersonal relationships where a person will find the opportunity to recover her transcendence. If the Other is at all well disposed towards her, this recovery will be positively encouraged.

As already suggested, however, there are an increasing number of relationships in the modern world where a recovery of subjectivity appears to be impossible. In the relationship between a person and a CCTV camera, for example, a stable situation exists in which there is no possibility of returning the look. The transcendence of a person's transcendence by a camera cannot be reversed; a person cannot become Other for the camera-Other and so regain her transcendence. It is not possible to stare down a camera.

People were, of course, publicly and permanently shamed long before modern, digital mass communication technology emerged, but today such shaming is far more common because of the pervasiveness of social media. The ruthless things people say *en masse* about a person on social media, often in response to something judged to be inappropriate that person said themselves, either on social media or as reported on social media, can reduce that person to a permanently disgraced and humiliated object before the entire world. A relatively minor *faux pas*, or even the polite expression of a tenable but heterodox opinion, can instantly provoke the outrage of thousands of censorious keyboard warriors determined to permanently *cancel* the transcendence of whoever dared to offend or contradict them. So-called *cancel culture*, modern ostracism, aims at the complete destruction of a person's career and reputation, his or her reduction to a permanently despised object.

Everyone is at risk of having their transcendence transcended by cancel culture. Even people with a moralising zeal for cancellation have inadvertently fallen foul of the censoriousness of other neo-Puritans. As with all witch hunts, the accusing finger is fickle and can abruptly point at anyone, even those who pride themselves on their political correctness. Douglas Murray, in his book, *The Madness of Crowds: Gender, Race and Identity*, gives the example of *Vox* writer David Roberts who tweeted, surely with some justification, about 'sedentary, heart-diseased, fast-food gobbling, car-addicted' Americans negatively judging destitute refugees, only to find himself accused by those who usually agreed with him of 'suburbo-phobia', of 'fat-shaming' and holding 'problematic' views. Roberts spent the rest of the evening 'frantically trying to save his career in dozens of remedy tweets' that culminated in him 'apologising sincerely for only being "half woke" and blaming his upbringing' (*The Madness of Crowds*, p. 241).

The power of social media as a weapon wielded by the self-righteous and easily offended to look at, judge, shame, and ruin people is well summarised by Murray, who argues that we now live in 'A world where nobody knows who is allowed to give alleviation for offence but where everybody has a reputational incentive to take it and run with it. A world in which one of the greatest exertions of "power" is constantly exerted — the power to stand in judgement over, and potentially ruin, the life of another human being for reasons which may or may not be sincere' (*The Madness of Crowds*, p. 182). More on the problems social media can cause in our relations with others in my final chapter, 'Lowering the Temperature'.

Sartre characterises interpersonal relations as a ceaseless, irresolvable power struggle. Like Arthur Schopenhauer and Friedrich Nietzsche before him, he is of the opinion, as has already been said, that conflict is the essence of all human relationships and that this ceaseless internecine warfare is essentially hellish. Conflict may involve a struggle to dominate the transcendence of the Other and render it a transcendence transcended. This is the most familiar form of power struggle. Alternatively, for masochists, it will involve conflict over who gets to be dominated. More on masochism in the next chapter, 'Concrete Relations With Others'.

Reservations, qualifications, and opposing views to Sartre's position and the extent to which he is correct to claim that the essence of all relationships is conflict, are all explored in detail in Chapter 4: 'Is Hell Other People?'

Finally, some people assume that identifying the phenomenon of being-for-others solves the age-old problem of *proving* that other minds exist; that Sartre is claiming there must be other minds if a person can experience herself in the mode of being-for-others.

In fact, Sartre maintains that the abstract problem of other minds is impossible to solve. Even if he did not hold that the problem is unsolvable, however, he would nonetheless agree that the problem is unsolvable via an appeal to the phenomenon of being-for-others. To feel embarrassed, for instance, a person need only believe there is a mind behind an apparent judgemental look. She need not know there is a mind there, anymore than a motorist need know a speed camera is on in order to feel her driving is under scrutiny.

If, in order to experience embarrassment, a person need only suppose she is seen by another, then embarrassment can arise when that supposition is false. The existence of embarrassment cannot remove the problem of other minds, because it is possible that the belief in the Other that induces embarrassment could be false on every occasion. On the grounds that the supposed for-itself of the Other is not on principle an object of knowledge that experience can confirm or deny the existence of, Sartre holds that the problem of other minds is impossible to solve by any means whatsoever.

If the Other on principle and in its 'For-itself' is outside my experience, the probability of his existence as *Another Self* can never be either validated or invalidated; it can neither increase nor decrease, it cannot even be measured; it loses therefore its very being as probability and becomes a pure fictional conjecture. (*Being and Nothingness*, p. 274)

Rather than undertake to prove the existence of other minds, Sartre shows that the existence of other minds cannot be realistically doubted given a person's own experience of herself as embarrassed, ashamed, proud, and so on before the Other. He holds that although the existence of the Other cannot be proven, it is constantly suggested by those structures of a person's being that cannot be described purely in terms of her being-for-itself, but must be further described in terms of her being-for-others.

It is, in fact, only when we try to prove the reality of the Other that doubts about his existence start to worry us. 'If I do not conjecture about the Other, then, precisely, I affirm him' (*Being and Nothingness*, p. 275). Expressing the same thought as Sartre, Ludwig Wittgenstein writes: 'My attitude towards him is an attitude towards a soul. I am not of the *opinion* that he has a soul' (*Philosophical Investigations*, iv, p. 178).

Although sceptics are right to insist that the reality of the Other cannot be proven, even sceptics will repeatedly find themselves affirming the reality of the Other pre-reflectively in the way they behave in everyday situations and in the way they experience their own being as ashamed, offended, flattered, grateful, proud, and so on.

THE BODY

To fully understand Sartre's concept of being-for-others we need to explore his remarkable view of the human body as that which exists in one way for oneself and in another way for others or from the point of view of others.

To state the obvious, the human body is essential to the human condition. Therefore, any account of the human condition that overlooks the body is incomplete. Sartre's distinction between being-for-itself and being-for-others provides an ideal basis for considering the body because these two modes of being are the essential ontological features of the body, just as they are the essential ontological features of consciousness.

At the heart of Sartre's view of the body is his focus on the radical difference between the way a person's body exists for them and the way it exists for others:

> These two aspects of the body are on different and incommunicable levels of being, they cannot be reduced to one another. Being-for-itself must be wholly body and it must be wholly consciousness; it cannot be *united* with a body. Similarly, being-for-others is wholly body; there are no 'psychic phenomena' there to be united with the body. There is nothing *behind* the body. But the body is wholly 'psychic'. We must now proceed to study these two modes of being which we find for the body. (*Being and Nothingness*, p. 329)

Humans are objects. The body is an object among other objects, subject to the same physical laws as all objects. Heidegger refers to this material being as being-in-the-midst-of-the-world. This is a person's being considered from the point of view of other people. This, however, is only one of a person's ways of being; a way of being logically subsequent to the transcendent way of being Heidegger refers to as being-in-the-world. While a person is in the mode of being-in-the-world, her body is not an object for her.

Now, to say a person's body is not an object for her when she is in the mode of being-in-the-world, when she is a pure being-for-itself that transcends the world, is not to say her body mysteriously ceases to be an object from the point of view of others. That would amount to the bizarre claim that when she is in the mode of being-in-the-world her body somehow disappears or ceases to exist.

The claim is rather that when she is in the mode of being-in-the-world her body is in a certain sense invisible to her, that she is oblivious to her body as a thing. Although it happens to be the case that a person can see and touch her own body, it is not essential to her being-in-the-world that she can do this. It is quite possible to imagine a conscious creature that is unable to see or touch its own body that lives its whole life oblivious to the reality of its embodiment.

One could easily conceive of bodies which could not take any view on themselves; it even appears that this is the case for certain insects which, although provided with a differentiated nervous system and with sense organs, cannot employ this system and these organs to know themselves. (*Being and Nothingness*, p. 381)

Wittgenstein makes the same point as Sartre, simply taking the human eye as his famous example. 'Nothing *in the visual field* allows us to infer that it is seen by an eye' (*Tractatus Logico-Philosophicus*, 5.633).

Although a person can see her eye in a mirror, the fact that the eye in the mirror is the same eye that is seeing its reflection cannot be inferred directly from the eye in the mirror — the eye *in the visual field*. To infer that the eye in the mirror is the eye seeing its reflection a person must know about mirrors and the phenomenon of reflection. If a person had never encountered a mirror before, she would mistake her reflection for another person.

Even when a person knows from experience that the eye in the mirror is the eye seeing the eye in the mirror, the eye in the mirror and the eye seeing the eye in the mirror remain ontologically distinct. The eye in the mirror, though she knows it is her own and nobody else's, remains other. It is an object in the visual field. She sees it only as an object. She does not and cannot see her eye seeing.

Making essentially the same point as Wittgenstein, Sartre imagines a creature physically constituted such that one of its eyes can see its other eye:

Nothing prevents me from imagining an arrangement of the sense organs such that a living being could see one of his eyes while the eye which was seen was directing its glance upon the world. But it is to be noted that in this case again I am the *Other* in relation to my eye. I apprehend it as a sense organ constituted in the world in a particular way, but I cannot 'see the seeing'; that is, I cannot apprehend it in the process of revealing an aspect of the world to me. Either it is a thing among other things, or else it is that by which other things are revealed to me. (*Being and Nothingness* p. 328)

An eye seeing itself in a mirror or one eye seeing the other eye directly, both examples make the point that consciousness is not a psychic phenomenon magically attached to the body that can be observed deep within eyes in the form of a seen seeing. Rather, a person's body, as it is for the person herself, is wholly psychic; it *is* the for-itself.

The body is the immediate, inescapable situation of the for-it-self, a situation that the for-itself continually surpasses towards future situations. The body is a contingent yet indispensable given that the for-itself continually transcends. The for-itself is nevertheless continually reclaimed by the body because the body is the very possibility and ground of the transcendence of the for-itself. The for-itself is that which continually surpasses the body without ever being able to render the body finally and completely surpassed. 'The body is what I nihilate. It is the in-itself which is surpassed by the nihilating for-itself and which reapprehends the for-itself in this very surpassing' (*Being and Nothingness*, p. 333).

If the for-itself surpassed the body once and for all instead of being a continual surpassing of it, a continual transcending of it, the for-itself would immediately cease to be. This is because the body is the immediate and ever-present situation of the for-itself. For the for-itself, to be and to be situated are one and the same.

> The body is not distinct from the *situation* of the for-itself since for the for-itself, to exist and to be situated are one and the same; on the other hand, the body is identified with the whole world inasmuch as the world is the total situation of the for-itself and the measure of its existence. (*Being and Nothingness*, p. 333)

The body is the immediate and ever-present situation of the for-itself that the for-itself perpetually negates and surpasses. Existing as the surpassing negation of the body, the for-itself absolutely requires the body in order to realise itself as that which is nothing beyond the surpassing negation of the body.

In temporal terms, the for-itself, as a project towards the future, renders the body past or surpassed. The body, however, remains as an immediate past touching upon the present that the for-itself requires in order to continually launch itself towards the future. The for-itself requires the body as the future requires the past.

> Thus the body, since it is surpassed, is the Past. . . . In each project of the For-itself, in each perception the body is there; it is the immediate Past in so far as it still touches on the Present which flees it. This means that it is at once *a point of view and a point of departure* – a point of view, a point of departure which I *am* and which at the same time I surpass toward what I have to be. (*Being and Nothingness*, p. 350)

That the for-itself perpetually surpasses the body towards the future fulfilment of its projects has implications for the *instrumental status* of the body. Sartre's explanation of the instrumental status of a person's body, as it is for the person himself, focuses on the example of a person writing.

From the point of view of other people, a person writing utilises his hand as an instrument in order to utilise his pen as an instrument. For himself, however, he does not utilise his hand, he utilises his pen in a hand that is himself. His hand is surpassed towards the project of writing and as such is not an object-hand. His hand is not acted upon by the for-itself; it is the for-itself acting in the world.

> I do not apprehend *my* hand in the act of writing but only the pen which is writing; this means that I use my pen in order to form letters but not *my hand* in order to hold the pen. I am not in relation to my hand in the same utilizing attitude as I am in relation to the pen; I *am* my hand. That is, my hand is the arresting of references and their ultimate end. The hand is only the utilization of the pen. (*Being and Nothingness*, p. 347)

The human world can be conceived as an infinity of potential systems of instrumentality. For a particular, potential system of instrumentality to emerge as an actual system of instrumentality there must be an 'arresting of references' (*Being and Nothingness*, p. 347) to which the entire system refers. Any system of instrumentality, in order to be a system of instrumentality, must refer back to that for which it is a system. Now, in the case of the person writing, the hand is not an instrument in the system, but that to which an entire system of instrumentality refers. The system of instrumentality emerges by virtue of its orientation towards the hand in action, the for-itself in action. The hand in action arrests the system, determines it, orientates it, and gives it meaning. At the same time, the system gives meaning to the activity of the hand.

> The hand is at once the unknowable and non-utilisable term which the last instrument of the series indicates ('book to be read - characters to be formed on the paper – pen') and at the same time the orientation of the entire series (the printed book itself refers back to the hand). But I can apprehend it — at least in so far as it is acting — only as the perpetual, evanescent reference of the whole series. (*Being and Nothingness*, p. 347)

What Sartre says of the hand also applies to consciousness. A person's consciousness, which for other people is amid the instrumentality of the world, is for the person himself the meaning and orientation of the system of instrumentality that he discloses through his activity.

Just as the for-itself surpasses the hand and makes it vanish as an object, so it can surpass the tool the hand is manipulating and make it vanish, too. When a person has learnt to use a tool well, the tool is forgotten while in use and surpassed by the task for which it is being used. It exists in the manner of what Heidegger refers to as *ready-to-hand*. The tool becomes an extension of the person's embodied consciousness as he acts towards his goals.

> My body always extends across the tool which it utilizes: it is at the end of the cane on which I lean and against the earth; it is at the end of the telescope which shows me the stars. (*Being and Nothingness*, p. 349)

When a person prods meat with a fork in order to discover whether or not it is cooked, he feels the texture of the meat there at the end of the fork, at which moment he does not feel the fork in his hand. Tools tend only to remind a person of their independent existence when they fail, or when he fails to manipulate them correctly. That is, when they suddenly cease to be an instrument for him and instead present themselves as an obstacle. Here they present themselves in the mode of what Heidegger refers to as *present-at-hand.*

For instance, I only really notice the instrumental system I am using to type these words when it presents itself to me as obstinate due to malfunction or user error. When both it and myself are functioning correctly, I forget it as I forget my body. When the set-up is running well, I give no thought to my hands, the mouse, or the keyboard. Even the screen is essentially unseen as I gaze instead at what is *on* the screen. All the physical elements of this personal computer have ceased to be objects for me to become instead the transcended, surpassed moments of my overall project of writing. As the professor who first taught me about existentialism says, 'Whilst I am typing this I am not conscious of my fingers, but only of what I want to say. My fingers are not even the instruments I use to write with. . . . When the body is working efficiently it is not noticed' (Anthony Manser, *Sartre: A Philosophic Study*, p. 13).

Fittingly, I had just typed the words above when there was a power cut that instantly crashed my PC. I suddenly became painfully aware of the failed instrumental system, now a huge obstacle rudely opposed to me, which only a moment before had been smoothly facilitating my transcendence as though a part of me. The most recent changes and additions to the document I was working on were unsaved and so obliterated. Trying to remember unsaved changes and additions is bad enough when the instrumental system is working again, but on this occasion the computer absolutely refused to reboot when the power was restored.

Finding all ways of acting in the instrumental world barred by difficulty, I spontaneously and non-reflectively willed the transformation of the world from a world governed by causal processes to a world governed by *magic.* That is, a world where causal processes no longer apply, and it seems vaguely possible to achieve one's goals through the kind of desperate wishing that is losing one's temper and throwing things.

In *Sketch for a Theory of the Emotions*, Sartre argues that anger and other purely emotional behaviours are *magical behaviours* that we resort to when the world has become too difficult for us to deal with practically and instrumentally. Emotion, he says, is a spontaneous attitude to a situation that aims to magically transform that situation in such a way that it suddenly no longer presents an insurmountable difficulty or threat to the consciousness of the person concerned.

A younger more volatile me would have kicked the PC or even thrown it out the window, causing myself even more technical problems. Instead, I pathetically fumed around the house for a few minutes, swearing profusely and punching things that can take being punched, like cushions and walls.

Once I had calmed down and accepted for the millionth time in my life that losing one's temper is seldom useful, I switched my transcendence from being that of the writer striving to complete this book, to that of the amateur computer engineer repairing a PC without losing important files. The only solution, which took hours of painstaking, eye-straining work, was to return the machine to factory settings and reinstall all applications and personal files. This could only be done after the hard disk had been physically removed from the PC, important files copied and saved to another PC using a hard disk enclosure which I had to go out and buy, then fitted back into the PC.

When I finally got back to my Word document the next day — fortunately very little had been lost — I saw that document (this document) very much as the tiny tip of a vast pyramid of instrumentality. A system composed not only of my electronically complex PC, the culmination of centuries of human technological progress with its 'brain,' screen, keyboard, and mouse but also the power cables outside strung across the country on pylons all the way back to the power station, the highly trained power distribution engineers with their much bigger computers and so on and so on.

With my task of writing, I was orientating this entire industrial complex towards myself, making it refer back to me, arresting its references with my project. I was making my chosen transcendence entirely dependent upon national infrastructure without giving it a second thought, *until* it abruptly and shockingly ceased to be a ready-to-hand system of instrumentality *for me* and became instead uselessly and infuriatingly present-at-hand.

A person's body is her consciousness in the sense that she is not a passive awareness in the world but a being who *acts* towards the future by physically working through an endless series of tasks and projects. Her body is absorbed by her consciousness, although this form of words tends to suggest that consciousness and body are distinct phenomena that can exist separately but happen to be united. To say that consciousness is embodied is not to argue, as Descartes does in his *Meditations*, that consciousness happens to be carried around inside the body, but rather that embodiment is consciousness' only way of being-in-the-world. The existence of each and every embodied person is unnecessary, but given that a person exists, it is absolutely necessary that they be embodied.

> It [my body] is therefore in no way a contingent addition to my soul; on the contrary it is a permanent structure of my being and the permanent condition of possibility for my consciousness as consciousness of the world and as a transcendent project toward my future. (*Being and Nothingness*, p. 351)

Sartre's existentialism is anti-metaphysical. As such it rules out ghosts: disembodied consciousnesses. The for-itself is not transcendent in a metaphysical sense. Its transcendence is only the temporal transcendence of the immediate in-itself of the body and the particular situation of the body. No body, no transcendence. No transcendence, no being-for-itself.

To advance our main aim of understanding being-for-others, it is worth considering two criticisms that have been levelled against Sartre's view of the body. They both argue that Sartre's distinction between the body as it is for oneself and the body as it is for others is too sharp. In drawing such a sharp distinction, Sartre arguably misrepresents a person's relationship with his own body and underestimates the importance of embodiment in the experience of others as subjects.

The first criticism claims that Sartre misrepresents a person's relationship with his own body when he insists that in the transcendent mode of being a person is oblivious to his own body. Recall Sartre's example of the spy. According to Sartre, when the spy is engrossed in spying, he is a pure consciousness of things. It is only when the spy believes he is seen that he becomes aware of his body. This is in keeping with Sartre's general view that a person's embodied self is disclosed to him through others.

> The unreflective consciousness does not apprehend the *person* [its own embodied self] directly or as *its* object; the person is presented to consciousness *in so far as the person is an object for the Other.* (*Being and Nothingness*, p. 284)

Now, some critics have argued against Sartre that it is not only via others that a person experiences his embodied self. There is also a *non-thetic* consciousness of embodiment that does not require others. A continuous general awareness of embodiment that falls short of the direct self-conscious focus on embodiment referred to as *thetic* consciousness of embodiment. As with driving a car, we need not be and are mostly not *thetically* conscious of ourselves as driving, thetically conscious of the various purposeful movements of our limbs and so on. We are mostly musing on other matters as we roll along. But we are *non-thetically* conscious, generally aware, that we are driving, otherwise we would be completely unaware that we are driving, an oblivious state likely to have serious consequences. Sartre denies *non-thetic* consciousness of embodiment when he writes, 'I am for myself only as I am a pure reference to the Other' (*Being and Nothingness*, p. 284).

As Sartre's critics point out, however, the presence of non-thetic consciousness of embodiment is strongly suggested by Sartre's own example of the spy. Before the spy becomes ashamed, he is jealous. When jealous, the spy is not, according to Sartre, aware of his body, because jealousy, unlike shame, is not jealousy before someone. A person is jealous of someone, not jealous before someone. Sartre's critics agree that jealousy is not jealousy before someone. They do not agree, however, that prior to the advent of his shame, while he is only jealous, the spy is oblivious to his body.

Even though jealousy is not before someone, it reveals my body to me as much as shame does. Just as when a person is ashamed, he experiences himself as having a thumping heart, clammy palms, and a flushed face; when he is jealously spying on his unfaithful beloved he experiences himself as having a stealthy posture, bated breath, a sinking, despairing feeling in his stomach and a desperate, seething anger in every muscle. The key point is that regardless of whether or not emotional states are before someone, every emotional state discloses our embodied self to us.

So long as a person is conscious, his body is always made known to him one way or another because every conscious experience has its accompanying bodily state of which the person is immediately and pre-reflectively aware.

Kathleen Wider, in her book *The Bodily Nature of Consciousness*, even argues that pre-reflective bodily awareness is the basis of consciousness. In Sartre's view, without non-thetic consciousness the for-itself cannot be conscious because to be conscious is to be conscious of being so. For Wider, this non-thetic consciousness is fundamentally bodily awareness; what she calls *bodily self-consciousness*. Consciousness, she argues, is rooted in the presence of the body to itself as presence to the world.

> The body must be present to itself in being present to the world. So there must be a kind of consciousness of the body, what I will call bodily self-consciousness, and this must form part of our awareness of the world. The most basic form of self-consciousness must be bodily awareness. (*The Bodily Nature of Consciousness*, p. 115)

As to the second criticism, Sartre's one-time close friend Maurice Merleau-Ponty argues in his 1945 book *Phenomenology of Perception* that Sartre undervalues the importance of embodiment in the experience of the Other as a subject. As we saw, Sartre claims that the Other must exist for me, as I must exist for the Other, as either transcendent subject or transcended object. The Other exists for me as a subject only when he transcends my transcendence and reduces me to an object.

The problem with this account, Merleau-Ponty argues, is that it overlooks the fact that the Other exists for me most often as an *embodied consciousness*. I am mostly aware of the Other as a subject, not because experiencing my own embodiment indicates a subject who has succeeded in transcending me and reducing me to an object, but because I experience a living, acting, embodied subject before me: a subject incarnate. I do not experience him either as an Other or as a body; his Otherness and his embodiment are one and I experience him as such.

To be aware of another person as angry, for example, is not only to be aware that he poses a threat to me; it is to be aware of him as embodying anger. His anger is not reducible to his bodily state in so far as his anger is inspired by and directed towards something external to his body, but neither does his bodily state merely indicate his anger. There is a very real sense in which his red face, clenched fists, and rolling eyeballs are his anger. If I witness these bodily states, I witness his anger, not the outward signs of a private, subjective anger taking place within him.

Recall what was said earlier about the intentional object of hatred. The appearances of hatred, both physical and behavioural (the two are closely bound), are not manifestations of an underlying hatred *in itself*; they are the hatred. Regarding anger, Sartre acknowledges as much when he writes:

> These frowns, this redness, this stammering, this slight trembling of the hands, these downcast looks which seem at once timid and threatening — these do not *express* anger; they *are* the anger. But this point must be clearly understood. In itself a clenched fist is nothing and means nothing. But also we never perceive a *clenched fist*. We perceive a man who in a certain situation clenches his fist. (*Being and Nothingness*, p. 370)

Alas, the kind of valuable insight into the meaning and significance of embodied consciousness revealed in the above passage does not sway Sartre from his problematic insistence that a person's experience of another person as a subject inevitably involves him experiencing himself as an object for that person. Sartre insists on treating what is only one way of experiencing others — others as an objectifying threat — as though it were the only possible way people can, over time, experience one another as subjects.

CHAPTER 3

Concrete Relations with Others

OUR ACCOUNT OF BEING-FOR-OTHERS HAS SO FAR MOSTLY GIVEN THE bare bones of the phenomenon, a generalised account, but really there is no such thing as being-for-others in general. Being-for-others exists entirely in the myriad cases of being-for-others that occur, the countless concrete instances of actual, diverse interpersonal encounters and interactions. As Sartre is fond of pointing out, there are no universal essences beyond the ever-increasing sum of particular cases; there is nothing beyond the existential series.

Hence, to fully understand Sartre's concept of being-for-others, we need to consider what he calls *concrete relations with others*, the personal, tangible, existential dynamics of intimacy. In one of the most vigorous, brilliant, and fascinating sections of *Being and Nothingness* (pp. 383–52), Sartre considers the nature of being-for-others in specific, concrete situations such as romantic and sexual relationships. It is worth exploring in detail his intriguing thoughts on what is sometimes called *sexistentialism*, both for their own sake and because further light will be shed on our abiding question: Is hell other people?

In Sartre's examination of concrete relations with others he mainly focuses on the extremes, the most intense forms of human interaction: love, sexual desire, sadism, masochism, and hate. There is undoubtedly much to be learnt about the human condition from exploring these fascinating phenomena, and much of what Sartre says about them is surely correct. Arguably, however, he is inclined to make them too representative, too much the model of *all* human interaction, largely overlooking the myriad everyday human contacts that are far less con-flictual, far calmer and friendlier, far more companionable, sociable, mutually supportive, and fun.

To be fair, Sartre closes his lengthy analysis of the stormy dynamics of concrete relations with others by considering *being-with* (*Mitsein*), the phenomenon of *being-with-others*, the phenomenon of *we*. Here he recognises that there are situations in which a person is in *community* with the Other rather than in *conflict* with him. *Being-with-others* is explored later in this chapter, while the viability of Sartre's primarily conflict-focused thesis of human relationships is the main concern of our next chapter.

Finally, in introducing this chapter it is important to point out that Sartre's account of romantic and sexual relations in *Being and Nothingness* is largely heteronormative. He talks mainly of relations between a man and a woman. I have largely followed him in this convention for no other reason than ease and consistency of explanation, usually having the term 'the lover' refer to a man, and the term 'the beloved' refer to a woman. It is vital to note, however, that almost whenever a couple is referred to in this chapter, the lover could alternatively be a woman and the beloved could alternatively be a man, or both lover and beloved could alternatively be men, or both lover and beloved could alternatively be women. It does not matter; the interpersonal dynamics Sartre explores remain the same be the romantic and sexual pairing heterosexual, homosexual, or lesbian. As I say in so many words towards the end of this chapter, homosexuality allows for the full range of interpersonal perceptions that Sartre considers, or as the philosopher Thomas Nagel puts it, 'Nothing rules out the full range of interpersonal perceptions between persons of the same sex' (*Mortal Questions*, p. 50).

LOVE

At the heart of Sartre's examination of concrete relations with others is his analysis of the phenomenon of *love*. Sartre's analysis of love focuses on romantic or erotic love, what is often called 'being *in* love', as in that familiar distinction we often come across in movies and novels, 'I still love him, but I'm no longer *in* love with him.'

Sartre has little or nothing to say about other phenomena that are also often referred to as love of another, such as strong, platonic affection for family, friends, children, and animals. As to love of chocolate and other such treats we claim to love, forget it; such love does not feature in Sartre's analysis. Some people may think they have a passionate, even romantic relationship with chocolate, they may dream of those cloying chocolate worlds presented to us by advertisers, but as far as I am aware, nobody ever threw themselves in the river for loss of a bar of Cadbury's Dairy Milk.

As we know from common experience, our own and that of others, being in love is a complex emotional roller coaster. All our fickle feelings are bound up with the beloved and their fickle feelings for us. The very value of our existence moment by moment is dependent on how they look at us, what we read from and into their looks, what we estimate their current judgements of us to be and so on.

To be in love with someone and to be loved by them is the ultimate feeling, the most sought-after state, the one that makes us feel most truly alive and at the centre of everything. Yet love is fraught with dire risks to our sense of well-being, to the value we place on ourselves, perhaps for the rest of our lives. Being in love is heaven on earth. It is also the risk of a kind of hell on earth, searing flames of rejection all too slowly subsiding to the embers of a painful yearning that can glow for a lifetime. As the poets and singers are fond of telling us, only love can break your heart. Sartre, for his part, is no less gloomy, arguing that the ideal of romantic love, perfect unity with the Other, is doomed to failure.

Romantic love is of course essentially other-related, and it is very much as an aspect of being-for-others that Sartre explores the phenomenon. Zeroing in on the million-dollar question regarding the phenomenon of romantic love, he asks, 'Why does the lover want to be *loved*?' (*Being and Nothingness*, p. 388). To understand why it is that the lover wants to be loved is to understand what love is.

The lover is not satisfied with the mere physical possession of the Other. The lover may have contrived to have the Other physically close to him at all times, locked up in his castle tower or down in his castle dungeon, but if the lover does not possess the *consciousness* of the Other, if the Other does not choose to direct her consciousness towards the lover in a particular way, the lover will be dissatisfied.

In desiring to possess the consciousness of the Other, the lover does not want to *enslave* the Other. He does not want to possess a robot-thing whose apparent passions flow mechanically in his direction, but rather a genuine Other who chooses at each moment to be possessed by him. The lover wants to be loved because he wants to possess the *freedom* of the Other, not as an enslaved freedom that would no longer be a freedom but as a freedom that remains free even though it is possessed because it continually *chooses* to be possessed:

> The total enslavement of the beloved kills the love of the lover. The end is surpassed; if the beloved is transformed into an automaton, the lover finds himself alone. Thus the lover does not desire to possess the beloved as one possesses a thing; he demands a special type of appropriation. He wants to possess a freedom as freedom. (*Being and Nothingness*, p. 389)

Sartre takes an example from the novel *In Search of Lost Time* by Marcel Proust. Marcel installs Albertine in his home, makes her financially dependent on him and is able to possess her physically at any hour of the day. Yet, 'Through her consciousness Albertine escapes Marcel even when he is at her side, and that is why he knows relief only when he gazes on her while she sleeps. It is certain then that the lover wishes to capture a "consciousness"' (*Being and Nothingness*, p. 388).

Various characters in Shakespeare's *A Midsummer Night's Dream* fall in 'love' as the result of a magic love-juice from the flower love-in-idleness (wild pansy) dropped on their eyes by the fairy Puck, but as in all such fairytales this chemically and psychologically induced false love is contrasted with real or true love, with love that is freely chosen. Titania: 'My Oberon, what visions have I seen! Methought I was enamoured of an ass' (*A Midsummer Nights' Dream*, Act 4, Scene 1).

It is important to the lover that the choice to be possessed be constantly renewed by the beloved. The lover will be dissatisfied with a love that continues to be given through loyalty to an oath, for example. Lovers are deeply insecure and constantly demand pledges of love, but as Sartre points out in this excellent passage, lovers are nonetheless irritated by pledges because they want love to be determined by nothing but the freedom of the Other:

> Who would be content with a love given as pure loyalty to a sworn oath? Who would be satisfied with the words, 'I love you because I have freely engaged myself to love you and because I do not wish to go back on my word.' Thus the lover demands a pledge, yet is irritated by a pledge. He wants to be loved by a freedom but demands that this freedom as freedom should no longer be free. He wishes that the Other's freedom should determine itself to become love — and this not only at the beginning of the affair but at each instant — and at the same time he wants this freedom to be captured *by itself*, to turn back upon itself, as in madness, as in a dream, so as to will its own captivity. (*Being and Nothingness*, p. 389)

The lover may not even want to deliberately seduce the beloved into loving him, through kind, attentive and romantic gestures, because a love that is *brought about* by him is a love determined by something other than the freedom of the beloved. Hence the lover may even be inclined to test the love of the beloved with challenging, 'difficult to love' behaviour. Ideally, the lover wants to be loved by a freedom that is no longer free, not because this freedom has been enslaved or causally determined but because it continually wills its own imprisonment, perhaps against its own better judgement.

In wanting to possess the beloved, the lover wants to be nothing less than the whole world for the beloved. He wants to be the meaning and purpose of the beloved's world, that around which and for which the beloved's entire world is ordered. The lover wants to be an object for the beloved, but not the object that he is for those who do not love him, an object alongside other objects, a mere *being-in-the-midst-of-the-world*, but rather a sacred object that symbolises an entire world in which the freedom of the beloved consents to lose itself.

The lover does not demand that he be the *cause* of this radical modification of freedom but that he be the unique and privileged occasion of it. In fact he could not want to be the cause of it without immediately submerging the beloved in the midst of the world as a tool which can be transcended. That is not the essence of love. On the contrary, in Love the Lover wants to be 'the whole World' for the beloved. (*Being and Nothingness*, p. 389)

The lover wants to be chosen as the limit of the beloved's transcendence. He wants to be that towards which the beloved transcends the entire world, without ever being that which the beloved transcends. Ultimately, the lover wants to cease being a contingent and indeterminate being subject to his own shifting evaluations and the evaluations of those who transcend him, and instead assume for himself the absolute, un-transcendable value he believes he would have for the beloved if the beloved chose to truly love him.

According to Sartre, romantic love is doomed to fail because what the lover wants is unachievable. It is impossible for the lover to possess the freedom of the beloved while the beloved remains free, because as soon as the beloved loves the lover she experiences him as a subject and herself as an object confronted by his subjectivity. The lover wants to possess the transcendence of the beloved as a transcendence while at the same time transcending it, but in taking possession of the transcendence of the beloved he will inevitably negate it and reduce it to a facticity, a mere inert *given* of his situation. Transcendence is always the transcendence of facticity and the lover can only transcend the beloved as a facticity and not as a transcendence.

Moreover, in seeking to take possession of the transcendence of the beloved, the lover runs the risk of being possessed by the transcendence of the beloved and being reduced to a facticity. The lover wants the freedom of the beloved to elevate him to an absolute value, but he is playing with fire in that the freedom of the beloved may suddenly look upon him with indifference or contempt and reduce him to an object among other objects. Maybe an object far less valued than the furniture surrounding him, because, unlike the table and chairs, he is despised.

It is important to stress that the lover is Other for the Other and that everything that has been said of the lover applies to the Other as well. The lover desires the Other to love him and thereby make him an absolute value. But if the Other loves the lover, it is only because she wants him to make her an absolute value. Conflict — the essence of all human relationships according to Sartre — is inevitable.

For Sartre, to love is to want to be loved. So when one person loves another he does not in fact want, as the Other wants him to, to make the Other an absolute value. Instead, his love consists in wanting the Other to make him an absolute value. Sartre wisely notes that love is the demand to be loved. The lover 'is the captive of his very demand since love is the demand to be loved' (*Being and Nothingness*, p. 397). As a pure demand, love can never supply what is demanded of it.

Not surprisingly, these themes, the convolutions of the fraught dialectical dance of romantic love, are further exposed by an exploration of the psycho-physical dynamics of sexual desire.

SEXUAL DESIRE

Sartre argues that sexual desire is not simply sexual instinct. A person could not experience sexual desire (or anything else) if he did not have a body, and sexual desire as we all know very much involves the body, but sexual desire is not generated by the body, or more specifically the sex organs, as a demand for sex, orgasm, or procreation.

Viewed objectively, sexual desire appears as an appetite like hunger that seeks satisfaction from a particular object. From the internal perspective of being-for-itself, however, sexual desire differs radically from hunger. Hunger is a physiological urge that the for-itself becomes conscious of. Hunger is *for* consciousness, in so far as to be hungry is to be conscious of being hungry, but unlike sexual desire, hunger is not a state or condition of consciousness.

Unlike hunger, sexual desire is a radical modification of consciousness that troubles it and defines it to its core. Sexual desire renders our entire consciousness 'troubled water' (*Being and Nothingness*, p. 409). Just as troubled water, as opposed to calm water, is water 'given as a clogging of the water by itself' (*Being and Nothingness*, p. 409), so sexual desire is a clogging of consciousness by itself. Sexual desire is consciousness itself 'hungry' for a certain relationship with the body of the Other that will bring about a certain relationship with its own body.

Sexual desire is an attempt to make the Other exist as flesh for me and for herself. In Sartre's terms, sexual desire is an attempt to realise the *incarnation* of the body of the Other as flesh (*Being and Nothingness*, pp. 412–13). But, the critic will ask, isn't the Other already incarnated, given that the Other is made of flesh?

Certainly, the Other's body is made of flesh, yet it is not primarily as an object that the Other exists for herself or for others. The Other's flesh is usually concealed, not only by her clothes but by her movements. Even a person who is naked can conceal their flesh as mere flesh with movements that are sufficiently graceful. I will return to the theme of grace shortly. The Other, for herself, is not flesh but a being in action who transcends her body towards her possibilities. Sexual desire aims to divest the Other's body of its actions, its transcendence, and its possibilities so as to reveal the inertia and passivity of the Other's body to them and to the one who desires them. This divesting and revealing is achieved through the sexual *caress* which, through the pleasure it gives the Other, 'causes the Other to be born as flesh for me and for herself' (*Being and Nothingness*, p. 412).

Sartre was an enthusiastic student of the caress. By his own admission, he liked to spend hours in bed with women, caressing and fondling them all over and familiarising himself with the individual charms and peculiarities of their bodies. He also liked to gaze lingeringly at their physical beauty, which he identified closely with their sensibility. He described himself to de Beauvoir, as she notes, as 'more a masturbator of women than a copulator' (*Adieux: A Farewell to Sartre*, p. 302). His main pleasure lay in ardently and expertly caressing and embracing women rather than in penetration.

Sartre notes that it is possible for a person to caress the Other with his eyes alone. To look at the Other with desire is to caress her and seek to incarnate her as flesh. The person who caresses does so to reveal the Other as flesh, but he does not want his caressing to take hold of her or act upon her. Instead, he wants his caressing to be a passive placing of

84

his body against the Other's body. He wants the very studied gentleness and passivity of his caresses to reveal his own passive flesh to the Other and to himself.

> The caress is designed to cause the Other's body to be born, through pleasure, for the Other — and for myself — as a *touched* passivity in such a way that my body is made flesh in order to touch the Other's body with its own passivity; that is, by caressing itself with the Other's body rather than by caressing her. This is why amorous gestures have a languidness which could almost be said to be deliberate; it is not a question so much of taking hold of a part of the Other's body as of placing one's own body against the Other's body. (*Being and Nothingness*, p. 412)

So, the lover desires to caress the Other's body in such a way that in caressing the Other's body he is caressed by the Other's body. The person who caresses seeks to incarnate the Other as flesh so as to incarnate himself as flesh, and to incarnate himself as flesh so as to incarnate the Other as flesh. He makes the Other enjoy his flesh through her flesh so as to compel her to be her flesh and so on. This is what Sartre famously calls '*double reciprocal incarnation*' (*Being and Nothingness*, p. 413). Ultimately, sexual desire is the desire for double reciprocal incarnation.

To achieve double reciprocal incarnation would be to possess the Other's transcendent freedom as an incarnated consciousness by possessing the flesh that the Other's transcendent freedom has determined itself to be. Like romantic love, with which it is closely associated, sexual desire aims at the unachievable possession of the Other's transcendence as a transcendence rather than as a transcendence transcended:

> Such is the impossible ideal of desire: to possess the Other's transcendence as pure transcendence and at the same time as *body*, to reduce the Other to his simple *facticity* because he is then in the midst of my world but to bring it about that this facticity is a perpetual appresentation of his nihilating transcendence. (*Being and Nothingness*, p. 416)

Sartre, as we have seen, made an in-depth study of Husserl. 'Appresentation' is a key term in the phenomenology of Husserl, referring to the capacity a presentation to consciousness may have to motivate the experiential positing of something else as present besides the actual presentation. Sartre is saying that the lover wants the presentation of the facticity of the beloved's body to also be the continual presentation of their transcendent freedom.

According to Sartre, the ultimate goal of sexual desire, double reciprocal incarnation, is impossible to achieve. A person cannot at the same time incarnate the Other's body and be incarnated by the Other's body. If the Other's body incarnates his body, he will become lost in the enjoyment of his own incarnation. His own incarnation will become the object of his consciousness, and he will neglect and forget the incarnation of the Other.

Sexual desire is the desire for a mutual caress, but caressing, for all its striving after the mutual caress, remains touching and being touched. As the old saying goes, 'There is always one who kisses and one who is kissed.'

Sartre argues that it is, not least, sexual pleasure itself that brings about the failure of the *ideal* of sexual desire. The more a person feels sexual pleasure in the incarnation of his own body by the Other, the less he will focus on his desire for the Other. In focusing on his own sexual pleasure he will lose sight of the Other as Other and no longer strive to possess her as an incarnated consciousness.

The failure of sexual desire to achieve its ultimate goal of double reciprocal incarnation almost inevitably leads to the emergence of some level of *sadomasochism*. Sartre describes *sadism* and *masochism* as 'two reefs on which desire may founder — whether I surpass my troubled disturbance toward an appropriation of the Other's flesh or, intoxicated with my own trouble, pay attention only to my flesh and ask nothing of the Other except that he should be the look which aids me in realising my flesh' (*Being and Nothingness*, p. 426). Indeed, sexual desire founders so often and readily upon these two reefs that 'normal' sexuality is, Sartre argues, 'sadistic-masochistic' (*Being and Nothingness*, p. 426).

With particular regard to sadism, as soon as a person neglects his own incarnation and focuses on the incarnation of the Other, as soon as he surpasses the facticity of his own body towards the possibility of acting on the Other, of *taking* the Other, he has already oriented himself in the direction of sadism.

With particular regard to masochism, as soon as a person neglects the incarnation of the Other and focuses on his own incarnation, as soon as he wants to be constituted as a facticity for the transcendence of the Other, to be acted on by the Other and *taken* by the Other, he has already oriented himself in the direction of masochism.

Let us consider Sartre's views on sadism and masochism more closely.

SADISM

The phenomenon of sadism emerges when sexual desire inevitably fails to achieve its unachievable goal of double reciprocal incarnation. A person whose sexual desire is not sadistic wants to exist as flesh for himself and for the Other; he also wants the Other to exist as flesh for herself and for him. In short, he wants to achieve a double reciprocal incarnation of the flesh. The sadist no longer wants to achieve a double reciprocal incarnation or had no desire to do so in the first place, being incapable of that desire or having an aversion to it. The true sadist has a horror of his own incarnation, argues Sartre, 'a horror of troubled disturbance *for himself* and considers it a humiliating state' (*Being and Nothingness*, p. 421).

The sadist refuses to be incarnated while at the same time he seeks with a cold, dry, and barren passion to possess the incarnation of the Other. He completely denies his own facticity in his efforts to transcend the transcendence of the Other and expose and possess the facticity of the Other.

> The sadist has reapprehended his body as a synthetic totality and centre of action; he has resumed the perpetual flight from his own facticity. He experiences himself in the face of the Other as pure transcendence. (*Being and Nothingness*, pp. 420–21)

As the sadist refuses to incarnate the Other through his own incarnation, he must incarnate the Other by using them as a tool. To make a tool of the Other is to make an object of the Other, and it is as an 'instrumental-object' that the sadist wants the Other to realise her incarnation.

Thus sadism is a refusal to be incarnated and a flight from all facticity and at the same time an effort to get hold of the Other's facticity. But as the sadist neither can nor will realise the Other's incarnation by means of his own incarnation, as due to this very fact he has no resource except to treat the Other as an instrumental-object, he seeks to utilize the Other's body as a tool to make the Other realise an incarnated existence. (*Being and Nothingness*, p. 421)

Sartre, in his description of sadism, contrasts the graceful with the ungraceful or obscene. A graceful body that has poise and moves with ease and precision is perceived as an instrument that manifests a person's freedom. A person who is naked conceals the facticity and obscenity of their flesh if their movements are sufficiently graceful. An ungraceful or obscene body, on the other hand, one that lacks poise and is awkward and laboured in its movements, is perceived as an instrument that manifests a person's facticity. An ungraceful, naked body is, so to speak, more naked and obscene than a graceful naked body for not being clothed in grace.

The supreme coquetry and the supreme challenge of grace is to exhibit the body unveiled with no clothing, with no veil except grace itself. The most graceful body is the naked body whose acts enclose it with an invisible visible garment. (*Being and Nothingness*, p. 422)

It is the obscene, graceless, instrumental-object body that manifests facticity that the sadist desires to incarnate, rather than the graceful body that manifests freedom. Sadism aims to destroy grace because it is a manifestation of the Other's freedom. Sadism triumphs in the destruction of grace, the destruction of freedom. The more ungraceful the sadist can render the body of the Other through the violence and pain he inflicts, and the humiliating, obscene postures he forces the Other to adopt, the more he will feel that he has enslaved the Other's freedom.

Pain is a facticity that invades consciousness. It is through the pain that the sadist inflicts on the Other that he forces the Other to identify herself with the facticity of her flesh. The sadist uses violence to force the Other into an 'incarnation through pain' (*Being and Nothingness*, p. 421). In pain the Other is incarnated for herself and for the sadist. The sadist enjoys the possession of the Other's flesh that he achieves through violence while also enjoying his own 'non-incarnation'.

> [Sadism] enjoys its own non-incarnation. It *wants* the non-reciprocity of sexual relations, it enjoys being a free appropriating power confronting a freedom captured by flesh. That is why the sadist wants to make the flesh present to the Other's consciousness *differently*. He wants to make it present by treating the Other as an instrument; he makes it present in pain. (*Being and Nothingness*, p. 421)

In his state of non-incarnation, the sadist is a free transcendence, he is all action, he feels powerful as he skilfully brings instruments of torture to bear upon the body of the Other in order to capture the freedom of the Other in pained flesh. The consciousness of the Other is ensnared in pain, and as the sadist is the cause of this pain, he feels he has ensnared the freedom of the Other. Sadism, however, like romantic love, sexual desire, and masochism, like all attempts to gain possession of the freedom of the Other, is doomed to failure.

The sadist wants to incarnate the flesh of the Other by using the Other as an instrument, but to apprehend the body as an instrument is very different from apprehending it as flesh. Instruments refer to other instruments, to systems of instrumentality, they are utilizable, they have potential, they indicate the future. Flesh revealed as flesh is an 'unutilizable facticity' (*Being and Nothingness*, p. 426) without potential; it is simply there in its contingency referring to nothing beyond itself. The sadist can utilize the flesh of the Other as an instrument to reveal flesh, but when the flesh *is* revealed in all its unutilizable facticity, suddenly no instrument remains for the sadist to possess through utilization.

The sadist strives for possession by utilization, but his very utilization of the flesh of the Other eventually incarnates flesh that cannot be utilized and, therefore, does not allow possession by utilization. The sadist realises his failure to possess the Other at the very moment he achieves complete mastery over the Other because in mastering the Other and reducing her to pained, contingent flesh, to a non-instrument, there is nothing left for him to utilize.

When the incarnation is achieved, when I have indeed before me a panting body, then I no longer know how to *utilize* this flesh. No goal can be assigned to it, precisely because I have effected the appearance of its absolute contingency. It is *there*, and it is there for *nothing*. (*Being and Nothingness*, p. 426)

The sadist could utilize the flesh of the Other to satisfy himself sexually, to achieve orgasm through intercourse and so on, but as this would involve the incarnation of his own flesh by the flesh of the Other it would not be sadism as defined. As noted, the non-incarnation of the flesh of the sadist is central to the phenomenon of sadism. In giving way to the desire for the incarnation of his own flesh he would cease to be sadistic. It is always possible that the project of sadism will be undermined by the emergence of desire within the sadist for the incarnation of his own flesh. 'Sadism is the failure of desire, and desire is the failure of sadism' (*Being and Nothingness*, pp. 426–27).

The project of sadism also fails because the freedom of the Other that the sadist strives to possess remains out of reach. The sadist's actions aim at recovering his being-for-others, but the more he acts upon the Other, torturing and inflicting pain, the more the Other slips away from him into her consciousness of being assaulted. The Other is not a being he has possessed but a being lost to him in her preoccupation with her own suffering.

The sadist discovers the failure of his sadism most acutely when the other looks at him and thereby transcends his transcendence. As a transcendence transcended, he experiences himself as an object for the subjectivity of the Other. The look of the Other alienates his freedom and reduces him to a being-in-the-midst-of-the-world. Suddenly, he is no longer even actively a sadist. 'Being-in-the-act-of-looking' is cancelled out, replaced by 'being-looked-at' (*Being and Nothingness*, p. 428). Unable, inevitably, to escape the inescapable circle, the sadist comes full circle. The mere gaze of the Other triumphs over all his sadistic cruelty, torture, and violence. 'This explosion of the Other's look in the world of the sadist causes the meaning and goal of sadism to collapse' (*Being and Nothingness*, p. 428).

Just as Sartre's war experiences made him interested in the theme of cowardice, so they made him interested in the relationship, the power struggle, between torturer and tortured. He explored this power struggle in *Men Without Shadows*, the play that followed *In Camera*. Completed in 1946 but set in 1944, *Men Without Shadows* considers the plight of a group of French Resistance fighters captured and tortured by forces loyal to the pro-German Vichy regime. You might be forgiven for thinking that there is not much of a power struggle in this relationship, that the power is all on the side of the torturer, and from a purely physical point of view that is largely true. Psychologically, however, the tortured person can still gain power and ascendency over the torturer.

If the purpose of the torture is to extract information, then the tortured person wins the battle of wills if he refuses to disclose information. But even if he discloses information, the tortured person can still look at the torturer and reduce him to an object, take the measure of what he is and is not, transcend his transcendence.

One character in *Men Without Shadows*, Lucie, is tortured and raped but does not crack. She becomes obsessed with her relationship with her torturers, even to the exclusion of her love for another Resistance fighter, Jean. Her only desire is to be tortured again, so she can once again transcend her torturers by shaming them with her silence and dignity. She says, 'All I want is for them to come for me again, and beat me, so I can keep silent again, and fool them and frighten them' (*Men Without Shadows*, Act 2, p. 214).

We have all seen films where a bully simply cannot wipe the defiant grin off the bloodstained face of his victim and, as a result, grows more and more angry, violent, and ridiculous. Though the bully is the one throwing the punches, there is a very real sense in which the victim, or so-called victim, maintains the upper hand. He maintains his dignity, his essential ascendency, while the bully is belittled by his own loss of dignity, his out-of-control temper and his thwarted desire to dominate.

There is an important sense in which a victim is not a victim if they refuse to accept and internalise their victimhood. This is why Big Brother's dominance of Winston Smith in George Orwell's *Nineteen Eighty-Four* is so shockingly absolute. Big Brother knows that true ascendency is not achieved by simply forcing a person's compliance. They must be broken within. They must genuinely surrender their will to the will of the Other. They must inwardly accept the dominance of the Other and moreover approve of it. The struggle the tyrant ultimately wants resolved in his favour is not his struggle with his rebellious subject but his rebellious subject's struggle with himself. The final lines of Orwell's dystopian masterpiece are given to the chilling expression of precisely this idea:

> O cruel, needless misunderstanding! O stubborn, self-willed exile from the loving breast! Two gin-scented tears tricked down the sides of his nose. But it was all right, everything was all right, the struggle was finished. He had won the victory over himself. He loved Big Brother. (*Nineteen Eighty-Four*, p. 311)

As long as his victims defiant look remains, however, the sadist, the torturer, the tyrant, has lost the battle and is bound to experience 'the absolute alienation of his being in the Other's freedom' (*Being and Nothingness*, p. 427).

Orwell means to leave us in no doubt that Winston Smith's utter subjugation is irreversible. That is the true horror of his novel, more so even than that 'picture of the future' we conjure up when we 'imagine a boot stamping on a human face – for ever' (*Nineteen Eighty-Four*, p. 280). In real life though, a character like Winston Smith could possibly overcome his brainwashing and broken spirit and rise again. Or if not him, other rebels. Importantly, Big Brother's power is not in fact absolute because it *depends* on Smith's subjugation and the subjugation of millions like him. The tyrant exists only by virtue of the tyrannised, the master only by virtue of the enslaved person:

> [The sadist] discovers then that he cannot act on the Other's freedom even by forcing the Other to humiliate himself and to beg for mercy, for it is precisely in and through the Other's absolute freedom that there exists a world in which there are sadism and instruments of torture and a hundred pretexts for being humiliated and for forswearing oneself. (*Being and Nothingness*, p. 427)

Ultimately, Big Brother wants total power over the people. As Inner Party member O'Brien says, 'But always — do not forget this, Winston — always there will be the intoxication of power, constantly increasing and constantly growing subtler' (*Nineteen Eighty-Four*, p. 280). However, if the people were entirely reduced to the mere puppets the oppressive methods of the Inner Party aim at, there would be no genuine, self-willed persons left for the Inner Party to enjoy having power over. A child may enjoy tyrannising over his toys because he imagines them to be real, but this is not real power; it is only pretend power that would not begin to interest or intoxicate most adults. Real power is possible only where there is resistance, where there is free transcendence to be transcended.

O'Brien recognises this difficulty, recognises that it is essential to the genuine power of Big Brother to go on meeting with resistance. Only in defeating and humiliating endless new waves of opposition, only in transcending the free transcendence of each new generation of heretics, can Big Brother enjoy real power. Real power being the *exercise* of power over every new opposing will, 'victory after victory, triumph after triumph' (*Nineteen Eighty-Four*, p. 281). The power of Big Brother depends on devouring freedom and defiance. That is, on there always being freedom and defiance to devour. Oppression and defiance are locked in a dialectical relationship; each requires the other in order to exist. O'Brien tells Winston, 'The heretic, the enemy of society, will always be there, so that he can be defeated and humiliated over again' (*Nineteen Eighty-Four*, p. 280).

It can be argued that no power is absolute, not only because the power of the master *relies* on the subjugation of the enslaved person, but also because every power is dependent on facticity, on a set of circumstances favourable to it that can never be entirely controlled and which will inevitably alter sooner or later, change being the only constant in life. The Third Reich, for example, referred to by the Nazis as the 'The Thousand Year Reich', lasted just twelve years.

'Everything gives way and nothing stands fast' (Heraclitus, quoted in Plato, *Cratylus*, 402a, *Plato: Complete Works*, p. 120). Everything falls apart and entropy is one of the fundamental laws of the universe. All power is, therefore, relative and every power-relationship inherently unstable. In real life, totalitarian regimes are seldom as confident in their power as the leaders of Orwell's Big Brother regime are, and if they are as confident, such confidence is eventually exposed as hubris.

In real life, so far in history, so-called absolute dictators are for a time unassailable, hence their formidable reputations, then they eventually die, or fall from power then die. Many meet an untimely and sticky end, assassinated or obliged to escape justice by committing suicide. You can compile your own extensive list. And even if they die peacefully of old age while still in power, their regime eventually crumbles and succumbs to a new order.

The growing worry today, however, is that the surveillance and security technology that makes Orwell's utterly and eternally repressive society possible is no longer the stuff of science fiction. Indeed, we now have far more potent, sophisticated, and varied surveillance technology available than even Orwell envisaged.

I warn elsewhere in this book that modern surveillance technology, which includes social media, is creating an Orwellian world in which at all times there is a look that cannot be returned, a harsh judgement that cannot be countered. This stable transcendence, because it is always lurking and cannot be reversed, makes it increasingly difficult for people to find a space, an opportunity, to regain their transcendence and fully recover their subjectivity.

The information technology we have unleashed, which is increasingly a power over and against us, is creating a human world characterised by increasing objectification and reification. So much of our will is being sapped by our largely willing participation in this alienation by media. When all is media, what is mediated? Representations of real life, people will say.

However, if living increasingly consists of people *filming* themselves living, people increasingly consuming and interacting with media even as they stumble along the street oblivious to real life, people spending more and more time 'acting' in the virtual reality of computer games, people increasingly choosing to 'meet' in virtual reality rather than down the pub (a trend exacerbated by the social distancing that was required to combat COVID-19), people always considering and evaluating even the most personal, intimate, and once-private details of their lives in terms of how these details are to be presented on Facebook, people addictively obsessed with their online connectedness and their social media selfie-self, then what remains of real life?

As the singer-songwriter Róisín Murphy said on BBC *Newsnight* in response to a question about the loss of nightclubs due to COVID-19 lockdown measures, 'I'm concerned that we are going to lose our kids in the matrix' (*Newsnight*, BBC 2, 6 October 2020).

In rounding off this section on sadism, having digressed somewhat, let us return to the theme of torture. Sartre was a big fan of the novels of William Faulkner. Faulkner's writings helped inspire Sartre's 1946 play *The Respectable Prostitute*, about racial segregation and racial violence in the United States. Sartre says in *Being and Nothingness* that 'nobody has better portrayed the power of the victim's look at his torturers than Faulkner has done in the final pages of *Light in August*' (*Being and Nothingness*, p. 427).

In that novel, the 'good citizens' of Jefferson, Mississippi, hunt down the African American Joe Christmas and castrate him. Although they master Joe's body and destroy him physically, the serene power of his dying look will master and haunt them, triumph over them, and arrest their freedom for the rest of their lives.

> But the man on the floor had not moved. He just lay there, with his eyes open and empty of everything save consciousness, and with something, a shadow, about his mouth. For a long moment he looked up at them with peaceful and unfathomable and unbearable eyes. . . . [His blood] seemed to rush out of his pale body like the rush of sparks from a rising rocket; upon that black blast the man seemed to rise soaring into their memories forever and ever. They are not to lose it, in whatever peaceful valleys, beside whatever placid and reassuring streams of old age, in the mirroring face of whatever children they will contemplate old disasters and newer hopes. *It will be there, musing, quiet, steadfast, not fading and not particularly threatful, but of itself alone serene, of itself alone triumphant.* (William Faulkner, *Light in August*, p. 407)

MASOCHISM

The phenomenon of masochism, like the phenomenon of sadism, emerges when sexual desire fails to achieve its goal of double reciprocal incarnation, or when sexual desire makes no effort to achieve or is not interested in achieving that incarnation.

As said, Sartre argues that to want to be loved is to want to possess the freedom of the Other while the Other remains free and Other — a free subject. It is, however, impossible to possess the freedom of the Other while the Other remains free because as soon as the Other loves me she experiences me as a subject and herself as an object confronted by my subjectivity.

My inevitable failure to possess the Other as a free subject and identify with her in that way may lead me to attempt the obliteration of my freedom as an obstacle to my hoped for unity with the Other. I may attempt identification with the Other by surrendering my freedom to hers and allowing her to possess me as an object. This new attempt to identify with the Other is masochistic.

A person who resorts to masochism will attempt to become for the Other a mere object without subjectivity. He will attempt to engage himself wholly in his objective being. He will attempt to deny his transcendence with the intention of becoming a pure facticity for the transcendence of the Other. The masochist wants to become a transcendence transcended by the Other to the extent that his transcendence is utterly annihilated by the freedom of the Other.

> Now it is *my* transcendence which is to be denied, not his. This time I do not have to project capturing his freedom; on the contrary I hope that this freedom may *be* and *will* itself to be radically free. Thus the more I shall feel myself surpassed towards other ends, the more I shall enjoy the abdication of my transcendence. Finally I project being nothing more than an *object*; that is, radically an *in-itself*. (*Being and Nothingness*, p. 400)

As a mere object for the Other, the masochist will feel ashamed, but he will love his shame as the measure of his objectivity. The more ashamed, naked, helpless, and debased the masochist becomes before the Other the more of an object he will feel himself to be.

In desiring to be an object for the Other, the masochist desires to be an object for himself. In fact, he wants to be an object for the Other in order to satisfy his desire to be an object for himself. Sartre argues that the masochist does not in fact attempt to fascinate the Other with his objectivity, he attempts to fascinate himself with his objectivity for the Other. 'Masochism is an attempt not to fascinate the Other by means of my objectivity but to cause myself to be fascinated by my objectivity-for-others' (*Being and Nothingness*, p. 400). Masochism may appear even to the masochist as a final and utterly selfless attempt to fascinate the Other through a total surrender to the Other, but in so far as the masochist aims ultimately to fascinate himself with his objectivity for the Other he is acting selfishly and, indeed, *using* the Other.

The masochist wants to be constituted as a facticity by the Other so as to experience his own transcendence as nothing. The masochist's project of seeking to be for himself the mere object that he is for the Other is not least a project of seeking to escape the anxiety he feels as a free transcendence that is burdened with having to make choices. As an *attempt* at abdicating transcendence masochism is a species of *bad faith*.

Bad faith is a central and multifaceted Sartrean phenomenon that he considers in many places in his writings, but most particularly in Part 1, Section 2 of *Being and Nothingness* (pp. 70–94). Sartre's vast writings are replete with characters exhibiting bad faith in a rich variety of forms, but essentially bad faith is the for-itself seeking to avoid the anxiety that arises from its inability to be anything in the mode of simply *being* it, the anxiety that arises from its always having to *choose* itself and always having to be *responsible* for its choices.

Bad faith involves treating the *choice* not to choose as though it were not a choice. It involves seeking to fool myself that I had no choice in a given circumstance and, indeed, that I did not make a choice. Objects have no choices and make no choices. It is not a free choice on the part of a thermostat, for example, to switch on the heating when a certain atmospheric temperature is reached. So, one way of seeking to escape the burden of choice, the burden of freedom, is to pretend to myself that I am only an object *acted upon*, like the thermostat. Importantly, as regards masochism, it certainly aids this pretence to a pure objectness, that appears also as an escape from anxiety, to have another person treat me as an object.

However, in the very act of *wanting* the Other to treat me as an object I am of course displaying desire, will, and choice. In so far as masochism is *choosing* to be an object that does not have to choose, choice is already present and remains present. To choose not to choose is already to have chosen. Or as Sartre puts it in seeking to sum up why the ideal goal of bad faith — the avoidance of self-responsibility — is unachievable, 'Freedom is the freedom of choosing but not the freedom of not choosing. Not to choose is, in fact, to choose not to choose' (*Being and Nothingness*, p. 503).

Masochism is and must be, as Sartre points out, and as you may have already worked out for yourself, doomed to failure. To attempt to fascinate himself with his objectivity for the Other, the masochist must be conscious of himself as an object for the Other. If he is conscious of himself as an object, then he is not that object but rather the transcendence of that object. He can only *aim* at being the object he is for the Other through a transcendence that always places him at a distance from being the object that he is for the Other. The harder he tries to be his objectivity the more he will assert his subjectivity.

> It is useless for the masochist to get down on his knees, to show himself in ridiculous positions, to cause himself to be used as a simple lifeless instrument. It is *for the Other* that he will be obscene or simply passive, for the Other that he will *undergo* these postures; for himself he is forever condemned to *give them to himself*. It is in and through his transcendence that he disposes of himself as a being to be transcended. The more he tries to taste his objectivity, the more he will be submerged by the consciousness of his subjectivity — to the point of anguish. (*Being and Nothingness*, p. 400)

Furthermore, the masochist's project of fascinating himself with his objectivity for the Other actually uses the Other as an instrument. As Sartre points out, 'Even the masochist who pays a woman to whip him is treating her as an instrument and by this very fact posits himself in transcendence in relation to her' (*Being and Nothingness*, pp. 400–401). Thus the masochist's objectivity escapes him. In seeking to be his own objectivity, he finds the objectivity of the Other and thus, in spite of himself, releases his own free subjectivity. As said, masochism is doomed to failure.

Interestingly, Sartre argues that this failure is what the masochist ultimately wants, because above all he has a love of failure. Paradoxically, the masochist at least succeeds in failing. Masochism says Sartre is a 'vice' (*Being and Nothingness*, p. 401), in so far as all vice is fundamentally the love of one's own failure. Here's how Skye Cleary puts it in her excellent book *Existentialism and Romantic Love*:

> And yet, Sartre supposes that failure is actually the goal anyway. So, ironically, one succeeds in and enjoys failing. With the failure of masochism — a strategy of assimilating oneself into the beloved — one throws oneself back into trying to appropriate the beloved, and this is sadism. (*Existentialism and Romantic Love*, p. 109)

Cleary recognises, as does Sartre, that the for-itself in love has a propensity to move to and fro between masochism and sadism, between the desire for objectification and the desire to objectify.

HATE

Although they may not always seem like it, especially to those with a fluffy, Valentine's Day view of romance, masochism and sadism are very much aspects of love. Although they can become extreme, distasteful, and destructive, they nonetheless aim at some form of intimate union with the Other. Hatred, on the other hand, is the abandonment of any attempt to realise union with the Other. The person who hates does not want his freedom to be a transcendence of the Other; he wants to be free of the Other in a world where the Other does not exist.

Sartre argues that any act on the part of the Other that puts a person in the state of being subject to the freedom of the Other can arouse hatred. A person who is subjected to disrespect, from great cruelty to mild disregard, is likely to respond with hatred, but a person who is shown kindness and consideration may also respond with hatred rather than the expected gratitude. Both callous acts and kind acts, in subjecting a person to the freedom of the Other, prevent that person from ignoring the Other.

> This is the reason, moreover, why gratitude is so close to hate; to be grateful for a kindness is to recognize that the Other was entirely free in acting as he has done. . . . I, myself, have been only the excuse for it, the matter on which his act has been exercised. (*Being and Nothingness*, p. 433)

Individuals who have found themselves the object of charity, for example, individuals whose need of charity 'ought' to make them grateful, often grow to hate charity and the charitable precisely because they are not free to refuse what the charitable are free not to give them. Hate, as life and art teach us, is often born of wounded pride. Charity wounds the pride of the dignified who hate to be indebted. This is not to say that to accept charity is necessarily undignified, but rather that anyone with any dignity is likely to suffer wounded pride at the receipt of charity. Pride is also wounded by insults that are either outrageously unfair or piercingly accurate. Either way, insults subject us to the freedom of the Other flaunted with maximum arrogance.

To hate is to 'pursue the death of the Other' (*Being and Nothingness*, p. 432). This is not to say that hatred must involve actively plotting the death of the Other, and usually it does not, otherwise murder would be far more common than it is. Rather, the person who hates seeks to realise for himself a world in which the hated Other does not feature and has no significance — past, present, or future. To hate is to want the death of the Other, but moreover it is to want that the Other had never existed.

Hatred should not be confused with contempt. Not least, there is often humour in contempt as displayed by ridicule, but hate, though it often struggles to disguise itself as contempt by pretending to laugh at the Other, takes the Other very seriously and is not amused. Hate is utterly grudging respect in which the one who hates takes no pleasure.

Hate does not abase the Other, and to hate is not to have contempt for some particular aspect of the Other such as his appearance. To hate is to resent the existence of the Other in general. 'What I hate in the Other is not this appearance, this fault, this particular action. What I hate is his existence in general as a transcendence-transcended' (*Being and Nothingness*, p. 432).

To hate the Other is to perceive him as a hate-object, as a loathed transcendence transcended, but the Other as hate-object remains nonetheless an object haunted by a transcendence that the person who hates prefers not to think about or acknowledge. This avoided transcendence lurks as a potential threat to the freedom of the person who hates; it threatens to alienate him and the hatred by means of which he strives to be free of the Other:

> I experience [the transcendence of the hated Other] as a perpetually fleeing character in the Other-as-object, as a 'not-given', 'undeveloped' aspect of his most accessible empirical qualities, as a sort of perpetual threat which warns me that 'I am missing the point'. This is why one hates *right through* the revealed psychic but not the psychic itself; this is why also it is indifferent whether we hate the Other's transcendence through what we empirically call his vices or his virtues. (*Being and Nothingness*, pp. 432–33)

In hating, the person who hates strives to be free of the Other, strives to inhabit a world in which the Other does not exist and has never existed as a free transcendence. But the very fact that he hates the Other implies that he recognises the freedom of the Other. Hatred strives to deny the freedom of the Other by projecting the non-existence of the Other, but precisely because hatred is a striving to deny the Other it is an implicit affirmation of the Other. 'Hate implies a recognition of the Other's freedom. But this recognition is abstract and negative' (*Being and Nothingness*, p. 432).

Seemingly consistent with Sartre's analysis of hatred is the view that hatred fuels itself in so far as this implicit affirmation of the Other is given grudgingly and is, therefore, resented. I hate the Other all the more because my hatred of him obliges me to recognise his freedom. I blame the Other for the fact that my hatred of him cannot be the pure denial of him I wish it to be.

Hatred fails as an attempt to abolish the Other because it cannot help being an implicit affirmation of the Other. Even if the hated Other dies or is killed by me, he is not abolished for me. Death does not make it that the Other had never existed, and for my hatred to attempt to triumph in the death of the Other requires me to recognise that he *has* existed. I desire the death of the hated Other in order to be free of him, but with his death what I was for him becomes fixed in a past that I am as having-been-it. The fact that I cannot influence what I was for the Other once he is dead means that he continues to alienate me from his grave.

Hatred is hatred of the Other as Other. As the hatred of otherness hatred is, as Sartre points out, hatred of all others in one Other. 'Hate is the hate of all Others in one Other. . . . The Other whom I hate actually represents all Others. My project of suppressing him is a project of suppressing others in general' (*Being and Nothingness*, p. 433). Hate is a revolt against one's being-for-others in general.

However, even if a person could entirely suppress or destroy all others — as tyrants attempt to do — he would not thereby reclaim his being-for-others or free himself from others. Once a person has been for others, he will be forever haunted by his awareness that being-for-others is an inescapable aspect of his being. To have been for-others is to have to be for-others for life, or in the peculiar situation of *In Camera*, for all eternity.

> He who has once been for-others is contaminated in his being for the rest of his days even if the Other should be entirely suppressed; he will never cease to apprehend his dimension of being-for-others as a permanent possibility of his being. He can never recapture what he has alienated; he has even lost all hope of acting on this alienation and turning it to his own advantage since the destroyed Other has carried the key to this alienation along with him to the grave. What I was for the Other is fixed by the Other's death. (*Being and Nothingness*, p. 434)

INDIFFERENCE

Indifference, as Sartre describes it, is an attitude towards others in which a person is wilfully blind to the being of the Other as a transcendence and thereby to his own being-for-others. Although Sartre does not use the term, certainly in *Being and Nothingness*, his indifferent person exhibits *schizoid personality disorder* (SPD) as described by clinical psychiatrists, most notably the Scottish psychiatrist and existentialist R. D. Laing.

Laing developed Sartre's philosophical psychology and his theory of *existential psychoanalysis* and applied it in the clinical setting. Sartre knew and respected Laing's work and even wrote an introduction to Laing's 1964 book *Reason and Violence*. In this book, Laing summarises the approach to psychology and personal history adopted by Sartre in *Saint Genet* (1952) and other works. *Saint Genet* is an existential psychoanalytic biography of Sartre's friend, the writer Jean Genet. Laing's best-known work, *The Divided Self: An Existential Study in Sanity and Madness* (1960), explores psychosis, schizophrenia, and the schizoid personality from the perspective of existential phenomenology.

SPD is generally described by psychiatrists as an eccentric personality disorder characterised by distance, detachment, apathy, emotional coldness, indifference to social relationships, unadventurousness, and a secretiveness likely to conceal an elaborate inner fantasy world.

SPD should not be confused with *schizophrenia*, a complex mental illness basically characterised by episodic or ongoing *psychosis*: difficulty in determining what is and is not real. Nonetheless, the psychologist Michelle L. Esterberg and her associates argue that SPD is an important risk factor for psychosis and can be 'difficult to distinguish from the prodromal [early] phase of schizophrenia, given the strong phenomenological similarities between the two syndromes' ('Cluster A Personality Disorders', p. 517), not least because both syndromes involve a significant detachment from reality.

The indifferent or schizoid person does in fact comprehend that the Other exists and that he is himself a being for the Other, but he practices *evading* this comprehension through a blindness maintained in bad faith. That is, he constantly strives to *ignore* the existence of the Other and his existence for the Other by trying to wholly *distract* himself, by all too deliberately pouring himself into complex projects, workaholism, or elaborate internal fantasies that seem to offer an escape from social reality, social demands, and social responsibilities. He avoids confronting his *being-in-situation*, certainly as far as the existence of the Other is concerned.

Sartre argues in his *War Diaries* and elsewhere that embracing one's being-in-situation, dealing positively with one's circumstances rather than seeking to turn a blind eye to their reality, is *authentic* — authenticity being the opposite, the overcoming, of bad faith. The indifferent person does not realise his blindness to the reality of the Other as a fixed state; he continually makes himself blind by employing the ongoing, evasive, reality-denying tactics of bad faith.

Although the term 'ignorance' is often used to describe the disposition of *not knowing* or being *unaware*, ignorance is in fact a form of knowing and awareness, even wariness. Peter can only *ignore* Paul if he knows Paul is there. To ignore someone is to know all too well they are there, yet at the same time to behave, or try to behave, as though they are not there. A person who ignores another is not *deceiving* himself that the other person is not there; rather he is *pretending* he is in a world in which the other person is not there.

A person — a lover, for example — may desire the presence of his beloved so he can provoke her interest in him by ignoring her. At other times, however, to strive to ignore someone is to strive in vain to be in an alternative reality where that person does not exist.

So, *ignoring* and being *unaware* are not the same, which is why Sartre's indifferent person is not autistic. Due to a genetic condition that affects brain development and hence social development, a person with autism will find it difficult or impossible, depending on the severity of their condition, to be aware of the existence of the Other as another consciousness and point of view on the world. Nonetheless, indifference can resemble a degree of autism and might even be loosely described as 'self-willed autism'. As with schizophrenia, Esterberg and her associates note that SPD 'has been shown to be phenomenologically similar to autistic-spectrum disorders, especially Asperger's disorder' ('Cluster A Personality Disorders', p. 517).

Interestingly, Esterberg and her associates argue that 'the social deficits and anxiety evidenced in those with SPD stem more from paranoid fears about others rather than the lack of desire for close relationships' ('Cluster A Personality Disorders', p. 217). Persons with autism may have little or no interest in close relationships; it simply not being in their 'make-up' to desire them. This is not the case with the schizoid person who may well 'deep down' desire close relationships but strongly resists acknowledging that desire out of fear, anxiety, and paranoia. So, paradoxically, the indifferent person is actually anything but genuinely indifferent. His indifference is a strained performance aimed first and foremost at convincing himself and reducing his immediate anxieties.

R. D. Laing argues that the schizoid person is *ontologically insecure*. Whereas the *ontologically secure* person has a strong, coherent, and stable sense of themselves in relation to the world and others, the ontologically insecure person has a fragile, incoherent, and disintegrating sense of themselves in relation to the world and others.

The ontologically insecure person, Laing argues, has a nagging *engulfment anxiety*. Their self-identity is so fragile that any relationship in which they might be loved, understood, or even *seen*, is perceived as threatening to engulf and overwhelm their autonomy and selfhood. Hence they detach themselves from others, in many cases constructing a 'false self', a protective *front*, that they present to the world, all the while feeling the 'real them' lies cowering behind. Describing the deep ontological insecurity he observed in his own psychiatric patients — an insecurity that presents a barrier to its treatment by psychotherapy — Laing writes:

> To be understood correctly is to be engulfed, to be enclosed, swallowed up, drowned, eaten up, smothered, stifled in or by another person's supposed all-embracing comprehension. It is lonely and painful to be always misunderstood, but there is at least from this point of view a measure of safety in isolation. (*The Divided Self*, p. 45)

Sartre says the indifferent person practices 'a sort of factual solipsism' (*Being and Nothingness* p. 402), acting as if he were alone in the world. Solipsism is the belief that the only mind that exists is one's own. Most commonly, solipsism is the view that there are no other minds *and* no external world. The indifferent person engages with the Other as an instrument or avoids the Other as an obstacle. He has 'an implicit comprehension of being-for-others; that is, of the Other's transcendence as a look' (*Being and Nothingness*, p. 402), but he is willing only to acknowledge the Other's function or lack of function. He strives to evade even imagining that the Other can look at him, that he can be an object for the Other's subjectivity, that the Other can render him a transcendence transcended.

He looks at the Other's look as a modification of the mechanism that the Other is for him, as something that expresses what the Other is as a facticity rather than what he himself is for the Other. For the sake of appearing 'normal' he may sometimes risk looking the other in the eye, as people find a person 'weird' who *always* averts his gaze during a social encounter. But he certainly does not look at the Other looking at him in order to stare the Other down and render him a transcendence transcended. He has perfected a studied indifference towards the transcendence of the Other and is averse to any battle of wills with the Other.

> I practice then a sort of factual solipsism; others are those forms which pass by in the street, those magic objects which are capable of acting at a distance and upon which I can act by means of specific conducts. I scarcely notice them; I act as if I were alone in the world. I brush against 'people' as I brush against a wall; I avoid them as I avoid obstacles. (*Being and Nothingness*, p. 402)

The indifferent person appears to have discovered a way of no longer being threatened by the Other's transcendence, but in fact it is because he is so threatened by the Other's transcendence that he persists in his indifference. In feigning indifference to the Other, he resists appearing shy, timid, or embarrassed before the Other, and so, at least to the casual observer, may well come across as self-confident. But his self-confidence is not a confidence before the Other as Other — he will not allow the Other to exist for him in that way — it is rather a confidence in his practiced ability to manage the instrument or obstacle that the Other is for him.

Indifference, then, is premised upon a deep insecurity, even paranoia, and involves a profound isolation. The indifferent person is alienated by his alienation of the Other. In cutting himself off from the Other, he is cut off from what he could be for the Other and from what the Other could make him be.

His indifference to the transcendence of the Other means that he can neither transcend the Other's transcendence to become a subject for the Other, or be transcended by the transcendence of the Other to become an object for the Other. He can only be the unjustifiable subjectivity that he is for himself. He is stuck with himself, unable to find in what the Other makes of him any relief from the contingency and meaninglessness of his existence.

'Hell is other people!' exclaims Sartre, or rather the Sartre character Garcin, meaning, as we know by now, that it is hell to exist for the Other and to be at the mercy of the Other's judgements. In his analysis of indifference, however, Sartre recognises the hellishness of refusing to exist for the Other and his judgements by isolating oneself in one's own subjectivity. He recognises the hellishness of a loneliness that is self-imposed and purely psychological, existing 'in the mind' even when there are people around disposed to social interaction.

Being-for-others is a source of distress and irritation, but it is also a source of relief and pleasure. Only by acknowledging the existence *of* the Other, and in so doing his existence *for* the Other, can a person feel valued, proud, charmed, flattered, and so on. In allowing himself to be reduced to an object by the Other's look, he may also be pleased to discover that he is a delightful or fascinating object for the Other. In so far as a person can enjoy thinking and feeling he is beautiful, for example, he can only do so by laying himself open to the appreciative looks of the Other and submitting himself to their objectifying compliments regarding his physical appearance.

Interestingly, some dictionaries now define 'objectify' as 'degrade to the status of a mere object', but often the objectification of persons by the look of the Other does not in any way aim at degradation. A human object admired aesthetically is no mere object, and certainly not a degraded one, but a treasured, alluring *subject incarnate* that mesmerises, excites, and entices with its physical presence. Who does not want to be, at times, such a sacred object for the Other?

So, the Other is a source of many positive as well as many negative evaluations, but the Other cannot be a source of *any* evaluations unless his otherness is admitted. The indifferent person refuses to *admit* otherness, to acknowledge it or to permit it, and in so doing refuses one of life's greatest pleasures, the pleasure of being charmed by the Other.

The view that the Other can be a source of positive as well as negative evaluations, that there can be concord with the Other as well as conflict, will be further explored in the next chapter, in answering our central question, 'Is hell other people?'.

BEING-WITH-OTHERS

The German word for 'being-with' is '*Mitsein*'. Sartre follows Heidegger in using the term 'Mitsein' to refer to the phenomenon of *being-with-others*, to the phenomenon of *we*.

Sartre repeatedly argues that conflict is the essence of all human relationships, that each being-for-itself struggles to transcend the transcendence of the Other and reduce him to a transcendence transcended. Nonetheless, there are passages in his writings where he at least qualifies this stark view, moments where he recognises it for what it is: an incomplete account that makes no reference to situations in which a person is in *community* with the Other rather than in conflict with him.

It can be argued that Sartre does not contradict himself by doing this because he maintains that conflict is a fundamental, enduring *ontological* feature of being-for-others, whereas community spirit is merely a temporary *psychological* phenomenon. As Cleary says, 'Whereas being-*for*-others is ontological, Sartre claimed that "we" is a psychological concept' (*Existentialism and Romantic Love*, p. 105).

Not least, being-with-others often requires submergence in an *us* as opposed to a *them* as opponent and/or hate object — Sartrean conflict at the group level. Given that 'my enemy's enemy is my friend', conflict with individuals on my side can be temporarily suppressed or ignored for the greater collective good. As Winston Churchill once said to his personal secretary John Colville, 'If Hitler invaded Hell, I would make at least a favourable reference to the Devil in the House of Commons.'

Being-with-others, according to Sartre, is always as temporary, unstable, and doomed as any pact with the Devil, because although people can achieve a sense of togetherness by striving in concert towards a common goal, everyone ultimately has their own perceptions and experiences of the striving as well as their own priorities, misgivings, and further objectives regarding the goal before and after it is achieved.

> Even though people identify with each other in the sense of common actions or aims, everyone's experiences and goals are different, and this difference is alienating. The prerequisite for honestly exploring the idea of 'we' is to know who the other is, and this one cannot know beyond doubt. I cannot grasp another's subjectivity; I cannot know anything about how others see me. (*Existentialism and Romantic Love*, p. 105)

Sartre considers how it is at all possible for there to be a *we*-subject in which a plurality of subjectivities at least appear to apprehend one another as transcendences-transcending rather than as transcendences-transcended. He argues that for the *we* to occur there must be a common action, a collective enterprise or an object of common perception that is the *explicit* object of consciousness.

For example, a member of an audience absorbed in watching a play is explicitly conscious of the play rather than the audience around him. In being explicitly conscious of the play, however, he is also implicitly or non-thetically conscious of being conscious of the play and of being a co-spectator of the play. His mental focus is on the words, actions, and characters of the play, but he is also generally aware that he is watching a play as a co-spectator:

> The best example of the 'we' can be furnished us by the spectator at a theatrical performance whose consciousness is exhausted in apprehending the imaginary spectacle, in foreseeing the events through anticipatory schemes, in positing imaginary beings as the hero, the traitor, the captive, *etc.*, a spectator, who, however, in the very upsurge which makes

him a consciousness of the spectacle is constituted non-thetically as consciousness (of) being a *co-spectator* of the spectacle. (*Being and Nothingness*, p. 435)

Earlier we compared non-thetic consciousness to being broadly aware that one is driving a car even though one is mentally focused on something else. Non-thetic consciousness is consciousness of being conscious but not consciousness explicitly reflecting upon itself as an intentional object, what is called *thetic self-consciousness*.

In offering another example of the *we*, Sartre imagines himself on the pavement outside a café. Knowing Sartre's penchant for cafés and the fact that his office was mostly cafés during the war years when he wrote *Being and Nothingness*, he was probably sitting outside a Parisian café when he came up with this example. Sartre observes the other patrons and they observe him: 'We remain here in the most ordinary case of conflict with others (the Other's being-as-object for me, my being-as-object for the Other)' (*Being and Nothingness*, p. 435).

Suddenly an incident occurs in the street, a collision between two vehicles.

> Immediately at the very instant when I become a spectator of the incident, I experience myself non-thetically as engaged in 'we'. The earlier rivalries, the slight conflicts have disappeared, and the consciousnesses which furnished the matter of the 'we' are precisely those of all the patrons: 'we' look at the event, 'we' take part. (*Being and Nothingness*, p. 435)

Being-with can only occur in this implicit, non-thetic way; it cannot be the explicit object of consciousness. If a spectator makes his fellow spectators the explicit object of his consciousness, rather than the shared experience of the play or the collision, he will cease to be a co-spectator with them of the play or the collision and they will cease to be his fellow spectators. His being-with them as part of a *we* will be lost as they become the object of his consciousness and he transcends their transcendence.

If you have ever observed a notable incident — a fire, a car accident, an arrest — with others, you will recall your excited sense of the shared *we* experience that Sartre describes. You may also recall that it does not last long. As soon as you begin to discuss the incident with the stranger next to you, those 'slight conflicts' which characterise interpersonal relations reappear.

She saw the incident differently from you, and if it involved cops and robbers she is supporting the side you are opposed to. She has heard a different story to you as to the causes of the incident, so begs to differ with your account. You, being you, believe you are already apprised of more background detail than she is but struggle to explain what you know without implying that you think she is stupid. She is a bad listener. She is an idiot. This tedious conversation with her is spoiling your voyeuristic enjoyment of the incident, even, ironically, your sense of a shared experience. Perhaps you do not identify with this portrayal, in which case slight conflict between you and me. And so it goes.

I will return to the phenomenon of being-with-others in the next chapter and seek to show that at times there can be significantly more to it than Sartre allows.

SEXUAL PERVERSION

For the final section of this chapter, I want to consider the influence of Sartre's theory of concrete relations with others on the fascinating theory of *sexual perversion* put forward by the American philosopher Thomas Nagel in *Mortal Questions* (1979), his landmark collection of philosophical essays. Nagel was professor of philosophy at New York University from 1980 to 2016. Nagel's theory is worthy of consideration because, on the one hand, it reveals an important direction in which Sartre's ideas have travelled — not least his core idea of *double reciprocal incarnation* — while, on the other hand, it increases our understanding of the dimensions of being-for-others by giving us a means of schematising and evaluating some further aspects of sexual desire.

Nagel undertakes to defend the idea of sexual perversion, to argue that it is an intelligible idea, albeit one that is often confused, particularly by moral considerations. He wants to identify 'exactly what about human sexuality qualifies it to admit of perversions' (*Mortal Questions*, p. 39).

Sexual perversion, if there be such thing, must in some sense be *unnatural*, a claim that demands a definition of natural, non-perverted sex. With a little help from Sartre, Nagel provides a definition of natural, non-perverted sex which we will explore in due course.

Sexual perversions, Nagel argues, must be 'unnatural sexual *inclinations*' (*Mortal Questions*, p. 39), rather than just unnatural practices related to sex adopted for reasons other than sexual inclination. He takes the example of contraception. Although an intentional perverting of the sexual and reproductive functions, contraception cannot be described as a *sexual* perversion. 'A sexual perversion must reveal itself in conduct that expresses an unnatural *sexual* preference' (*Mortal Questions*, p. 39). Although some people might have a fetish with regard to the use of contraceptive devices, this is not the usual reason for their use.

Sexual perversion has nothing to do with reproduction going astray in any living thing. Sexual perversion is 'a concept of psychological, not physiological, interest' (*Mortal Questions*, p. 39). Hence, we do not apply the concept to lower animals and plants, however their reproductive functions may deviate from what is natural and normal.

If higher animals can be sexually perverted it is because they are psychologically, not anatomically, similar to humans. Thus, it might be possible to have a sexually perverted dolphin, as dolphins are highly intelligent, self-aware, and so on, but not a sexually perverted sheep. Sheep are simply too dim-witted to think of it. Although sheep are the clichéd object of one form of human sexual perversion, they are not themselves perverted.

While on the sordid subject of sheep molestation, it must be noted without further delay that sexual perversion cannot be defined in terms of social disapproval or custom. Adultery and fornication, for example, although frowned upon by many societies, are not considered unnatural practices but rather objectionable practices in religious or ethical terms. A sexual act can be highly immoral but not actually *sexually* perverted, such as a man having consensual sex with his adult daughter, or it can be sexually perverted but not immoral, such as intercourse with a sex doll. Incest is widely held to be immoral because it can harm individuals and society in various ways, whereas intercourse with a sex doll is a private practice that does not harm anyone.

The English moral philosopher John Stuart Mill makes harm to others a central principle of his utilitarian moral theory. According to Mill, although we may disapprove of certain activities that other people get up to, we have no reasonable grounds for judging as immoral any activities other people get up to that do no harm to anyone beyond themselves, and therefore no right to seek to prevent such activities. This is known as Mill's *harm principle*. 'The only purpose for which power can be rightfully exercised over any member of a civilised community, against his will, is to prevent harm to others' (*On Liberty*, p. 14).

The key question here, of course, is always whether or not a certain act does in fact harm others. Private recreational drug use, for example, may harm others if addiction causes a person to neglect his children, but it is hard to see any real harm to others in a person privately indulging in intercourse with a sex doll or any other inanimate object that is his exclusive property.

Some feminists argue that the use of sex dolls — almost exclusively men using 'female' dolls — encourages men to disrespect women, to sexually objectify them and perceive them as submissive and so on. Add to this sex dolls that represent women of 'barely legal' age and sex dolls that are programmed to resist in order to fulfil rape fantasies, and we seem to have possible grounds for arguing that the use of sex dolls, or at least the use of some sex dolls by some people in some situations, can in fact lead to harm to others and is therefore immoral.

To argue convincingly that sex doll use is immoral in Mill's terms and therefore ought to be outlawed, the feminists would have to prove that men who use sex dolls are *more likely* to disrespect women, sexually objectify them, and sexually abuse them as a result of sex doll use than they would be if there had been no sex doll use. It appears, however, that it is as impossible to prove this as it is to prove the opposite: that men who use sex dolls are *less likely* to sexually abuse women as a result of sex doll use than they would be if there had been no sex doll use. It has been claimed by some that sex doll use allows some men to harmlessly satisfy and so eliminate otherwise dangerous sexual desires. It is surely impossible to design realistic experiments that might credibly support hypotheses that there are cause-effect relationships to be found here.

It is certainly very difficult if not impossible to *generalise* about men who use sex dolls, their motivations, and the effect their sex doll use has on their behaviour towards women. To take an individual hypothetical case instead then, a man might sexually assault a woman having previously used a sex doll, but this still does not prove the existence of a cause-effect relationship, even if the doll was a lookalike of the woman he went on to sexually assault. What is significant and disturbing is the psychological reality of his dangerous desire, the desire that *led* him to acquire a lookalike doll and so on, not the existence or use of the doll as such. If he is abusive towards women, it is likely he will also be 'abusive' towards his sex doll, but it seems it cannot be demonstrated that it is owning and using the sex doll that renders him abusive towards women.

It is important to stress that most men who use sex dolls do not become rapists, just as most rapists do not use sex dolls. There is no credible evidence that sex doll use inspires men to rape. Men who rape are primarily obsessed with power over real women, not with constructing elaborate fantasies involving dolls. Not least, there are men who are very tender and considerate towards their personal sex doll. So-called sex dolls are often, more accurately speaking, expensive and sophisticated *companion dolls* for men who have lost partners.

There is even, so I have heard, a Bambi sex doll. Yes, that Bambi. We may find all sex doll behaviour weird, creepy, even offensive, but taking offence at eccentric behaviour is not necessarily the same as being harmed by that behaviour. The subject of sex dolls, it seems, is surprisingly complex, and I can do no more here than offer these few reflections as my limited contribution to further discussions.

Before presenting his psychological account of sexual perversion Nagel first considers a sceptical argument that denies the existence of any sexual perversion at all. The argument runs that sexual desire, like hunger, is an appetite which may have various objects. Some objects of sexual appetite are more common than others, but none are in any sense *natural*. If sexual appetite is satisfied by the generation of certain pleasant sensations in the various erogenous zones of the body, it is conceivable that almost anything might provide these pleasant sensations, even if it is the case that an object elicits sexual arousal and provides sexual pleasure only as a result of association and conditioning.

We may be unable to empathise with certain sexual preferences of others or condemn certain sexual practices such as sadism on extraneous ethical grounds, but once a desire is observed as sexual then that is all that can be said about it. A desire is either sexual or it is not and cannot be seen as imperfect or perverted. Arguably, 'Sexuality does not admit of imperfection, or perversion, or any other such qualification — it is not that sort of "affection"' (*Mortal Questions*, pp. 40–41).

It is worth stressing that to deny there is sexual perversion is not to deny that some sexual activities are immoral. There are good grounds for arguing that some sexual activities are immoral regardless of whether or not there is sexual perversion — paedophilia, for example. Adults having sex with children is immoral because it is the coercive exploitation of a powerless person, who is too young to give genuine consent, by a person in a position of power who is old enough to be responsible for their actions. Kant argues in his *Groundwork of the Metaphysic of Morals* that it is always unethical to exploit others as a mere, unconsenting means to one's own ends and goals rather than respect them as *ends in themselves*, as people with their own ends and goals. More on Kantian ethics in our final chapter.

If there is sexual perversion, then some sexual perversions may increase a person's propensity to perform certain immoral sexual acts. This, however, still does not make the perversion itself immoral, anymore than poverty is immoral because it may increase a person's propensity to steal. A particular perverted sexual desire may have a range of acts that will satisfy it, some of which are immoral and some of which are not. Also, as we have seen, there are immoral sexual acts which are not perverted by any sensible measure of perversion, and sexual acts which are arguably perverted but not immoral by any sensible ethical standard. Matters will doubtless become clearer when Nagel's account of sexual perversion has been outlined in full.

The crucial point in all this is that it is always unhelpful and mis-leading to confuse and conflate the two distinct concepts 'perverted' and 'immoral'. Indeed, it is this conflation that has long impeded efforts to gain both a clearer understanding of the nature of sexual perversion and the nature of sexual ethics.

The sceptical view of sexual perversion, resting as it does upon the notion that sexual desire is simply an *appetite*, rules out the possibility of a *psychological* account of sexual perversion. Nagel's ingenious response to the sceptical position is to note that 'it should make us suspicious of the simple picture of appetites on which the skepticism depends' (*Mortal Questions*, p. 41). Challenging this oversimplified picture, he argues that even the standard appetites such as hunger and thirst can in fact be perverted.

What would constitute a gastronomic perversion? Desire to eat an inappropriate substance such as paper might seem a little odd but lacks the 'psychological complexity' (*Mortal Questions*, p. 41) to be considered a perversion. On the other hand, if a hungry individual sought satisfaction by eating cookbooks, or would only eat living animals, or would only eat by having food forced down his throat through a funnel, then perversion might seem a more appropriate label. Why is this? Well, as Nagel says:

> What helps is the peculiarity of the desire itself, rather than the inappropriateness of its object to the biological function that the desire serves. Even an appetite can have perversions if in addition to its biological function it has a significant psychological structure. (*Mortal Questions*, p. 41)

Just as hunger is an attitude to objects in the external world, so too is sexual desire. Sexual desire, however, is usually directed at persons rather than omelettes, and for that reason it is far more complicated. This complexity 'allows scope for correspondingly complicated perversions' (*Mortal Questions*, p. 42).

Nagel goes on to consider the complex psychological interchange that he believes takes place in the *natural* development of sexual attraction. As will be seen, Nagel holds that it is *fixations* and *hang-ups* relating to the various stages of the natural development of sexual attraction that constitute the all-important psychological basis of sexual perversion. In developing his theory of natural human sexual interactions, Nagel draws on the ideas of Sartre explored earlier in this chapter.

According to Sartre, as we have seen, sexual desire is one of the main ways, although not the only way, in which an embodied consciousness seeks to come to terms with the existence of the Other. As we discovered, the ultimate purpose of sexual desire, the ideal goal of sexual interaction, is *'double reciprocal incarnation'* (*Being and Nothingness*, p. 413): both parties existing simultaneously as subject and object, as subjects incarnate, for the Other and for themselves. That is, at one and the same time, Romeo existing as a subject incarnate for Juliet and for himself, and Juliet existing as a subject incarnate for Romeo and for herself.

For Sartre, double reciprocal incarnation is doomed to failure because a person cannot at the same time incarnate the Other's body as flesh and be incarnated as flesh by the Other's body. If he focuses on the incarnation of the Other, he cannot do so without neglecting and forgetting his own incarnation. If the Other's body incarnates his body, he will become lost in the enjoyment of his own incarnation. His own incarnation will become the object of his consciousness, and he will unavoidably neglect and forget the incarnation of the Other. If Sartre is right about this, then it is not really possible to have a model of successful and completely fulfilled sex, in comparison to which other sex is unsuccessful, incomplete, and perverted. Thus, Sartre's view, 'cannot admit the concept of perversion' (*Mortal Questions*, p. 44).

Nagel disagrees with Sartre that sexual desire cannot achieve its ultimate purpose. I will let that disagreement go rather than try to settle it. What matters here is that, despite their disagreement, Sartre's thesis is pivotal to Nagel's thesis because of the *attempt* at 'perfect sex' that Sartre considers. It is Sartre's key notion of *double reciprocal incarnation* that Nagel relies on to develop his theory of sexual perversion. Nagel's view is, therefore, *related* to Sartre's 'but it differs from Sartre's in allowing sexuality to achieve its goal on occasion and thus in providing the concept of perversion with a foothold' (*Mortal Questions*, p. 44).

Mutual sexual desire, says Nagel, involves 'a complex system of superimposed mutual perceptions — not only perceptions of the sexual object, but perceptions of oneself' (*Mortal Questions*, p. 44). Nagel separates out the elements of this mutual perception by considering its development, by considering the various stages which ideally move a couple towards double reciprocal incarnation.

To clearly separate the elements involved, Nagel takes a somewhat artificial situation, although it should be assumed that the various levels of perception described can be present in all instances of sexual attraction and activity, from seeing to touching to full-on sex between any two human adults.

Romeo and Juliet are sitting at opposite ends of a cocktail lounge with many mirrors 'which permit unobserved observation, and even mutual unobserved observation' (*Mortal Questions*, p. 45). Romeo notices Juliet and is immediately sexually attracted to her. At this stage, he is aroused by an unaroused object. Soon Juliet notices Romeo — although not yet that Romeo has noticed her — and begins to exhibit 'the subtle signs of sexual arousal, heavy-lidded stare, dilating pupils, faint flush, etc' (*Mortal Questions*, p. 45). Romeo senses these signs, and his arousal, which is nonetheless still solitary, is increased by them.

But now, by calculating the lines of reflection, Romeo realises that Juliet's aroused stare is directed at him. Romeo now senses Juliet sensing Romeo. This is an important development, because Romeo is now not only aware of himself through his own arousal but also through the arousal of Juliet his presence is causing. This stage is further separable from the first because it is often the case that a person's sexual arousal does not begin until he becomes aware that his presence is arousing the Other.

A further development occurs when Juliet senses that Romeo senses her. Romeo is now in a position to notice and be aroused by Juliet's arousal at being sensed by him. Nagel says of Romeo that he has become, 'conscious of his sexuality through his awareness of its effect on her and of her awareness that this effect is due to him' (*Mortal Questions*, p. 46).

Once their interactions become fully reciprocal as described, it is impossible to conceive of further types of mutual perception. When the relationship between Romeo and Juliet advances, the same mutual perceptions, which to begin with are all visual, will take place in more involved and sexually intimate ways. Physical contact and ultimately sexual interaction and intercourse with their 'far greater range of subtlety and acuteness' (*Mortal Questions*, p. 46) will be the natural extensions of these first visual exchanges.

Nagel stresses that in real life things do not happen in such an orderly fashion as they do in his hypothetical Romeo and Juliet scenario. He believes, however, 'that some version of this overlapping system of distinct sexual perceptions and interactions is the basic framework of any full-fledged sexual relation and that relations involving only part of the complex are significantly incomplete' (*Mortal Question*, p. 46).

We now have a general schema of the development and form of natural, human sexual interactions. If it is assumed that sexual relationships, unless somehow prevented, will progress towards this natural state of full-blown mutual awareness, shared affection, and emotional reciprocation, then a sexual perversion can be characterised as a psychosexual 'blockage' (*Mortal Questions*, p. 49) which thwarts this progression or causes it to deviate. Many familiar sexual shortfalls and deviations can be identified and described using this approach.

The desire for intercourse with inanimate objects, for example, is a desire 'stuck at some primitive version of the first stage of sexual feeling. If the object is not alive, the experience is reduced entirely to an awareness of one's own sexual embodiment' (*Mortal Questions*, p. 49).

Children and animals, although permitting an awareness of the embodiment of the Other, 'present obstacles to reciprocity' (*Mortal Questions*, p. 49). The object of sexual desire is unable to recognise 'the subject's desire as the source of his (the object's) sexual self-awareness' (*Mortal Questions*, p. 49).

As for the exhibitionist, he displays his desire and arousal without desiring to be desired in return. He wants the Other to be aware of his desire, possibly for it to shock and disturb her, but he does not want to be an object of desire for the Other. Even if he wants the Other to desire him, to admire him, he does not want to be the object of her sexual attentions. His life experiences may have made him fearful of such attentions and averse to them.

As for the voyeur, he 'need not require any recognition by his object at all' (*Mortal Questions*, p. 49). Indeed, we might distinguish between the genuinely perverted voyeur who does not want recognition from the Other, who is happy just to look in secret and whose arousal largely depends on knowing that he sees without being seen, and the incidental, non-perverted, although still possibly immoral voyeur, who looks because he is aroused and would rather like to advance towards a double reciprocal incarnation with the Other.

With regard to sadism, the Marquis de Sade himself claimed that 'the object of sexual desire was to evoke involuntary responses from one's partner, especially audible ones' (*Mortal Questions*, p. 50). Nagel argues that although inflicting pain is no doubt the most efficient way of achieving this, doing so 'requires a certain abrogation of one's own exposed spontaneity' (*Mortal Questions*, p. 50). It is the concerted effort to cancel one's own exposed spontaneity, to avoid any risk of one's own incarnation, that is the psychological essence of sadism, the attitude that makes it a perversion. 'The sadist's engagement is itself active and requires a retention of deliberate control which may impede awareness of himself as a bodily subject of passion in the required sense' (*Mortal Questions*, p. 50).

As for the masochist, he 'cannot find a satisfactory embodiment as the object of another's sexual desire, but only as the object of his control. He is passive not in relation to his partner's passion but in relation to his nonpassive agency' (*Mortal Questions*, p. 50). Fully reciprocal sex would require him to recognise his partner's passion even while making himself the passive object of that passion, and to recognise his partner's passion as partly resulting from his own willingness to be passive.

As a masochist, however, he does not want to recognise his partner's passion and certainly not that he himself is the cause of it. Sartre, as we have seen, argues that the masochist is not interested in fascinating the Other with his objectivity; he is interested only in fascinating himself with his 'objectivity-for-others' (*Being and Nothingness*, p. 400). The masochist is interested in his partner only as a *means* to fascinating himself with his objectivity-for-others.

Far from surrendering himself to his partner in full awareness of the value of that surrender to both of them, the masochist uses his partner as an instrument. Thus, the masochist succeeds only in achieving an appearance of passivity that is in fact the product of his own very active will. Masochism is not only a failure of natural, non-perverted sex, it is also its own failure.

To summarise, sadism and masochism are 'disorders of the second stage of awareness — the awareness of oneself as an object of desire' (*Mortal Questions*, p. 50).

As to anal sex and oral sex between consenting human adults, it is highly doubtful that they are perverted. These acts allow for the full range of interpersonal perceptions previously defined. They would only be perverted if combined with one of those desires that Nagel has already identified as perverted. Oral sex with an animal, for example, would be perverted, although the perversion would be the bestiality, not the oral sex as such.

The fallacy that anal sex and oral sex are in themselves perverted derives not from any psychological assessment of people who enjoy them but from an illiberal moral evaluation. The fallacy that these acts are perverted also derives from concerns that they are less hygienic than genital sex and are, therefore, unhealthy practices that help spread sexually transmitted infections and so on. These concerns are not entirely unfounded, although that in no way implies that anal sex and oral sex are perverted. As the Better Health Channel Website of the Victoria State Government puts it, with regard to oral sex, 'Many experts say oral sex is not safe sex. It may be "safer sex" than genital sex without a condom . . . but oral sex without a condom still carries the significant risk of catching or passing on sexually transmitted infections (STIs).'

The notion of perverted sex is as often confused with the notion of 'dirty sex' as it is confused with the notion of immoral sex. Moreover, given that cleanliness is still considered by many to be next to godliness, 'dirty sex' is still widely confused with immoral sex. 'Dirty sex', in the opinion of some particularly prudish people, is any sexual activity apart from missionary position intercourse. This can be considered dirty too — not least because it is enjoyable — but unfortunately it is necessary for reproduction. Hence, some exceptionally strict and repressed religious groups stipulate the interposition of a bed sheet, with a strategically positioned hole, between the naked bodies of the participants.

Nagel does not consider masturbation, probably because although masturbation is sexual it is not sex and cannot therefore be perverted sex. This picture is somewhat complicated by the fact that sexual partners might watch each other masturbate as part of their natural sexual interactions. Masturbation here, then, refers to solitary masturbation. Masturbation is sometimes described as 'sex with oneself', but this is really only a figure of speech in that it is impossible to be truly other to oneself to the extent that one can have sex with oneself. People can of course do all sorts of sexually stimulating things to themselves, but this can only be very loosely described as *having sex with* oneself.

If we allow, for argument's sake, that masturbation is a form of sex, then it could be described as sexually perverted in Nagel's terms as, except for an awareness of one's own arousal, it does not realise any of the mutual perceptions that together comprise what Nagel defines as natural, non-perverted sex.

Then again, a masturbator might arouse himself by *imagining* he is involved in various sexual activities that realise Nagel's full range of mutual perceptions. Alternatively, a masturbator might imagine himself involved in sexual activities that we have already defined as perverted. Perhaps, at a stretch, it can be argued that masturbation is perverted or not perverted, or at least more or less perverted, depending on what a person thinks about while masturbating. One can think about perverted or non-perverted sex while masturbating, or indeed at any time.

Neither does Nagel consider the masturbation stimulus material that is pornography. Looking at pornography, like solitary masturbation, is sexual but not sex. Therefore, like masturbation, looking at pornography cannot be perverted sex. If we allow, for argument's sake, that looking at pornography is a form of sex, then this activity does appear to be perverted in Nagel's terms, as it is a kind of sexual relationship with another person that is not and cannot be reciprocated. A person looking at pornography is aroused by a sexy model but he cannot arouse the model or be aroused at her arousal at his arousal, other than in his imagination.

Much more can be said about the phenomenology of masturbation and pornography using Nagel's theory as a guide; about the relationship between the viewer and different kinds of pornography; about the level of voyeurism involved in looking at different kinds of pornography; and about the type and degree of perversion different kinds of pornography involve. Unfortunately, covering these topics adequately would run to many pages; they will therefore have to be considered as beyond the scope of this present work.

Homosexuality, because it allows for the full range of interpersonal perceptions, is not perverted under the terms of Nagel's phenomenological and psychological model: 'Nothing rules out the full range of interpersonal perceptions between persons of the same sex' (*Mortal Questions*, p. 50). Nagel does, however, raise the controversial issue of whether or not 'homosexuality is produced by distorting influences that block or displace a natural tendency to heterosexual development' (*Mortal Questions*, p. 50).

Having raised this controversial issue, Nagel says he does not know how to approach it. Addressing the complex question of what, if anything, makes a person homosexual, heterosexual, or bisexual is beyond the scope of his essay. He simply argues that, although clearly more extreme, the so-called distorted tendency to sexually prefer members of one's own sex may be no different in principle to the tendency to prefer large breasts or blond hair, tendencies that nobody would seriously call perverted. We might say it is simply a matter of 'whatever turns you on'.

Then again, as philosophers, psychologists, and scientists, we are still intrigued to know why a particular person is turned on by this and not that, by this person and not that person, by members of the opposite sex rather than by members of his or her own sex, by members of his or her own sex rather than by members of the opposite sex, by members of both sexes and so on. It makes no sense to conclude, as some people have, usually in the name of political correctness, that these preferences are *not* caused and *cannot* be caused by anything, be it biological, psychological, sociological, or biographical.

Finally, setting aside moral considerations, Nagel asks if non-perverted sex is necessarily preferable to perverted sex? It may be that sex which 'receives the highest marks for perfection *as sex*' (*Mortal Questions*, p. 52), sex which achieves or at least gets closest to achieving the holy grail of double reciprocal incarnation, is actually less pleasurable than certain perversions. As he says, 'if enjoyment is considered very important, that might outweigh considerations of sexual perfection in determining rational preference' (*Mortal Questions*, p. 52). Then again, perhaps there is nothing more enjoyable, stimulating, fulfilling, and sexy than reaching for, and perhaps briefly grasping, the holy grail of double reciprocal incarnation.

It is time now to directly address the central question we have long been approaching and preparing the ground to answer: 'Is hell other people?'

CHAPTER 4

Is Hell Other People?

NOT REALLY

If you have read to this point rather than jumped to it, then you will already be aware that enough has been said previously at various points along the way to offer an answer to our billion-dollar question without further ado: *Hell is not other people! Not really.* What follows here at length is simply further justification of that repudiation.

'Hell is other people!' is only true in the artificial and limited context of Sartre's play *In Camera*, in which the maxim appears, spoken by the eternally damned character Joseph Garcin. As we saw in Chapter 1 when we examined *In Camera* in detail, hell in the play is literally being trapped in a small room forever with other people. 'There's no need for red-hot pokers' (*In Camera*, p. 223) because hell is being endlessly subjected to the judgement of others, endlessly seeking in vain to determine the opinion of others and endlessly being unable to know what others really think of one.

The context is deliberately contrived and highly dramatised to throw into the sharpest relief Sartre's many interesting psycho-philosophical points about the downsides, the negatives, the anxieties and tortures, of being-for-others. It is a context that allows little or nothing to be said about the upsides, the positives, the pleasures and rewards, of being for-others.

Outside of the play, 'Hell is other people!' is an inaccurate dysphemism, a strained metaphor, a *conceit* in the literary sense of being an elaborate figure of speech. Many people are delighted to be shocked by this figurative device and to shock others with it, especially these days on social media. They are thoroughly seduced by its boldness and ostensible perspicacity. As with all conceits, however, 'Hell is other people!' can start to perplex and annoy if you examine it closely and carefully.

Even within the play, as was also pointed out in Chapter 1, hell is not *simply* other people. Hell is three particularly unpleasant people, the eternal, claustrophobic confinement, the inability to sleep or even to blink, the lack of periodic darkness, and the lack of any distractions or relief from one another. It is even the depressing furniture. Sartre's hell is bad in all these ways from the outset, although arguably anything would become hellish if it went on forever.

Even the most pleasant and interesting people would eventually become unbearable if you had to spend an eternity in their company with absolutely no me-time. Although, of course, you would be obliged to bear them, having no choice but to do so, no choice to escape them even by committing suicide.

Still, if you were given a choice, as Garcin is, between an eternity of suffering the anxiety, frustration and shame of your being-for-others, or the eternal agony of burning forever in a more traditional hell, you would probably choose the former, as Garcin does (*In Camera*, p. 219). So, there is actually a deeper hell than the one in which Garcin, Inez, and Estelle find themselves. Namely, the sempiternal spit-roast. Hell, strictly speaking, refers to a place, to a situation, that *cannot be worse*, so maybe even in the play, hell is not other people after all. And if hell is not other people even in Sartre's clever but unrealistic and ultimately preposterous play, then hell is highly unlikely to be other people in the real world.

In the supernatural horror film *The Exorcist*, the possessed child Regan says to the priest, 'Your mother sucks cocks in hell Karras, you faithless slime!'. Reflecting on this the comedian Andy Field reasons that although he does not wish his mother in hell, he hopes that if she goes to hell she sucks cocks for all eternity as that would not be so bad as burning forever (*Stand Up for Live Comedy*, BBC Three, 19 October, 2020). It is a crude example, but nonetheless a sophisticated line of reasoning that neatly supports my general point.

At best 'Hell is other people!' is a great slogan, a great piece of hyperbole, a shameless overstatement that is used, indeed overused, even abused, to advertise Sartre's fascinating theory of being-for-others. It is a dubious *bon mot*, an unjustifiable universal, categorical statement that unhelpfully over-emphasises the conflict, slight or considerable, that undoubtedly characterises much human interaction.

Certainly, it is a soothing mantra to mutter when that early rising neighbour of yours, the one who loves his power tools, fires up a chainsaw at seven in the morning just when you were trying to enjoy a lie in. The git has managed once again to transcend your transcendence from a distance without even realising it, to rain on your humble, quiet parade with his grand, noisy one. What you would like to do to him in that moment, if you could only be bothered to get out of bed, cannot be repeated here as it would amount to hate speech. What you would like to say to him, if you were not so prudent as to realise that it would not be a good idea to openly fall out with him. You would have to live with the tension and embarrassment, on top of all the other irritations, of having *had words* with him. Your very middle-class restraint makes you even more angry and frustrated.

Feeling this way is bad enough, but it is not hell if we understand that hell is by definition the worst of places, traditionally an underworld where the souls of the damned burn forever in fire and brimstone. Brimstone, by the way, is sulphur, which burns with a particularly suffocating and irritating odour. Your chainsaw-wielding neighbour is making your life a sort of misery in that moment, but, to be fair, he is not subjecting you to eternal punishment.

You still have some autonomy, various means of escape, various avenues of transcendence. You could pop in your trusty earplugs and put a pillow over your head; you could take the opportunity to get up early and go out for the day or make your own noise mowing the lawn; or you could simply try to be less annoyed and doze through the noise until it ends. After all, it is your irritation, the feeling that you have been slighted by the overactive bastard yet again, that is keeping you awake, more than his actual noise. Your irritation is probably even *amplifying* the volume of his noise in your own head, as tinnitus sufferers amplify the noises they hear in their ears by obsessively dwelling upon them.

I do not have bad neighbours as bad neighbours go. They do not surround me and submerge me as a sort of human equivalent of fire and brimstone. In fact, they are very good neighbours compared to how bad neighbours can be. Friendly, at least to my face, and will always help in a crisis. And if there is a serious, ongoing bone of contention they will cooperate in trying to reach an amicable solution. But what if you've got so-called Neighbours from Hell like those you see on TV documentaries? People with little or no restraint and zero diplomacy, who for whatever reason are hell-bent on making your life a constant misery in as unreasonable and spiteful a way as possible? People who love putting out fire with gasoline?

I have a friend whose neighbour kidnapped his beloved cat and kept it hidden in her flat for two weeks while he, distraught, searched high and low for it, made posters and organised search parties. He suspected all along the cat was in her flat, given that she had an impressive track record of doing nasty, unneighbourly deeds, but he did not have any actual, concrete evidence on the basis of which the police could search her property. In the end, the situation got too hot even for her wickedness to handle and she made out the cat had miraculously turned up in her property, drifted in through the window of her flat after two weeks of supposedly prowling about the locality undiscovered despite the extensive search and rescue efforts. To her credit, she did not kill the cat, even fed it and of course eventually returned it.

There are plenty of stories of people killing their neighbour's cats out of anger, malice, or desire for revenge. But still none of this is actually hell. It is bad enough, as we say, but it could be a lot worse. To repeat, hell, strictly speaking, refers to a place, a situation, that *cannot be worse*.

So, what about terrible situations created by the deliberate actions of other people that are quite accurately referred to as 'hell on earth'? A child taken by a psychopathic sex predator, slave ships, concentration camps, gas chambers, battle trenches, 9/11, war-torn Ukraine, the ongoing Arab-Israeli conflict, the Nanjing Massacre — a massacre so appalling that according to the classic TV series *The World at War* even the Nazis were shocked by what the Imperial Japanese Army did to the Chinese. In each of these cases it is certainly other people who make these hells on earth. Surely, these cases give us grounds for asserting that hell is indeed other people.

We cannot deny the ring of truth to 'Hell is other people!' when we see footage of Putin's spiteful obliteration of Mariupol or Bashar al-Assad's chemical weapons attacks on his own civilian population, babies coughing up their corrupted lungs in wrecked hospitals. Indeed, we cannot deny the ring of truth when we see such images. That is, the trust-inspiring sound, tenor, or impression of being truthful. However, 'Hell is other people!', as was suggested right at the outset of this book, remains a sweeping generalisation.

Examples of infamous atrocities, terrible though they are, do not allow us to assert that 'Hell is other people!' because they are, thankfully, not all the human world amounts to. Despite the stark impression that our relentless, catastrophising, twenty-four-hour media cycle likes to give us of a thoroughly troubled human world, most of the time, in most places, atrocities are not taking place. People are getting along with each other reasonably, boringly well — but as good news is no news, we do not often hear about it.

Sartre's famous maxim — Garcin's famous maxim — needs qualifying and moderating to make any real sense, even if qualifying and moderating it destroys it as a neat catchphrase and memorable slogan that might or might not be a useful first approximation towards understanding a complex philosophical theory of human relationships. Let us *unpack* 'Hell is other people!' then, as philosophers like to say. Indeed, let us take it apart and reassemble it with structural improvements, so that it is more sensible, meaningful, and useful, if far less striking.

THE PROPOSITION

What Sartre actually wrote in his play *Huis Clos* was *'L'enfer, c'est les Autres'*. *'L'enfer'* means 'hell'. *'C'est'* translates to 'this is'. *'Les autres'* translates to 'others'. So, the literal translation into English of *'L'enfer, c'est les Autres'* is 'Hell, this is others'. This can be abbreviated in English, without any change of meaning, to 'Hell is others'. To make it clearer in English that 'others' here is referring to *other people*, the sentence is most commonly written as 'Hell is other people!'. The purpose of this *petite leçon de français* has simply been to dispel any doubts that 'Hell is other people!' is a fair and accurate English translation of what Sartre wrote in French, a translation that captures precisely what he meant.

'Hell is other people!' is a sentence, a statement, a proposition. The addition of the exclamation mark in English does not make it an exclamation in the grammatical sense — pedants say exclamations must begin with 'what' or 'how' — but an exclamatory statement/proposition.

A proposition states something about something. A proposition contains a subject term and a predicate term. The predicate term tells you something about the subject term. In the proposition 'The sky is blue', for example, the subject term is 'sky' and the predicate term is 'blue'. The predicate denotes a quality or property belonging to the subject. There are two main types of propositions: *analytic* and *synthetic*.

In an analytic proposition, the idea expressed by the predicate term is already contained in the subject term. An *analysis* of the subject term, provided you know what it *means*, reveals the idea expressed by the predicate term without having to resort to empirical evidence; without having to sense how the world is. In the analytic proposition 'A father is a male parent', for example, the idea 'male parent' is contained in the idea 'father', or to put it another way, it is exactly the same idea differently expressed.

Basically, 'male parent' *means* 'father', 'father' *means* 'male parent'. A father is a male parent, a male parent is a father. Thus, in an analytic proposition, subject term and predicate term are entirely interchangeable. The proposition 'A father is a male parent' does not tell you anything new if you already know what 'father' means. All analytic propositions have the form 'A is A' or 'A is not A'. 'A is A' is a tautology or truism, while 'A is not A' is a contradiction. A tautology is *necessarily* true on purely logical grounds, while a contradiction is *necessarily* false on purely logical grounds.

Now, in light of the above analysis, it can be said that 'Hell is other people!' is not an analytic proposition. The idea 'other people' is not contained in the idea 'hell'. I can think of hell or hellishness, of an utterly terrible state of affairs, without having to think at all of other people.

Maybe every hell must be hell *for someone*, for people, but this is not the same as saying hell *is* people. Equally, I can think of other people without having to think at all of hell or hellishness. 'Hell is other people!' is not a tautology, it is not a necessary truth, although in many respects it parades as one, or rather, it is frequently and incorrectly put forward as though it were one by its many adherents.

If 'Hell is other people!' is not an analytic proposition, then it must be a synthetic proposition. In a synthetic proposition, the idea expressed by the predicate term is not contained in the subject term and cannot therefore be analysed out of the subject term. The predicate term expresses a different idea to the subject term. Synthetic propositions bring different concepts together, *synthesise* them together, in order to say this subject has this property. The subject will also have other properties expressed by other synthetic propositions. 'The sky is blue' is a synthetic proposition, as is 'The sky is air', as are other propositions we might use to describe the sky. 'The sky is blue' claims the sky has the property of being blue. 'The sky is blue' is not a necessary truth. The idea 'blue' is not contained in the idea 'sky'. 'Sky' does not *mean* 'blue' and 'blue' does not *mean* 'sky'.

If I think of the sky, I may well think of it as blue, but I might equally think of it as red or grey or, indeed, imagine it as any colour I like. A person blind from birth will, arguably, have no concept of colours, having never seen them, and so will not think of the sky as having any colour at all. The proposition 'The sky is blue' is a *contingent* truth — as opposed to a necessary truth. The truth of the proposition 'The sky is blue' depends on how the sky itself is. 'The sky is blue' is generally true because clear, daytime sky is blue or looks blue. The truth or falsehood of a synthetic proposition is not a matter of logic; it is a matter of empirical evidence. The evidence of sensory experience, perhaps committed to memory or recorded somehow, determines whether any given synthetic proposition is true or false.

Now, what can we say about the synthetic proposition 'Hell is other people!'? On the basis of all that has just been said about synthetic propositions, you might be forgiven for thinking that 'Hell is other people!' is asserting that the subject 'hell' has the property 'other people'. But hold on, which is the subject term here and which is the predicate term? As said, in an analytic proposition subject and predicate are interchangeable, but 'Hell is other people!' is not an analytic proposition, it is a synthetic proposition.

'Hell has the property of being other people' seems confused, just as 'Sky has the property of being blue' does not seem confused. This confusion seems to be arising from treating 'hell' as the subject term. But what reason is there to treat 'hell' as the subject term, other than that it comes first in the proposition? Normally, the subject term is stated first in a synthetic proposition, but there are grammatical formulations of synthetic propositions in which the predicate term is stated first. Is 'Hell is other people!' such a formulation? The answer to this question lies in doing some very basic analysis.

Children studying grammar learn that the subject term is what the sentence, the proposition, is *about*, whereas the predicate term tells us something *about* the subject term. Take the synthetic proposition 'Grass is green'. It is self-evident which is subject and which is predicate here, self-evident that the proposition is *about* grass, not least because it makes no sense to say 'Green is grass'. Green is a colour, a quality, a property, you cannot have green without there being something which is green, in this case grass. Green must, so to speak, inhere in some subject, be a property of some object.

Now, it is possible to think of synthetic propositions in which 'hell' is clearly the subject term. 'Hell is hot', for example. As with 'Green is grass', it makes little or no sense to say, 'Hot is hell'. Hot is a quality, a property, an attribute; you cannot have hotness without there being something that is hot. Hotness must inhere in some subject, in this case hell.

In the synthetic proposition 'Hell is other people!', 'hell' is not really referring to a place, to a thing, to a subject that has properties, but rather to a property, a quality, an attribute. Namely, the attribute of hellishness, as in 'very bad', 'unpleasant', 'terrible', 'horrible', 'the worst thing imaginable' and so on. And to what are these attributes said to belong? Answer: *other people*. The subject term of the proposition 'Hell is other people!' is not in fact 'hell' but 'other people'. In 'other people' we have a clear subject, or rather collection of subjects, that can be claimed to have hellish properties. The dramatic, rhetorical formulation, 'Hell is other people!' conceals what is really being claimed, that '*Other people are hell!*'.

Admittedly, 'Other people are hell!' does not seem much of a swap around for all the process it took to get here. However, we do now seem to have a proposition that is more straightforward and honest. A proposition that lays all its cards on the table, rather than a pseudo-analytic proposition that puffs itself up as it tries to fool us, almost at the level of feeling rather than thought, that 'hell' and 'other people' are synonymous.

'Other people are hell!' is already less rhetorically powerful than 'Hell is other people!', even with the retention of the exclamation mark, but it is nonetheless a more meaningful, more logical, even a more grammatical formulation. It reveals what is really being asserted, and as such allows us to cross-examine the assertion, to disagree with it, to qualify it, and to reformulate it in the light of reason and experience.

'Other people are hell!' is still far too categorical a statement, and far too negative. It flies in the face of a vast amount of everyday, positive experience of other people being many other things besides hellish, including things that are very much the opposite of hellish. If it is at all true that at least some other people are sometimes non-hellish, sometimes pleasant, sometimes kind, sometimes lovely, even sometimes heavenly, then we have to moderate our language.

We have to be less than categorical, only allowing ourselves to make such qualified, conditional claims as, 'Other people are sometimes hell' or 'Some other people are hell' or, most judiciously, 'Some other people are sometimes hell'. How mundane 'Some other people are sometimes hell' would look on a T-shirt or a mug, especially if underneath in small print was added, 'Although mostly other people are a mixed and moderate bag, far from hellish and far from heavenly. Often a bit irritating but okay really'.

This is how a great realist writer like Jane Austen portrays people, not particularly evil and mostly not particularly saintly. Her characters are full of forgivable, even attractive human foibles, often irritating to others but by no mean hell on Earth. Beautiful Emma Woodhouse, 'faultless in spite of all her faults' (*Emma*, p. 312), is a great example. Emma is a spoilt, immature, manipulative snob, but also capable of great kindness and sensitivity, of learning from her mistakes, of making moral progress. What a sparkling, engaging, incredibly convincing character Emma is.

Some people find Jane Austen boring, perhaps because her characters are so realistic, that is, so morally middle-of-the-road. Yet in many ways Austen is a far better, far more penetrating and accurate psychoanalyst of everyday being-for-others than old Sartre with his all too frequent *sturm und drang*.

We have come a long way from 'All other people are always hell'. Nobody is perfect, but surely the vast majority of people never reach anything like hellishness in their behaviour towards their fellow human beings. Maybe some people are hell for others, or certain others, all of the time, but that is only *some* people being very nasty to *some* people.

It might be objected that some people do encounter *all* other people as hell, perhaps because they have acute paranoia. For them, hell is other people. However, saying, 'For him, hell is other people', is not the same as making the universal claim that 'Hell is other people, for everyone!'. It simply states that there are some unfortunate people whose mental derangements are such that they encounter all others as hellish, even if most or all of those they encounter are not in reality devils and would not be judged to be devils by any sane person who encountered them.

So what have we got? What have we toned 'Hell is other people!' down to? Something like this: Perhaps some other people are hell all of the time, perhaps all other people are hell some of the time, but it sure as hell ain't true that all other people are hell all of the time. There is no convincing evidence for such a universal claim, and a wealth of evidence against it, some of it to be found within Sartre's own theory of being-for-others. A theory that is, nonetheless, time and again encapsulated in the all too famous maxim 'Hell is other people!', but should not be thus encapsulated, as it is ultimately unhelpful and misleading to do so.

Imagine Garcin, Inez, and Estelle are not dead, not trapped forever in a small room in hell, but, as would be far more realistic, far more *existential*, stranded for a considerable period of time on a small, unattractive desert island on Earth where there are no mirrors and it is difficult to sleep because of the insects. A situation not unlike the British TV series

I'm a Celebrity . . . Get Me Out of Here!, only without chirpy Ant & Dec to chivvy things along.

Garcin, Inez, and Estelle might subject each other to the same humiliations as they do in Sartre's dreary play, attempt the same futile justifications, try and fail to determine the Other's opinion of them. But in the end, just before they are rescued and can finally get away from each other and find more amicable company and surroundings, Garcin will swing round abruptly and declare with bitter laughter, 'Sometimes people can be so nasty, but Inez believing I'm a coward is probably not as bad as being penetrated by red-hot pokers.' Curtain.

CRITICAL CRITICS AND CRITICISMS

As we have repeatedly seen, Sartre's *conflict thesis* of human interaction is based on the claim that to experience the Other as a *subject* is always to experience myself as a transcended *object* for the Other. I therefore, according to Sartre, always experience the Other as a threat to my subjectivity, to my being-in-the-world as a free transcendence. As we also saw when considering the role of the body in Sartre's phenomenological ontology, Sartre's contemporary Merleau-Ponty disagrees with him on this point, arguing that my awareness of the Other as a subject is often not based on my experience of myself as an object for the Other.

Merleau-Ponty argues instead that I am most often aware of the Other as an *embodied consciousness*. Most often I do not experience the Other merely as a threatening look that has transcended and objectified me but as a living, breathing, acting, embodied subject there before me in all his sentient, reflective richness — a subject incarnate whose living embodiment and subjectivity are one and indivisible.

Now, if Merleau-Ponty is right — certainly his phenomenological description seems more in keeping with common experience than Sartre's — and I frequently encounter the Other as an embodied consciousness, then there is clearly an alternative, non-threatened and therefore non-conflictual way for me to encounter the Other. Merleau-Ponty's notion of embodied consciousness surely undermines Sartre's key claim that 'Conflict is the original meaning of being-for-others' (*Being and Nothingness*, p. 386).

In criticising Sartre's uncompromising view that 'Hell is other people!', his view that at the very least the essence of all human relationships is conflict, my old professor and PhD examiner, Gregory McCulloch, writes:

> What a sorry business this all is! But surely, even though there is undoubtedly something that rings true in Sartre's account, we at least sometimes manage better than this. Most people would not agree that sexual relationships have to be as fraught and unsatisfying as Sartre insists, and whether or not sexual relations are, as it were, at the bottom of all others, still many of us seem often to rub along rather more harmoniously than Sartre would have it, in and out of bed. (*Using Sartre*, p. 139)

McCulloch goes on to suggest that Sartre's insistence on the universality of conflict is largely if not entirely motivated by personal considerations. Sartre, he argues, is tempted to speak too much from his own experience and/or to play the novelist by over-emphasising one aspect of human nature. 'It is hard not to see here plain autobiography, and/or Sartre the novelist, intent on embodying a powerful though partial view of the human condition' (*Using Sartre*, p. 139).

Well, we explored Sartre's life in some detail, at least up to the time he wrote *Being and Nothingness* and *In Camera*. We explored his road to 'Hell is other people!'. As we saw, he lived through two world wars and experienced certain hardships, especially as a prisoner of war, but his suffering was never extraordinary. It was nothing, for example, compared to the torment of the victims of the Nazi Holocaust or the agonies of French Resistance fighters tortured for information. He took risks in resisting the Nazi occupation of France, he did his bit, but arguably the closest he ever came to the really sharp end of the French Resistance was writing about it. Life in general taught him that some other people are sometimes hell, but his own life certainly gave him no grounds for asserting categorically that hell is other people.

On the contrary, Sartre had a loving and mutually supportive relationship with his mother until she died in 1969 aged eighty-six. He had many good friends, despite famously falling out with some of them over politics; his students adored him; and his work gained him thousands of admirers. He loved being part of the social hustle and bustle of Paris, as much as he enjoyed taking holidays to other crowded cities with members of his devoted inner circle. He was seldom alone his entire life, in fact. Even when he undertook the essentially solitary activity of writing, which he did for several hours per day on most days of his life, he often did so in busy cafés or had de Beauvoir or some other woman in his study or close by.

Like most people, he was occasionally hurt in love, and the capricious Olga Kosakiewicz in particular drove him to distraction, to fits of jealousy, but his relationship with her was as much heaven as it was hell, an exquisite, amorous torture that he certainly craved. His *ménage à trois* with Olga and de Beauvoir helped inspire *In Camera* to some extent, but the threesome in the play is very much a far-fetched, gothic, nightmare version of the actual threesome, which was often a source of great pleasure and fascination to all parties.

McCulloch, then, is wrong to suggest that Sartre's bleak view is 'plain autobiography' (*Using Sartre*, p. 139), as there was little in Sartre's largely charmed life to inspire such a view, and a great deal to preclude it. McCulloch is right, however, to attribute Sartre's grimness to Sartre the novelist, the dramatist, the dramatiser, intent on presenting a powerfully bleak but partial view of the human condition. Recall Sartre's admission, made in his *War Diaries*, that his characters are far gloomier than he is because they lack the 'living principle' (*War Diaries*, p. 338) which he possesses. 'I stripped my characters of my obsessive passion for writing, my pride, my faith in my destiny, my metaphysical optimism' (*War Diaries*, p. 339).

It should be said that despite his gloomy characters and settings, Sartre's overall philosophy is uplifting, and I have argued at length in other books such as *How to Be an Existentialist* that existentialism is ultimately a positive, optimistic, and beneficial philosophy. A philosophy that outlines how it is possible for people to live a worthwhile life despite the tough, inalienable, existential truths of the human condition: our inability to be at one with ourselves, the impossibility of achieving complete contentment, the relentlessness of freedom and responsibility, constant anxiety, the omnipresence of other people, the inevitability of death, and so on. Indeed, a person's life can only reach its full potential if he confronts these existential truths courageously and responds to them constructively.

As I have also argued elsewhere, Sartre's fictional writing contributes greatly to the overall exposition of his philosophy, gives it a richness, humanity, and authenticity it would otherwise lack. Yet I have to acknowledge here that sometimes his fictional writing can confuse his philosophy, even throw some people off what is really important and of most value in it.

This is the case with 'Hell is other people!', a clever-sounding, would-be maxim which Sartre penned as a finishing flourish to a play he drafted in just a couple of weeks in 1944. I am tempted to say 'Hell is other people!' is a throwaway line, but it is not. Certainly not in the context of *In Camera*, which is certainly not a throwaway play, being a very good play in many respects, albeit one that needs to be taken with a large pinch of salt in the context of Sartre's philosophy as a whole.

It is worth noting that Sartre does not go as far as to assert in *Being and Nothingness* that 'Hell is other people!', despite the conflict-focused thesis of human relationships detailed in that mighty tome completed around the same time as *In Camera*. The phrase would not fit in *Being and Nothingness* without at least some qualifying and softening.

Arguing along similar lines to McCulloch, Marjorie Grene notes that Sartre ignores the evidence of certain concrete situations when he suggests that the look is always threatening. Grene simply and effectively invokes 'the testimony of experience' (*Sartre*, p. 154), inviting us to consider 'the rare but still indubitable experience of mutual understanding, of the reciprocal look of peers; or the look of mother and infant, where the one protects and the other is protected. In its immediate appearance there seems no internecine warfare here' (*Sartre*, p. 154).

Given that 'the testimony of experience' seems pretty irrefutable here, how are we to make sense of Grene's contra-Sartrean claim that the look is not always threatening and sometimes even benign and reassuring? Søren Overgaard, in his paper, 'The Look' (*Jean-Paul Sartre: Key*

Concepts, pp. 106–17), echoing Jonathan Webber in his paper, 'Bad Faith and the Other' (*Reading Sartre: On Phenomenology and Existentialism*, pp. 180–94), argues that in *Being and Nothingness* Sartre weaves together two distinct aspects of the look: the look as that which makes me aware of my being-for-others, and the look as that which ascribes to me a fixed nature ('The Look', p. 115). This seemingly unhelpful conflation of two distinct aspects of the look is possibly, says Overgaard, 'merely a consequence of Sartre's general decision to weave together phenomenological ontology and cultural critique' ('The Look', p. 115).

The former experience, the look making me aware of my being-for-others, need not involve conflict. The look can even be received, as Grene argues, as a look that is protective, reassuring, and kind. It is the latter experience of having been ascribed a fixed nature that underlies 'the alienation that [Sartre] finds in our experience of shame and the conflict that he finds in our interpersonal relationships' ('Bad Faith and the Other', p. 192).

It is not that the Other looks at me *per se* that stirs conflict, but rather that in looking at me *some* others ascribe to me a fixed nature such as idiot, voyeur, or bigot that I resent, or simply that in looking at me I *believe* they have. Alternatively, of course, I might believe that in looking at me they are ascribing to me a fixed nature I approve of, such as intelligent or daring, possibly the fixed nature I am in the habit of striving to ascribe to myself, in which case there is also no conflict.

Conflict arises when the fixed nature that is ascribed to me by the Other *conflicts* with the fixed nature I strive to ascribe to myself. 'The ascription to me of a fixed nature which is outside of my control . . . clearly conflicts with the project of seeing myself as having a particular kind of fixed nature' ('Bad Faith and the Other', p. 191). The look of another, perceived rightly or wrongly as being negatively judgemental, bursts the fragile bubble of self-delusion I craftily blow for myself by thought, word, and deed: the fantasy that I am good, wise, clever, brave, superior, and so on in the mode of *being* what I am. It is no wonder that the negative judgement of the Other makes me hostile towards him, makes me want to get the better of him, makes me want to recover my reputation, my status, my ego-bubble, both in my own estimation and in his.

Alternatively, I may simply want to annihilate him so that he can no longer take the measure of me. In annihilating him, however, I would not annihilate the fact, the memory, that he once took the measure of me. Indeed, his death would set his negative judgement in stone as something neither of us could ever change.

Both Overgaard and Webber rightly identify the role of bad faith in all this, for it is bad faith to seek to delude myself that I have any kind of fixed nature, bad faith to pretend to myself that there is no requirement to constantly *choose* who I am. As a being-for-itself I can never simply *be* what I am, I can only ever *aim* at being what I am, *play* at being what I am, without ever being able to become it once and for all.

Crucially, I can no more *be* what another person labels me as than I can *be* what I label myself as. So, it is a form of bad faith for me to believe or to take seriously that I am, for example, the idiot-*thing* another person would have me be. Webber suggests that to achieve authenticity, to rise above bad faith, is to no longer be susceptible to the belittling, fossilising judgements of others and to the conflict this susceptibility generates.

> Sartre's account of our relations with one another is an account of the lives to which we are condemned by the project of bad faith. Reading [*Being and Nothingness*] in this way makes sense of Sartre's recommendation of a radical conversion to authenticity: such a conversion will liberate us, he thinks, from the [interpersonal] difficulties detailed throughout *Being and Nothingness*. ('Bad Faith and the Other', p. 191)

So, in separating the look that makes a person aware of his being-for-others from the look that ascribes to him a fixed nature, Webber and Overgaard offer a reading of Sartre that helps us to make sense of Grene's simple but powerful observation — it being an observation of everyday life that anyone might make — that the look is definitely not always threatening.

Continuing to criticise Sartre's conflict-obsessed, hell-is-others thesis, Grene appeals to the findings of developmental psychology pointing out that 'human infants deprived of a family setting develop more slowly' (*Sartre*, p. 154).

Research psychologists have accumulated a wealth of evidence to support the view that personal attachment to others, and particularly to a primary attachment figure, most often although not necessarily the biological mother, is vital to a child's healthy physical, emotional, and cognitive development. Infants who do not enjoy a strong and contented attachment to a caregiver, one that goes well beyond the mere servicing of their basic physical needs, suffer a range of disadvantages that often impact negatively on the rest of their lives. The person who does not establish strong personal bonds as a child is more likely as an adult to experience relationship problems, to have learning difficulties, to suffer mental health issues, to underachieve and to fall into a pattern of antisocial and even criminal behaviour.

It is of course a matter of common knowledge that a difficult childhood, particularly one characterised by a lack of close, loving, nurturing relationships with adults, often leads to a difficult life. Developmental psychologists, however, have clarified and codified this common knowledge by studying the effects of insecure and non-existent attachment (privation) in a systematic and broadly scientific way.

Attachment theory, pioneered by such figures as John Bowlby and Mary Ainsworth, distinguishes between securely and insecurely attached infants on the basis of how the infants behave, under scientifically controlled test conditions, with their caregiver, when separated from their caregiver, and when introduced to strangers in the presence and absence of their caregiver.

Without going into the details of the tests, it has been repeatedly shown that sustained sensitive responding by the caregiver to all the physical, emotional, and intellectual needs of the infant produces *secure attachment*. The securely attached infant is comfortable with intimacy and interacts confidently with strangers. Importantly, the caregiver provides the securely attached infant with a *secure base* from which to independently explore the world and develop constructive relationships with other people. Not surprisingly, secure attachment, characterised by trust in others and outgoing behaviour, is closely linked to good subsequent cognitive and emotional development.

A lack of sustained sensitive responding by the caregiver to all the physical, emotional, and intellectual needs of the infant produces *insecure attachment*. The insecurely attached infant is not comfortable with intimacy and does not interact confidently with strangers. The insecurely attached infant lacks that all-important secure base from which to explore the world and the being of others, and as a result is far more likely to experience poor subsequent cognitive and emotional development.

It follows that it can be disadvantageous for a child to experience a disruption of attachment from their primary attachment figure, although this depends on a variety of factors. Most children show signs of distress on physical separation from their primary caregiver. Securely attached children tend to recover quickly from this *separation anxiety*, especially if they find themselves in a friendly environment with plenty of distractions, particularly other children. The novelty of the situation and the opportunity it affords for independent behaviour and socialisation is even good for their development when not too prolonged, and they trust, as the securely attached child tends to do, that their primary caregiver will soon return.

Prolonged disruption of attachment from the primary caregiver can have serious negative effects, although this depends on the environment in which the disrupted attachment takes place, not least in comparison to the child's usual environment. In the debate about whether nursery care is preferable to home care, psychologists have noted that a good nursery school is better than a bad home characterised by poor parenting.

Studies have shown that children subjected to prolonged disruption of attachment can become markedly withdrawn. They stop playing, cry a great deal, and even refuse food and drink. Clearly, in that order, these behaviours are detrimental to their healthy cognitive, emotional, and physical development. Even when returned to their primary caregiver they can continue to show signs of emotional trauma such as anger and shunning intimacy.

If the effects of insecure attachment and seriously disrupted attachment are bad, then the effects of *privation*, failure to form any attachment at all, are much worse. Privation is usually due to abusive or neglectful parenting or poor institutional care and is, fortunately, relatively rare. Social and emotional development are severely affected by privation which often produces *attachment disorder*, a recognised and distinct psychiatric condition which is listed in the *Diagnostic and Statistical Manual of Mental Disorders*.

Children suffering from attachment disorder have no preferred attachment figure due to severe neglect or frequent change of caregiver and exhibit an inability to react and relate to others positively or appropriately. There is even evidence to suggest that they can suffer from a condition called *deprivation dwarfism*: stunted growth due to lack of emotional care rather than poor nourishment. Psychologists have suggested that the production of growth hormones may be restricted by emotional disturbance.

Children with attachment disorder are unlikely to have a close friend or friends and tend to be disliked by other children, not least because they are often uncooperative, quarrelsome, and bullying. Attachment disorder can manifest as *inhibited*, where the child is shy and withdrawn and struggles to cope with social situations, or *disinhibited*, where the child is over-friendly and attention seeking. In the latter case, the child is frequently spurned by others who often find his advances indiscriminate and presumptuous.

There are many factors that lead to a person having a successful or unsuccessful life, a fulfilled or unfulfilled personal and social life and so on, and even children who suffer privation and attachment disorder can eventually recover and 'turn out well' as adults. However, given that children who experience the dire effects of privation at an early age often grow up also having to contend with poverty and poor education, their chances of having anything approaching a happy life are greatly reduced.

Attachment disorder, as is shown in the case of the disinhibited child, can sow the seeds of adult psychopathic and sociopathic conditions, characterised by impaired empathy, lack of remorse, lack of moral inhibition and excessive egotism, the last often a reaction to a deep sense of inferiority. These tendencies might lead a person to become the CEO of a multinational corporation or a leading politician, but particularly where education is lacking, they are more likely to lead to a chaotic life, abuse of self and others, criminality, or incarceration.

Perhaps the most important finding of developmental psychology in the area of attachment is that the relationship between the infant and its primary caregiver — some psychologists allow that this can be primary or main *caregivers* — serves as a *template* for all later relationships. Bowlby called this template the *internal working model*. The model is a mental representation of a person's relationship with their primary caregiver, ideally allowing them to successfully orientate themselves in their environment, particularly where significant others and their own being-for-others is concerned.

If, as an infant, a person has a close, loving, secure relationship with their primary attachment figure, where the caregiver is consistently sensitive and responsive to their signals (social releasers), then the internal working model is likely to be a good one. Going forward, it should facilitate healthy, positive, and constructive social *orientation*. It should provide an exemplar for intimate relationships that are far more likely to be successful than unsuccessful.

On the other hand, if an infant's attachment to a primary attachment figure is insecure or non-existent then their internal working model will be a bad one that leads to unhealthy, negative, and destructive social *disorientation*. The model is unlikely to be a useful exemplar for the formation of successful intimate relationships. Indeed, it is more likely to produce maladaptive behaviours and dispositions that make sustaining successful intimate relationships difficult.

We all know from experience of our own relationships and/or those of others, as well as from relationships portrayed in novels and films, what these maladaptive behaviours and dispositions are: insecurity, jealousy, possessiveness, impatience, intolerance, irascibility, quarrelsomeness, disloyalty, lack of empathy, and so on. All of them are destructive of intimate relationships, all of them are rooted to a significant degree in people's experience of, and their response to, less than perfect early attachments.

Adults with a good or relatively good internal working model are less likely to favour these destructive, maladaptive behaviours, having better strategies at their disposal, and if provoked into them can keep them under reasonable control. Adults with a bad internal working model are more likely to favour these maladaptive behaviours because as children they were not taught by positive example or afforded the opportunity to discover for themselves better conduct with which to respond to and deal with others. Long practice renders these infelicitous proclivities inveterate, to the extent that a person who is hooked on them is unlikely to have the personal insight or emotional strength to change them for the better without the help of a psychotherapist.

R. D. Laing also recognises the importance of early attachments to the quality and direction of a person's subsequent psychological development: 'It is out of the earliest loving bonds with the mother that the infant develops the beginnings of a being-for-itself. It is in and through these bonds that the mother "mediates" the world to the infant in the first place' (*The Divided Self*, p. 190).

For Laing, the infant who has the benefit of secure attachment to a primary caregiver is likely to grow up *ontologically secure*, whereas the infant who does not have the benefit of secure attachment to a primary caregiver is likely to grow up *ontologically insecure*. This distinction between ontological security and insecurity was outlined in the previous chapter when we considered the engulfment anxiety of the schizoid person. It is comparable to Bowlby's distinction between a good and a bad internal working model to the extent that to have a good internal working model is to be ontologically secure while to have a bad internal working model is to be ontologically insecure.

Laing says the ontologically secure person experiences 'his own being as real, alive, whole; as differentiated from the rest of the world in ordinary circumstances so clearly that his identity and autonomy are never in question; as a continuum in time; as having an inner consistency, substantiality, genuineness, and worth' (*The Divided Self*, p. 41).

The ontologically insecure person, on the other hand, is not blessed with such a sense of personal coherence and self-esteem. He feels 'precariously differentiated from the rest of the world, so that his identity and autonomy are always in question. He may lack the experience of his own temporal continuity. He may not possess an over-riding sense of personal consistency or cohesiveness. He may feel more insubstantial than substantial, and unable to assume that the stuff he is made of is genuine, good, valuable' (*The Divided Self*, p. 42).

For Laing, then, a secure sense of his own autonomous identity, primarily established in childhood, is required if a person is to relate well to a complex external world that invariably includes other people. Otherwise, as with the indifferent or schizoid person we considered in the previous chapter, all relationships will *threaten* him, not least with the loss of his fragile personal identity.

Far from other people being hell then, close, loving, personal relationships with other people from an early age are essential to our healthy emotional, cognitive, and even physical development, to our general well-being and ability to orientate ourselves satisfactorily in society for the rest of our lives.

Troubled, insecure personal relationships with those who raise us are harmful to our development, but this is not to say that we would be better off having no personal relationships at all. The evidence shows that there is probably nothing worse for a person's future prospects than privation, nothing worse than being cut off from others and having no closeness and intimacy with them. As John Donne wrote, 'No man is an *island*, entire of itself; every man is a piece of the *continent*, a part of the *main*' (*Devotions Upon Emergent Occasions*, Meditation 17).

If our adult relationships with certain other people become somewhat hellish, possibly as a result of mutual maladaptive behaviours acquired in childhood due to insecure or non-existent attachment, then the solution is probably not to end all close relationships with others and become a hermit. As the evidence strongly indicates, we have a fundamental, ongoing psychological need for intimate connections with others. Problems associated with close adult relationships might be removed by ending all close relationships — although even a hermit can feel jealous that his former lover is with another — but new torments, *isolation* and *loneliness*, will soon arise. Aristotle wrote, 'He who is unable to live in society, or who has no need because he is sufficient for himself, must be either a beast or a god' (*Politics*, Book 1, 1253a 27–29).

Actually, most beasts do not like to be alone either, with many non-human persons, chimps and dogs for example, and even domestic cats, being susceptible to attachment disorders comparable to those suffered by human persons. Even gods seem to love company, if the legends are to be believed.

Furthermore, in his isolation and loneliness, the memory of a person's closest relationships will continue to haunt him forevermore, very likely with ever increasing intensity. To repeat, 'He who has once been for-others is contaminated in his being for the rest of his days' (*Being and Nothingness*, p. 434). Poets know this all too well.

The poet and novelist Thomas Hardy married Emma Gifford in 1874. Perhaps because they were unable to have children, their relationship deteriorated. They lived for years under the same roof as virtual strangers. Yet after Emma died in 1912, the ageing Hardy found himself haunted for the rest of his days by the ghost, the memory, the loss, of Emma's beloved younger self.

> Woman much missed, how you call to me, call to me,
> Saying that now you are not as you were
> When you had changed from the one who was all to me,
> But as at first, when our day was fair . . .
>
> Thus I; faltering forward,
> Leaves around me falling,
> Wind oozing thin through the thorn from norward,
> And the woman calling.
>
> (Thomas Hardy, *The Voice*)

SARTRE AGAINST SARTRE

As we have seen, Sartre's central thesis in the area of being-for-others is that the basis of all human relationships is conflict. Melodramatically put, 'Hell is other people!'. As we have also glimpsed, however, there are times when he himself makes various claims that go against his central thesis — or claims that can be reasonably interpreted as going against his central thesis. I want now to round up these various Sartre against Sartre claims and consider them in turn.

Firstly, Sartre's own life is a testament to the implausibility of his conflict thesis, but this testament has already been considered in some detail elsewhere, so there is no need to say anymore about it here, notwithstanding a brief slide or two into a biographical point as I proceed.

Secondly, is the picture Sartre paints of sexual desire really so bad? Lovers are forever thwarted, he says, in their desire to achieve double reciprocal incarnation, but what lover gives this rather abstract notion any thought? Does even the most philosophical lover really care? Sex is sex, not philosophy, and most lovers are surely not such pensive perfectionists. They want the simple pleasures of the flesh that are undeniably delivered by relatively uninhibited sex with anyone they find attractive. They want intense orgasms and the release and relaxation from frustration that intense orgasms bring, rather than to attain the holy grail of double reciprocal incarnation.

And if sexual desire eventually collapses into a little sadomasochism, as Sartre claims it is bound to do, then as long as it is consensual and nobody gets seriously hurt, then that can be interesting and highly pleasurable too. As Nagel asks, is non-perverted sex necessarily preferable to perverted sex? His suggestion being that sex which obtains or at least gets close to the holy grail of double reciprocal incarnation may be less pleasurable than certain perversions. Sexual enjoyment may outweigh sexual perfection.

In the final analysis, there is nothing in Sartre's account of sexual desire that is particularly off-putting, and certainly nothing hellish. Indeed, reading his account is more likely to turn a person on, to make them crave all that turmoil and exquisite frustration. Arguably, Sartre's account of sexual desire is subtle, intellectualised erotica, or can be read as such.

Thirdly, as we have seen, Sartre's analysis of concrete relations with others considers the phenomenon of *indifference*, an attitude in which a person is wilfully blind to the being of the Other as a transcendence. Indifference is an effort to ignore the Other as a subjectivity. It is, as Sartre says, the practice of 'a sort of factual solipsism' (*Being and Nothingness*, p. 402). Indifference is an ongoing attempt at self-preservation, an ongoing effort to permanently defuse the challenge presented by the Other as a consciousness that I cannot ultimately control, a consciousness that is capable of judging me in ways I cannot ultimately determine.

Like all ignoring, which must by definition be aware that the ignored entity is there, indifference is actually anything but indifferent to the Other. Indifference aims at reducing immediate anxieties, but it is itself an anxiously maintained, strained coping strategy, a costly defence mechanism. The cost being that the indifferent person is continually stuck with himself, with his unjustifiable subjectivity, unable to find any respite from his contingency and meaninglessness in what the Other might make of him. In cutting himself off from the Other, the indifferent person cuts himself off from what he could be for the Other and what the Other could be for him, cuts himself off from a wealth of possible interpersonal pleasures and intrigues.

Indifference stems from deep insecurity and involves profound isolation and alienation. To escape the relative hellishness the Other can present, the indifferent person locks himself up each day in his own private hell, in his own dungeon of solitary confinement. The dungeon excludes the complications of being-for-others and offers a certain kind of miserable sanctuary, but it also precludes all the possible pleasures of being-for-others, such as feeling proud, admired, flattered, valued, respected, befriended, loved, and so on.

In his analysis of indifference, Sartre recognises that far from other people being hell, there is an intrinsic value to having relations with other people. He acknowledges that the dull, flat isolation and loneliness of indifference is not, on balance, preferable to the exciting roller coaster of intimacy. Many people are scared of roller coasters and refuse to ride on them. Most people who are scared of roller coasters, however, would really like not to be scared of them, as they know, even if they will not admit it to themselves or to others, that roller coasters offer terrific excitement and the thrill of feeling wholly alive.

As seen, Sartre's indifferent person exhibits *schizoid personality disorder*. Psychological research into this disorder reveals that the schizoid person, unlike the autistic person, actually desires close relationships but flees them due to paranoid fears about others. We might say, in simple terms, that the schizoid person is afraid of being hurt, just as people who are afraid of roller coasters are afraid of being thrown from the roller coaster or having some other terrible roller coaster accident. In being overcautious, however, they hurt themselves continually in an insipid yet extremely insidious way by failing to live their life to the full. That is, by failing to explore to the full the exciting possibilities of their being-for-others.

This is why, as Tennyson says, 'Tis better to have loved and lost than never to have loved at all' (*In Memoriam, A. H. H.*). The indifferent person, the person who *strives* to be indifferent but is not really so, loses every day at least the chance of love by giving himself no chance of winning it. The caring person, on the other hand, the person who is strong and brave enough to care and to go on caring despite having been hurt, is at least open to the kind of life-enhancing joy that only intimacy can bring. It is as true on the emotional plane as it is on the battlefield that 'Cowards die many times before their deaths; The valiant never taste of death but once' (Shakespeare, *Julius Caesar*, Act 2, Scene 2).

In our above analysis of indifference, we have spoken as though isolation and loneliness are always self-imposed, as though anyone can venture into the world and find great friendship and love if they simply put their mind to it and get out more. Certainly, many people who are isolated could make more effort to go out, meet others, and socialise. Undoubtedly, isolated people are often held back from socialising not by lack of opportunity but by pride, in so far as seeking to break out of their isolation and seek the company of others is felt by them to be a shameful admission that they are lonely. An isolated person may well think, I cannot be lonely if I choose to be lonely. Thus, he seeks to render his miserable, habitual isolation a *glorious* isolation. There are, however, many people who are not really in a position to break out of their isolation, certainly to any great extent.

This is particularly true of the elderly, especially those who are frail and live alone, very likely because their spouse, if they had one, is dead, and their children, if they have any, flew the nest long ago and have their own busy lives, often it seems on the far side of the world. The vast majority of elderly people no longer go out to work, and many of their old friends will have died. It is harder to make new friends when you are elderly, because disability and illness make it harder to venture out and meet new people. Hence, elderly people, due to their lack of health, energy, and mobility, often find it difficult to meet up with other elderly people. As to young people, most of them are obsessed with the company and approval of their peers and are generally not interested in spending time with older people.

Loneliness and isolation is an age-old problem, not just a problem of old age, and there are all sorts of reasons why a person of any age can become lonely and isolated. It is sad but true, for example, that people who are lonely and isolated are often shunned by others. They may come across as a little desperate for company when they find it, as too talkative, having not spoken to anyone for ages, as inattentive, having so much they want to offload. The other person may well fear that this lonely person, that nobody else seems to be interested in, will try to monopolise them, try to become their best friend, when they already have good friends of their own. They may well fear that there must be something weird and unsavoury about this lonely person, given that nobody else seems to want to befriend them. Thus, loneliness breeds loneliness, not least because loneliness itself is often perceived as a weird character trait by people who are popular.

It is important to note that loneliness is not only a negative psychological state of boredom, yearning, hopelessness, and depression. Loneliness is stressful and, therefore, increases a person's risk of cardiovascular disease and stroke. Memory and learning are often adversely affected and, in the elderly particularly, Alzheimer's disease and other forms of dementia are more likely to progress. Loneliness can often lead to alcoholism and substance abuse, as well as to obesity due to comfort eating. Ultimately, lonely, isolated people are at greater risk of committing suicide. All these factors mean that loneliness increases risk of premature death.

Of course, some people enjoy their own company and can quite happily spend days alone if they are occupied. However, few people would want to be marooned alone on a desert island indefinitely, even if they were as usefully occupied as Robinson Crusoe always was on his desert island — or had a volleyball with a face to share their thoughts with (as in the film *Cast Away*). Most people who enjoy their own company are confident that they can enjoy the company of others when they choose to.

True loneliness and real isolation arise when a person has no recourse to others. When she is confronted by a desolate future with no prospect of close personal contact. When she has, for example, no other company to look forward to, day after day, beyond perhaps a brief visit from a care worker. The amount of loneliness in this overcrowded world is truly shocking. Where do all the lonely people come from?

The key point is that it is not other people that the legions of the lonely dread but the lack of other people in their lives. Having nobody to talk to for days, weeks, even months on end, having nobody to share their thoughts and experiences with. And this dread grows as the years advance, because isolation and advancing years tend to go hand in hand. For most people, hell is not other people; hell is the prospect of living entirely or almost entirely alone and the fear of dying alone. For those all alone in bedsit land, the great fear is being found 'dead behind the door', when the flies and the stench finally indicate the presence of their corpse. It happens every day.

Sartre considers loneliness in *Nausea*, particularly the loneliness of the Autodidact, 'that poor humanist, whom men don't want any more' (*Nausea*, p. 228). He does not, however, treat loneliness as a general evil to the extent that he treats the existence and proximity of other people as a general evil. Arguably, loneliness is dismissed as something certain people such as the Autodidact *deserve* for having the effrontery to be so unattractive, irritating, and desperate for friendship with anyone.

Having declared early on in the novel that 'The Autodidact doesn't count' (*Nausea*, p. 16), Roquentin later takes rare pity on him after he is punched and thrown out of the library. Roquentin nonetheless views the desperate isolation and loneliness of the Autodidact as inevitable. 'But it was inevitable that one day he should find himself alone again. . . . Now he has entered into solitude — forever. . . . the long succession of days of exile' (*Nausea*, p. 228).

In contrast to the Autodidact, Roquentin's isolation is self-imposed and, therefore, comes across as far more noble and alluring. Nevertheless, one cannot help thinking that some decent company besides the creepy

Autodidact would help enormously with Roquentin's mental health issues. From the point of view of a psychiatrist, Roquentin certainly exhibits some of the symptoms of schizoid personality disorder, if not full-on psychosis, although he does make one failed attempt to break out of his self-imposed estrangement from humankind.

Roquentin visits his former lover Anny in Paris in response to her letter. It emerges that they have developed a similar, nihilistic view of the world. They are both in despair over the pointlessness of life and relationships, deeply troubled by the absurdity and superfluity of existence. They agree that they cannot help each other with their pessimistic attitude and the isolation it induces. Anny is kept by a wealthy man, but he means nothing to her. Their brief encounter ends and they part company, understanding that neither will ever attempt to cross the gulf of circumstances and nihilistic philosophy that separates them. Back in Bouville, Antoine thinks: 'Anny came back only to take all hope away from me. I am alone in this white street lined with gardens. Alone and free. But this freedom is rather like death' (*Nausea*, p. 223).

Suppose, however, that they had stayed together. They might at least have found in each other, in the love for one another that they clearly possess, a distraction from *the nausea*; some hope of pleasure, even if, as they believe, 'there are no perfect moments' (*Nausea*, p. 213).

So, Sartre, in most of his writings, does not recognise the evils of isolation and loneliness anywhere near as readily as he recognises the evils of irritating, overbearing company. Had Sartre been less surrounded by people, less loved by family, friends, and mistresses, had he more personal experience of the evils of loneliness and isolation, he might well have concluded that 'Hell is the complete lack of other people.' It would surely be a claim that had more truth in it, a claim that was more supported by evidence and testimony, than that questionable, threadbare platitude, 'Hell is other people!'.

The Urban Dictionary website once gave one of the definitions of 'Hell is other people!' as: 'A phrase with fresh meaning in 2020, when people all over the world are commanded by law to stay far away from each other, when the innocent presence of another human can cause your death.' This definition is of course referring to the COVID-19 pandemic that began in late 2019, the worldwide spread of a highly contagious coronavirus that to this day remains deadly to some, particularly to the elderly and those with underlying health conditions.

To limit the spread of the virus and prevent health services from being overwhelmed, particularly before the creation of vaccines, most governments around the world ordered people to *self-isolate* and *socially distance*, to stay indoors away from others if they were particularly vulnerable, and at the very least to keep a distance from others in public if they possibly could. Everyone was urged to obsessively wash their hands, and the wearing of face masks, another impediment to normal human interaction, became compulsory in most communal situations. Large public gatherings were prohibited, with sporting events, for example, taking place without spectators. Some people, especially healthy, young adults, were prepared to take the risk and crowd together whenever they could, on beaches, at illegal raves, and at political protests, such was their desperate need to be part of a crowd. Others were more cautious. For many months, they stayed out of one another's homes, a strategy that made visiting family and friends impractical. Following an almost total worldwide lockdown when the virus first peaked in the spring of 2020, some places in the world, when the measured rate of COVID-19 infection rose above certain levels, were still subject to periodic lockdowns of various degrees of severity as late as early 2023.

There is, indeed, a ring of truth to 'Hell is other people!' 'when the innocent presence of another human can cause your death', but above all it was found that the most widespread anxiety and burden of the pandemic at its height was the self-isolation and social distancing it required. Given that relatively few people in relation to the entire world population have even now actually contracted COVID-19, thanks largely to self-isolation, social distancing, and vaccines, and only a small percentage of those infected have died or even become particularly ill, COVID-19 *itself* was always on the margins of most people's experience. The self-isolation and social distancing, however, the difficulty and danger of mixing closely with others as people did so freely before the pandemic, became a global bad vibe that placed a great deal of strain on many people's mental health and sense of well-being.

Social distancing made all but the most unsociable and misanthropic of people realise how much they valued the company of others, how much they took the company of others for granted in the past, how much, almost like the Autodidact crushed into that shed with two hundred fellow humans, they wanted to squash into a jam-packed pub, restaurant, nightclub, or gig.

So, hell is other people in the sense that they can give you a deadly disease, but for most people the real misery of the pandemic at its height was the need to self-isolate and socially distance. Not being able to see friends and family so easily if they were not already a part of one's household, one's bubble, not being able to stay with them, not being able to sit close to them or hug them. Against Sartre, most people would agree that hell, relatively speaking, is not other people but self-isolating and socially distancing from them. For most of 2020, people had no precise idea when the insidious situation would end or what the full extent of the political, economic, social, and psychological damage would be. Fortunately, starting in late 2020, thanks to the ingenious efforts of other people called scientists, effective vaccines were rolled out across the world and the need to socially distance eventually began to reduce. So far.

Fourthly, *being-with-others*. As noted in Chapter 3, in highlighting the phenomenon of being-with, the phenomenon of community spirit, the phenomenon of *we*, Sartre acknowledges that it somewhat qualifies his central conflict thesis. He plays down the phenomenon of being-with, however, according it merely a *psychological status* that is superficial and temporary, rather than an *ontological status* that is fundamental and enduring.

Despite this playing down, Sartre cannot deny that being-with is a very real phenomenon when it occurs, one that at times entirely eclipses the sense of conflict that he claims elsewhere is always present between consciousnesses. Being-with certainly has the capacity to make other people, the presence of other people, far from hellish when it occurs, and that surely is all the ammunition we require to further attack the unconditional assertion that 'Hell is other people!'. Quite simply, other people are not always hell because it is possible to have a far from hellish and, indeed, sometimes quite heavenly sense of community and oneness with them.

Arguably, the examples Sartre gives in his chapter on concrete relations with others, watching a play together and seeing a car crash together (*Being and Nothingness*, p. 435), do not provide particularly intense or prolonged examples of being-with. The experience of being-with, in these examples, is portrayed as rather fragile and fleeting, with *opposition* poised to reassert itself over *co-existence* at any moment.

A better example of being-with is given earlier on in *Being and Nothingness*, better because it reveals that being-with can be more profound and prolonged than some random people simply happening to see a play or a car crash together. This is the example of *the crew* (*Being and Nothingness*, pp. 270–71), which Sartre takes from Heidegger. Being part of a competitive boat crew, especially if the role is chosen, has a far broader and deeper context than happening to be sitting outside a café alongside strangers when two vehicles collide in the street.

For the competitive boat crew, there is a unified and unifying physical effort towards a common goal. Each member has a gut feeling of admiration for his fellow athletes, for their commitment to the pursuit of that common goal, a respect that reaches back beyond this race to all the previous races and rigorous training they have suffered and endured together. Each is proud that he is *with* the others, *at one with them*. There is an *esprit de corps*, a camaraderie, a team spirit, a feeling of pride and mutual loyalty shared by all members of the group.

> It is the mute existence in common of one member of the crew with his fellows, that existence which the rhythm of the oars or the regular movements of the coxswain will render sensible to the rowers and which *will be made manifest* to them by the common goal to be attained, the boat or the yacht to be overtaken, and the entire world (spectators, performance, *etc.*) which is profiled on the horizon. (*Being and Nothingness*, pp. 270–71)

It can be argued that there is an *us* here only because there is a *them* as opponent, that there is still Sartrean conflict at the group level because the common goal is to beat the competition. But what if the crew are racing against the clock, or the crew in question is a mountaineering team, a band of brothers or sisters or both striving to conquer a great peak, the resistance of which is not the wilfully malign cruelty of an Other but the absolute, impersonal indifference of nature? What if the crew is a dance troupe striving to perfect their intimately interweaving moves and gestures, or a group of rescue workers racing against time to find survivors in the aftermath of an earthquake, or restaurant staff recognising that they have a mutual interest to pull together to get through a busy evening and earn their living?

In all these cases and countless others like them, the self is not transcended by other people, nor does it seek to transcend other people. Rather, the self is transcended by some collective, communal experience or enterprise in which the individual person becomes, or allows himself to become, submerged in an *us* that does not require conflict with a *them* in order to be maintained. The conflict, the battle, in all these cases, is *the team* striving to overcome the facticity and adversity of the world as it exists *apart from* other people, not a battle against other people. The staff of a good restaurant, as opposed to the staff of a bad one, are not battling against their customers, rather they are in a battle with Murphy's Law *on behalf of* their customers.

There are so many collective human activities and situations where cooperation and selflessness predominate, as opposed to competition and egoism, that a person could spend the greater part of their life absorbed in such activities to the almost total exclusion of interpersonal conflict.

Some people seem to come into conflict with others wherever they go. They are, for whatever reasons, divisive, antagonistic, confrontational, and belligerent. Some other people, for whatever reasons, unfortunately get picked on by the belligerent, despite or because of the fact that they are mild-mannered, timid, or simply defenceless. A great many people, however, are fortunate enough in their circumstances and relationships to sail through life experiencing so little conflict with others that they might struggle to comprehend why Sartre thinks conflict is fundamental to the human condition. Conflict for them is not something that as a rule characterises their interactions with other people, but rather something that happens to certain other people, mostly on television.

Profound, conflict-excluding *being-with* can also arise as a central and highly desirable feature of religious and/or drug experiences. In many cultures the two are often brought together by design, with psychoactive drugs playing a key role in religious rituals. For many people, religion is a drug, and for many others, recreational drugs are a religion. For people praising the Lord together, praying together, singing or listening to music together, dancing together or dropping Ecstasy together, the aim is to unite together to achieve a state of reverie amounting to a collective loss of self. This collective loss of ego frees them to become one with something higher, to come together as one on a higher plane of existence.

A good rave, for example, one with good music, good lights, good people, and good empathy-inducing Ecstasy, is felt by those loved-up people present to generate a harmonious, non-conflictual unity with others, a higher or even divine state of collective consciousness that comprises every individual consciousness yet synergistically transcends every individual consciousness. Here, being-with is the shared experience of euphoria. Here, being-with *is* euphoria, a *social euphoria* that absolutely cannot be realised without other people. Hence, it cannot be said that this feeling of social euphoria is *just* the effect of the Ecstasy. Ecstasy may be a necessary condition of this intense feeling of social euphoria, but it is not a sufficient one.

In fact, Ecstasy may not even be a necessary condition. There are people who insist that if one learns from the Ecstasy experience what emotional baggage needs to be relinquished in terms of the hang-ups, barriers, and defence mechanisms that suppress natural empathy, one can achieve the same ecstatic feeling of social euphoria *without* the Ecstasy. Indeed, without any drug at all beyond lights, music, dance, and cordial company. They may well be right. After all, Ecstasy, a chemical, cannot itself contain empathy, anymore than a knife can contain pain.

So, the reality of the phenomenon of being-with gives the lie, as so many things do, to the sweeping generalisation 'Hell is other people!'. In so far as being-with, in its highest, purest, religious and quasi-religious forms, is a state of collective social euphoria, then it can be said against

Sartre, or at least against Garcin and those chronic misanthropes who endorse his unrealistically pessimistic worldview, that at times other people are heavenly; that there are special occasions when being-for-others and the being of others is simply divine.

Lastly, it is worth noting that in the mid-sixties Sartre offered a clarification of the meaning of 'Hell is other people!'. In a commentary he gave that preceded a recording of *In Camera*, he said:

> 'Hell is other people!' has always been misunderstood. It has been thought that what I meant by that was that our relations with other people are always poisoned, that they are invariably hellish relations. But what I really mean is something totally different. I mean that if relations with someone else are twisted, vitiated, then that other person can only be hell. Why? Because . . . when we think about ourselves, when we try to know ourselves . . . we use the knowledge of us which other people already have. We judge ourselves with the means other people have and have given us for judging ourselves. Into whatever I say about myself someone else's judgment always enters. Into whatever I feel within myself someone else's judgment enters. . . . But that does not at all mean that one cannot have relations with other people. It simply brings out the capital importance of all other people for each one of us. (From the 2005 Imago Theatre Playbill for Sartre's *No Exit*)

Sartre seems to be speaking off the cuff here, providing a verbal introduction to help promote a recording of *In Camera*, so perhaps we should not be too hard on him. Some of what he says is of value, such as, 'Into whatever I say about myself someone else's judgement always enters.' It is a great Sartrean line. What he says overall, however, is not really a clarification of 'Hell is other people!'.

The basic problem is that he argues that what he *really* meant by 'Hell is other people!' is something very different from what he actually said, as though you can say one thing and mean another *and* expect others to know what you really meant and not misunderstand you. The great philosopher Sartre, of all people, should know that if you do not say what you mean you will not mean what you say. The maxim 'Hell is other people!' does not say what he claims it says in the above long quote; it does not say what he claims it means.

'Hell is other people!', as we have seen, is a categorical, unconditional proposition. It asserts that all people are hell all of the time. However, in his so-called clarification, Sartre says that we should not understand it as categorical and unconditional but as qualified and conditional, as not applying invariably to everyone all of the time but only if and when 'relations with someone else are twisted, vitiated'.

Sartre says, '*if* relations with someone else are twisted', ignoring the fact that 'Hell is other people!' entails that all relations with all other people are always twisted. In other words, Sartre is insisting that, 'Hell is other people!' should be taken to mean 'Relations with some people can be hellish'. Going by all that has been said in this chapter and elsewhere, the latter formulation surely contains more truth than the former, but it cannot be legitimately said that the latter formulation is synonymous with the former.

Edward J. Grippe, in his paper 'The Hell of Our Choosing' (*Ethics and Phenomenology*, pp. 117–44), makes the following point:

> Jeremy Wisnewski has noted the movement from the categorical in Sartre's explanation of his quote ['Hell is other people!'] and how it has been misunderstood to the conditional in his explanation of its meaning. Clash of the categorical sense of the relations with Others and the conditional. ('The Hell of Our Choosing' p. 138)

From the beginning to the end of his so-called clarification, Sartre incrementally dilutes 'Hell is other people!' until we arrive at the almost laughable assertion that '["Hell is other people!"] simply brings out the capital importance of all other people for each one of us.' Sartre is of course right that other people are of capital importance for each one of us, but 'Hell is other people!' is a very odd and misleading way of expressing that capital importance.

CHAPTER 5

Lowering the Temperature

GIVEN THAT SOME PEOPLE SOMETIMES FIND OTHER PEOPLE TO BE hellish, that interpersonal relations are frequently heated, inflamed and caustic, it is fitting and useful to consider how the temperature of such relations might be lowered from searing to pleasantly warm.

In seeking to lower the temperature, however, we do not want to cool relations between people too much. As it was for Goldilocks, too cold is as bad as too hot. People may have got very touchy on social media, but generally they appreciate a little spice in their real-life relationships, a modicum of cut and thrust, a twist of friendly sarcasm and humorous insult, a pinch of entertaining repartee and witty banter to reveal and reinforce familiarity and true friendship. As author Ziyad Marar says, 'Even criticism is necessary to living well. Without it we'd be playing tennis with the net down' (*Judged*, p. 2).

Without a little friendly mockery — as distinct from unfriendly bullying — social life would be as boring as tennis without a net, football without goals, cricket without stumps, or a wet weekend in Wigan with The Association of Painfully Nice People. Real friends can be sarcastic with one another, even outright insulting at times. What best buddies do not encourage and enjoy a little mutual teasing on occasion? It is all an integral part of their intimacy, revealing how well they know each other, how much they trust each other not to go *too* far, how much they understand and even value each others' faults and foibles. Ask people what they miss most about their schooldays, and many will reply, 'The way we used to take the piss out of each other'.

POLITENESS

Good relations between people in the normal, everyday run of things are maintained and improved by good manners and appropriate levels of politeness, all attuned to the situation and the degree of familiarity or unfamiliarity existing between the persons in that situation. For example, you may swear in front of at least some of your friends on some occasions, even at them, but you should never swear in front of, and certainly never at, your grandparents.

Good manners, they say, cost nothing but can yield great wealth. Bad manners may be free too, at the point of delivery, but can cost the Earth. 'She was very polite to me', says the floating voter who does not follow politics closely, about the charming politician who shook his hand, and his vote is secured. 'She was very rude to me,' says the same floating voter about another politician, and despite her worthy manifesto, his vote is lost forever.

Politeness and over-politeness can be a sign of sophistication, a sign that someone is untrustworthy, but politeness can also be genuine, even among politicians. There is no doubt that many politicians, of whatever wing, do have a genuine regard and warmth for people. We tend to hate politicians because of their policies, their prejudices, and their blunders, but few of them, unlike many of us, are actually misanthropes.

What are good manners? Basically, as most of us know, manners is 'please' and 'thank you'. Bad manners is not minding your Ps and Qs. 'What do you say?' prompts mother. 'Please', adds the child. 'What do you say?' prompts father. 'Thank you', adds the child. The 'please' and 'thank you' must be meant of course. A reluctant 'please' and a grudging 'thank you' are worse than no 'please' and 'thank you' at all.

We are all familiar with the snappy 'please' and the sarcastic 'thank you'. These are the worst of all, as bad as that phrase, 'with respect', which seems to say 'without respect' or 'I am struggling to respect you right now'. The nuances of language are complex and so much depends on the tone of voice in which something is said and the facial expression and body language with which it is said. So, what do a sincere 'please' and a sincere 'thank you' really reveal?

Well, 'please' shows *consideration* and 'thank you' shows *gratitude*. Manners can get very complicated. In many societies throughout history manners, etiquette and protocol have been raised to the level of a courtly art form. Yet the root and essence of all good manners is simply consideration and gratitude adjusted to the occasion and genuinely displayed. Consideration is a person's respect for and appreciation of the Other, while gratitude is a person's respect for and appreciation of the Other's respect for and appreciation of them. Manners, then, are a positive acknowledgement of the Other as Other, not a mere object but a subject who has feelings and autonomy. It is moral to be considerate and grateful, to recognise that the Other is broadly like myself: rational, motivated, proud, sensitive, susceptible and so on.

Gratitude is really an extension of consideration. It would be impossible for someone to be grateful but not considerate. Gratitude is an overt expression or display of consideration for the consideration of the Other when the Other's consideration is expressed through some kind word or deed.

Ideally, manners should be a two-way street, but the dignified, self-controlled, virtuous, diplomatic person will maintain his polite consideration for the Other, his respect for the Other, even when the Other is giving him no consideration in return and there are no obvious grounds for appreciation of the Other. This consideration of the Other, although initially unrequited, may win the Other over and thus establish a mutual consideration and regard, one that not only feels pleasant to both parties but could be beneficial to both parties going forward beyond that pleasant feeling itself.

It is true that if you smile at the world it tends to smile back, because a genuine smile shows genuine consideration for and recognition of the Other as Other. The genuine returned smile is not least an expression of heartfelt gratitude for that recognition.

In practice, good manners can take many forms depending on the situation in which they are required. It is good manners to eat with your mouth closed, for example, because eating with your mouth open repulses the Other and, therefore, shows a lack of consideration for his sensitivities. It is good manners, for example, to be on time for a meal the Other has prepared for you as this shows gratitude for his efforts. If your bad-mannered lateness could not be avoided, then a sincere apology restores good relations. If you cannot avoid the bad manners of eating with your mouth open, then eat alone.

Good manners should guide all our Other-related actions and words. For polite action, as for polite word, genuine consideration and gratitude are the foundation and essence. The person who keeps the principle of proper regard for others always in mind and applies it consistently will tend to have good relations with others. He or she will tend to be respected and liked, will be deemed by those refined enough to appreciate it to be gentlemanly or ladylike, will liberally spread that free yet sometimes scarce commodity, *goodwill*, thus increasing the level of concord in the world and decreasing the level of conflict.

OVER-POLITENESS

Over-politeness is, in a sense, a form of bad manners. In so far as it offends the Other and makes them uncomfortable it fails to show the Other due consideration. People are over-polite either because they have too much regard for themselves or too little regard for themselves. Jane Austen, the great analyst of manners, features characters of both types in her novels, even characters who are a comic blend of both types, as well as characters whose manners are honest, measured, and perfectly pitched.

Those with too much regard for themselves believe that politeness exists to be flaunted as a sign of their superior social status. 'Genteel', from the French *gentil*, once meant 'well-born' or 'well-bred', but 'genteel' came to refer to a person whose politeness, refinement, and respectability is exaggerated, affected, and condescending. The genteel person believes they are a cut above the people towards whom they are genteel and that those people need to be constantly reminded of this, hence the display.

In recognising the existence and importance of social hierarchy, the person given to displays of gentility will recognise that some people are socially superior to her. A monarch may have no social superiors, but then monarchs, being monarchs, do not generally need to *put on* airs and graces. Queen Elizabeth II, for example, was seen to be forthright and measured in her politeness rather than genteel. In the company of social superiors, the over-polite person may switch her over-politeness from genteel and condescending to obsequious and ingratiating. In the mixed company of perceived inferiors and perceived superiors she may be awkwardly and comically torn between the two.

Such is the character and behaviour of the clergyman, Mr William Collins, in Jane Austen's *Pride and Prejudice*. As the heir presumptive to the estate of the Bennet family, Mr Collins is in a sense their social superior. He prides himself so much on his scrupulous politeness towards the Bennet family, even though they are in his view beneath him, that his politeness is patronising. True to the definition of 'patronising', his efforts to be kind and helpful towards the Bennets betray his assumption of superiority over them.

He sees himself as doing the Bennets a great favour and honour, as selflessly fulfilling a noble obligation, when he proposes marriage to the second eldest daughter of the family, Miss Elizabeth Bennet, who is far and away his superior in intelligence, common sense, accomplishments, looks, manners, and virtues.

Mr Collins is hurt by Elizabeth's polite but outright rejection of his marriage proposal, not because he has a deep affection for her but because he considers himself to be a very good catch for her and because, in his view, he generously stooped to her social level with the very charitable offer of raising her and her family up through her marriage to him.

On the other hand, Mr Collins is obsequiously and sycophantically over-polite towards his benefactress and social superior The Right Honourable Lady Catherine De Bourgh. His behaviour in her presence is toadying and fawning, and even in her absence he speaks of her at every opportunity in absurdly deferential and reverential tones as a personage of the most refined taste and judgement. Collins is a snob. He views his connections to Lady Catherine De Bourgh and her splendid estate, Rosing's Park, as grand attainments to be constantly flaunted before his supposed inferiors.

Mr Collins is a wonderful, comic mixture of too much self-regard and too little self-regard, depending on who he is evaluating himself in relation to. Thus, he illustrates both *condescending* over-politeness and *obsequious* over-politeness. He is both excessively proud and excessively humble, often preposterously wrenched in both directions at once by the ambiguities of his social role. He lacks the self-knowledge and strength of character to hold himself together and be his own man:

> The subjection in which his father had brought him up had given him originally great humility of manner, but it was now a good deal coun- teracted by the self-conceit of a weak head, living in retirement, and the consequential feelings of early and unexpected prosperity. A fortunate chance had recommended him to Lady Catherine de Bourgh when the living of Hunsford was vacant; and the respect which he felt for her high rank, and his veneration for her as his patroness, mingling with a very good opinion of himself, of his authority as a clergyman, and his right as a rector, made him altogether a mixture of pride and obsequi- ousness, self-importance and humility. (*Pride and Prejudice*, p. 48)

The Bennet family do not despise Mr Collins, rather they see him as a silly man and rather hilarious, all but Mrs Bennet that is. As weak-headed in her own way as Mr Collins, and desperate for her five daughters to be married off, Mrs Bennet is angry with Elizabeth for rejecting him. Austen identifies Mr Collins' fundamental vice not as ava- rice or mean-spiritedness but simply as lack of common sense, echoing the wisdom of many great thinkers from Socrates to Christopher Mar- lowe that the only sin or evil is ignorance.

Some people are over-polite not because they are condescending or obsequious but because their lack of self-regard manifests itself as a lack of self-confidence. They doubt they can create a good impression on the Other and are not comfortable with what they think the Other thinks of them. Hence, they constantly seek to ingratiate themselves with the Other, offering too many compliments or compliments that ring false. They dance attendance on the Other, apologising all the time and laugh- ing nervously and apologetically after everything they themselves say, as if to say, 'I do not really mean anything I say, so please do not be offended if you disagree'.

In not feeling worthy of the Other's consideration, they will be embarrassed by the Other's generosity, and in their embarrassment will find it difficult to express the right level of gratitude. Not wishing to offend, to appear ungrateful, they will be over-grateful, protesting their gratitude too much and for so prolonged a period it will become strained and artificial and thus irksome to the Other.

To be fair, most of us struggle with gratitude, with really feeling it and displaying an appropriate level of it. As noted, kindnesses, favours, and gifts subject us to the transcendent freedom of the Other as much as the Other's selfish acts do. Indeed, giving can be a selfish act if it aims to establish superiority over the receiver. Some people prefer to earn or even to steal what they have rather than be given it, rather than need to feel grateful for it, obliged and indebted.

Sartre, in *Saint Genet*, his biography of Jean Genet, says that as a charity case everything Genet received as a child was a gift for which he had to be grateful. Others were free not to give him what he was not free to refuse. Hence, Genet felt that nothing he was given was really his. He turned to stealing in order to have a 'possessive relationship with things' (*Saint Genet*, p. 12). He stole to possess things for which he did not have to say 'thank you'. Ironically, only stolen things truly felt as though they belonged to him. Only loot was a genuine appropriation, an acquisition resulting from the exercise of his own free will.

Nevertheless, despite these reservations about gratitude, it should be kept in mind that if showing gratitude can be difficult and irksome, not being shown gratitude is downright infuriating.

The anxiously over-polite person is too self-conscious, concerned too much with himself and what the Other thinks of him to have any real consideration for the Other. His strained over-politeness creates the interpersonal tension he seeks to dispel, tension he then strains to dispel with yet more over-politeness. It can be impossible for the Other to break this vicious spiral of over-politeness, which can become an almost manic display, the manifestation of a deep neurosis. Consequently, the Other soon begins to find the over-polite person, the person who will just not stop being over-polite, exasperating.

Perhaps in trying to paint a picture of anxious over-politeness I have drawn a caricature, or at least an extreme case, but we all know from experience that people being over-polite, perhaps obliging us to be over-polite in return, can be an emotional strain. There is a distancing sort of formality in over-politeness that prevents one from relaxing.

How often people say things like, 'I enjoy his company. He is down to earth and easy going, not too polite and formal. I can be myself with him because he doesn't try *too* hard'. The most popular family I ever knew, their house always full of visitors, had the motto, 'If people don't like us how they find us, they can leave us'. Their consideration for others and for themselves consisted in 'being themselves', mostly polite and kind-hearted but without affectation.

Whereas the likes of Mr Collins are perhaps to be despised — it is to the credit of the Bennets that they do not despise him — the anxiously over-polite person is perhaps to be pitied. Their company, however, is undeniably wearisome, forcing people to seek the relief of escaping them. Aware of people's desire to escape them, they tend to mistakenly assume that the remedy is to be even more overwhelmingly polite next time they find themselves in company.

They are not unlike people who repeatedly lose friends because of their constant bullshitting, who then mistakenly assume that the way to win friends is to further increase the frequency and magnitude of their bullshit. Essentially, they cannot distinguish between making friends and trying desperately to impress others with exaggerated or entirely false claims about their achievements and adventures. It is remarkable how many people in this world fail to realise the simple truth that as a rule the best way to impress other people and win their regard is not to try *too* hard to impress them and win their regard.

In his book *An Astronaut's Guide to Life on Earth*, former commander of the International Space Station, Colonel Chris Hadfield — a man who definitely does not need to bullshit about his achievements — argues that it is better, particularly in a new situation, to be viewed as a neutral zero than a harmful minus one. 'Everyone wants to be a plus one, of course. But proclaiming your plus-one-ness at the outset almost guarantees you'll be perceived as a minus one, regardless of the skills you bring to the table or how you actually perform. This might be self-evident, but it can't be, because so many people do it' (*An Astronaut's Guide to Life on Earth*, pp. 181–82).

IMPOLITENESS

In defining politeness, we have already gone some way to defining impoliteness. Given that at heart politeness is thought and behaviour that shows consideration and gratitude, impoliteness is thought and behaviour that shows a *lack* of these virtues.

Firstly, to set them aside, it can be said that some people are more *abrupt* in their manner than others, or at least some other people find them to be so. Such people are not necessarily impolite, as they may be very considerate. Perhaps they simply find it difficult to be charming or feel that to be charming is to be dishonest and guilty of false flattery. Such people are certainly not guilty of being over-polite.

'Rude' means offensively impolite, but it also means roughly made or done, lacking sophistication. So, a person might be rude in the latter sense, without being rude in the former sense. Most of us know rough and ready people like this, and they are often featured as heroes in novels and films. They often emerge as the best people in the end, 'when you get to know them'. They are 'rough diamonds' and 'the salt of the earth', not least because they are honest and do not try to be ingratiating.

As to people who are rude in the former sense of offensively impolite, they fall into two broad camps: those who are deliberately rude and inconsiderate, and those who are rude and inconsiderate seemingly by nature. The existentialists say we all choose who we are to a significant extent, that we are all responsible for our words and actions, so perhaps everyone who is rude is *deliberately* rude. Yet it still seems possible to draw a distinction, based on everyday observation, between people who are making an effort to be rude and inconsiderate, and people for whom being rude and inconsiderate is effortless second nature, probably as a result of their upbringing. I will consider the latter type in due course.

It seems there are people, some moody teenagers for example, who are deliberately rude all the time because they are angry and frustrated with all other people all of the time. They have, as the expression goes, a permanent chip on their shoulder. More commonly, however, deliberate rudeness is a feature of temporary anger and frustration with the Other on the part of a person who is not generally disobliging and inconsiderate. Picture, for example, the pronounced and very deliberate rudeness of a normally mild-mannered, courteous, and civilised person provoked into road rage by what they perceive to be the inconsiderate actions of another road user.

Deliberate rudeness aims at making the Other feel my anger. It is also an attempt to make the Other feel as bad as they have made me feel. It is often the quickest and most easily available form of revenge, but it is also a crude weapon that tends to backfire. The deliberately rude person, especially the one who descends into angry insults, displays her loss of self-control to the Other and so loses her dignity. Her rudely angry efforts to annihilate the transcendence of the Other end up compromising her own transcendence, wounding her own ego. She makes a fool of herself in front of the Other, reduces herself to an embarrassing spectacle for the Other. She gifts the Other the opportunity to negatively objectify her, the opportunity to label her a ridiculous, obnoxious object.

It is always better to try to restrain oneself from being angry for trivial reasons, to develop the good habit of brushing aside small offences and insults and rising serenely above them. Minor effronteries are just not worth the time and effort required to address them. But when one is justifiably angry and feels one must show it, then controlled anger is almost always far more impressive and effective, and certainly always far more dignified, than anger that resorts to rudeness and aggression. Controlled anger exacts no price of personal embarrassment and the resulting clarity of one's expression of indignation *is* its effectiveness.

> Anybody can become angry, that is easy; but to be angry with the right person, and to the right degree, and at the right time, for the right purpose, and in the right way, that is not within everybody's power and is not easy. (Aristotle, *Nicomachean Ethics*, Book II, 1109a27; variant translation as quoted in Edith M. Leonard, *The Child at Home and School*, p. 203)

An excellent example of anger that is just right in all these ways is found in Jane Austen's novel *Emma*, one of her several masterful studies of manners and morality. Righteous anger displayed, so it happens, in response to an incident of exquisite rudeness that is both deliberate and heedless.

During a daytrip to Box Hill, Surrey, where for complex reasons a fractious atmosphere develops among the day-trippers, Emma Wood-house is unable to resist insulting poor, dull, wittering Miss Bates, when she (Emma) gets carried away playing a silly game in which people have to say one very clever thing, two moderately clever things or three very dull things:

'Oh! very well,' exclaimed Miss Bates; 'then I need not be uneasy. "Three things very dull indeed." That will just do for me, you know. I shall be sure to say three dull things as soon as ever I open my mouth, shan't I?' (looking round with the most good-humoured dependence on everybody's assent). 'Do not you all think I shall?'

Emma could not resist.

'Ah! ma'am, but there may be a difficulty. Pardon me, but you will be limited as to number — only three at once.'

Miss Bates, deceived by the mock ceremony of her manner, did not immediately catch her meaning; but when it burst on her, it could not anger, though a slight blush showed that it could pain her. (*Emma*, p. 299)

Mr George Knightley, who truly loves Emma (not least for her wit) but not blindly, he being older and wiser and a man of true virtue, is angry and disappointed with Emma's blatant rudeness towards Miss Bates. Mr Knightley can be said to embody to some extent the supreme Aristotelian virtue of *megalopsuchia* (greatness of soul or magnanimity), due to his strong will and self-control, his dignity, his unpretentiousness, his unshowy generosity, his solicitude, his impeccable manners, and so on. Although he greatly values Emma's 'open temper' (*Emma*, p. 232), Mr Knightley clearly feels that she too should be encouraged to aspire to megalopsuchia. I will return to Aristotle's ethics in some detail, as it has bearing on all that has and will be said in this chapter.

Later, when they are alone, Mr Knightley admonishes Emma with intense yet powerfully polite restraint. Rather than descend to ineloquent rudeness, he maintains his self-control and, therefore, his persuasiveness. He does not allow his anger to undermine his sole purpose in addressing Emma, namely her moral improvement.

When Emma unconvincingly protests that as a ridiculous woman Miss Bates deserved the insult, Mr Knightley reminds Emma in no uncertain terms that Miss Bates is her inferior in social standing and wealth, and her superior in age. That it is, therefore, utterly unbecoming of someone of Emma's superior rank and inferior age to resort to superciliously insulting such a person. Aristotle, for his part, argues that the magnanimous person is never haughty towards the humble because it is vulgar to use one's strength against the weak (*Nicomachean Ethics*, 1124b14–1125a4, p. 157). Mr Knightley insists that Emma ought to be courteous and compassionate towards Miss Bates at all times and above all exceedingly *tolerant* of her foibles and eccentricities. Knightley says:

> 'Were she a woman of fortune, I would leave her every harmless absurdity to take its chance; I would not quarrel with you for any liberties of manner. Were she your equal in situation — but, Emma, consider how far this is from being the case. . . . Her situation should secure your compassion. It was badly done, indeed! You, whom she had known from an infant . . . to have you now, in thoughtless spirits, and the pride of the moment, laugh at her, humble her . . . This is not pleasant to you, Emma — and it is very far from pleasant to me; but I must, I will — I will tell you truths while I can; satisfied with proving myself your friend by very faithful counsel'. (*Emma*, p. 303)

Emma is a decent, good-hearted, and normally very polite person and is mortified by her beloved Mr Knightley's acute analysis and eloquent criticism of her unbecoming behaviour; her deliberate rudeness motivated in part by her all too quick wit and spontaneity, in part by Miss Bates' undeniably ridiculous and irritating character and in part by the fractious atmosphere of the Box Hill trip.

The events on Box Hill bring about an existential *radical conversion* in Emma, a coming of age, a new fundamental choice of herself as a mature, responsible woman, in preference to an irresponsible youth. Emma learns her moral lesson well. 'She had been often remiss, her conscience told her so; remiss, perhaps, more in thought than fact; scornful, ungracious. But it should be so no more' (*Emma*, p. 304). After a wretched night feeling thoroughly ashamed of herself, Emma visits Miss Bates first thing in the morning and shows through her mature, contrite, and genuinely considerate manner, rather than through a direct apology that would only give Miss Bates more pain by directly recalling the incident, that she is truly sorry for her insult and that such a *faux pas* will never happen again.

Apologising is consideration that compensates for the fact that one was inconsiderate. The essence of a sincere apology is the *remorseful acknowledgement* that one acted thoughtlessly. An apology that is not genuinely penitent is not an apology; indeed, it is a further insult. It indicates that a person is only 'apologising' because it is in *their* interest to do so, perhaps to avoid punishment, as in the case of the impenitent student commanded by a senior teacher to apologise to a junior teacher for disruptive behaviour and insolence. In this case, the senior teacher surely affords the student a further opportunity to disrespect the junior teacher. An insincere 'apology' indicates that a person places no value on the person they are 'apologising' to. So often when people say 'sorry' they really only mean they feel sorry for themselves.

It is interesting then that both mainstream media and social media are constantly trying to *force* politicians and celebrities to apologise for something they have done or said, as though this forced apology were worth anything to anyone. It is also interesting how often people seem to be satisfied by these forced apologies, as though they cannot tell the difference between an apology freely and sincerely given and a cynical, career-salvaging apology issued under duress.

Psychologists Steven J. Scher and John M. Darley, in their article 'How Effective Are the Things People Say to Apologize? Effects of the Realization of the Apology Speech Act' (*Journal of Psycholinguistic Research* 26, pp. 127–40), consider the nature of apologising and strategies for doing so.

Firstly, they note that apologising is difficult. It takes courage to humble oneself before the Other, to deliberately place oneself at the mercy of their transcendence. Fear of apologising and reluctance to do so mean that the consequences of a regrettable incident can grow out of all proportion to the incident itself, destroying relationships and careers in the process and setting the conditions for serious conflict. A regrettable incident may be trivial; what is never trivial is that the person responsible showed no remorse.

As to strategies, the most important feature of apologising appropriately is, as said, to show genuine remorse. Show it as soon as possible, saying why you feel the need to apologise, and above all be honest with the other person. Admit responsibility and show *empathy* regarding how your inconsideration may have made the other person feel. This needs to be handled with care, as it is not empathic to blatantly *assume* you know how you made the other person feel. Make amends, perhaps with a gift or kind gesture, or by bringing about a situation that allows you to show you value the other person.

Sometimes it is enough to *offer* to make amends, but beware, empty promises do more harm than good. Do not give, or offer to give, more than what is appropriate and proportionate to your misdemeanour. Do not, for example, offer to have yourself flogged in the street because you forgot your wedding anniversary. A good way of making amends is to promise that whatever it was will never happen again, but you may need to show how you plan to change your behaviour so that it really does not happen again. Finally, make sure that it does not happen again, and if it does happen again, maybe it is time to have yourself flogged in the street after all.

Having been prompted by Emma Woodhouse to consider strategies for effective apologising, I feel I must also be prompted by Mr George Knightley to consider strategies for effective anger management.

Like apologising, controlling one's anger is difficult. Depending on natural temperament, physiology, age, hormone levels, diet, upbringing, life experiences and so on, some people find anger management more difficult than others. Mr Knightley makes it look easy, but he may have gone to great efforts in his life to become a gentleman for whom self-control is second nature. We have to be wary of the background we attribute to fictional characters when we are not actually informed by the author, but you take my point.

One of the main difficulties of controlling anger and preventing it from escalating into aggression and violence is that it tends to flare up most when our self-control mechanisms are already compromised. We may be tired and stressed, both of which reduce our patience with others. The first strategy of anger management may simply be to keep this in mind, to try to be particularly aware that we are far more prone to anger when we are tired and stressed. This could consist of telling ourselves that the last thing we need when we are tired and stressed is an ugly incident that makes us even more tired and stressed.

When I was a schoolteacher, I used to tell myself that if I could get through Friday without losing my temper, I would have a more relaxed and carefree weekend. That was the reward. Losing my temper over some petty, storm-in-a-tea-cup incident involving a rude, uncooperative child was not worth losing my weekend peace of mind for. The principle is, of course, generally applicable. It is *never* worth losing your temper, as doing so never helps the situation and because the most enduring feature of losing your temper with others is usually the embarrassment and anxiety you feel at having done so.

This is not to say that you should not feel and show anger when a situation truly justifies it. I have taught — tried to teach — more than a few children who were so self-centred, so insensitive to the impact of their disruptive behaviour, so disrespectful in their manner towards everyone, so unresponsive to reasonable requests calmly made, that a measured show of anger was the only way to break through their narcissism and make them cooperate. The trick of course, certainly if you want to keep your stress levels down, is to *pretend* to be angry — so much of teaching is a performance.

Unfortunately, it is hard to *pretend* to be angry when one is already *genuinely* angry with a situation, an unruly class for example, one can neither fully control or escape — a situation one can neither *fight* effectively or take *flight* from. Repeatedly finding oneself in a situation one can neither manage effectively or flee is a major cause of the physiological and psychological condition of chronic stress, as characterised by damagingly high cortisol levels, immunosuppression, depression, and so on. Existentially, of course, one is always free to abandon one's responsibilities, to walk out mid-lesson for example, but this would only create new problems and stressors, certainly in the short term.

I knew a real hard nut of a teacher, ex-army, who walked out on a very unruly maths class mid-lesson, climbed into his car, which was parked right outside the window of his room, and drove off. His pupils watched him go. Having a gap in my timetable I was despatched to cover those barely subdued rascals. Before the bell he swept back in declaring he would take the reins from there. Appreciating his plight, I scurried away. Apparently, the Head had persuaded him by phone to return, presumably with the inducement that if he returned *asap* the whole incident could be swept under the carpet. It was. I am not sure what the purpose of this anecdote is except to illustrate stress, fight-or-flight behaviour, and existential choice. I was also going to say, anger *mismanagement*, but perhaps it is an illustration of anger *management*, given that there are far worse things his anger might have led him to do.

To take another example of justified anger, injustice warrants anger and *ought* to be met with outspoken indignation and crusading action rather than timidity and passivity. Anger is an energy that can drive us to achieve great things for great causes. Where would humanity be if people did not repeatedly grow angry with injustice, oppression, and antisocial behaviour? Anger must be contained and directed, however, because power without control is a train wreck waiting to happen. As Mr Knightley and Aristotle teach us, righteous, controlled, measured, managed anger is almost always more effective and productive than flying off the handle and stomping about.

If you are angry about the illegal dumping of rubbish, for example, one of the most antisocial, inconsiderate, annoying, selfish, filthy, environmentally damaging, inexplicable, and unjustifiable activities on Earth, do not simply rant to equally appalled friends about it. Reduce your futile anger by directing it constructively. Join a litter picking group or report specific incidents of dumping to your local council, who ought to have a collection service. If they lack one, pressure them to set one up. It may annoy you to do this while the filthy dumpers relax without a care in the world — they seldom get caught, let alone prosecuted — but it is less annoying and more rewarding than doing nothing.

Anger is always *about* something, it is an *intentional* psychological state existing in relation to certain aspects of the external world, like a field gateway strewn with dumped household waste, car parts, and old plastic toys. Nonetheless, anger *in itself*, supposing we can divorce anger from its context for the purposes of explanation, has a *physiological* basis. I am angry *with* someone, but my anger is also my increased heart rate and blood pressure, my red face, and my trembling limbs. It is this suddenly increased metabolism that can cause someone to literally 'see red' when they are provoked to anger.

We could all go through life on sedatives that prevented us from becoming angry by inhibiting our metabolism, but as with all drugs there would be negative side effects, including the suppression of *all* our emotions, responses, and capacities. Moreover, sedatives will not clean up that gateway. Carefully prescribed sedatives may play a useful short-term role in cases where anger management issues are extreme, but in the long-term, for most people, self-help strategies that do not involve a chemical cosh are preferable.

Many strategies for managing anger recognise the physiological basis of anger and seek to deal with it at that level. 'Take a deep breath and count to ten' is probably the best piece of simple anger management advice that has ever been given or could ever be given, and several of the other more sophisticated strategies are essentially variations on that theme. Count to a hundred, take several deep breaths, walk around, ride your bike, repeat a pre-chosen mantra that you find soothing — not 'REDЯUM' — stretch and do other non-strenuous yoga-like exercises.

Basically, give yourself, your body, time and opportunity to calm down. Help yourself to find your neutral space rather than digging yourself deeper. Stop talking. Literally visualise a stop sign and obey it, especially if you have mired yourself in one of those interminable quarrels that invariably become ever more unreasonable, heated, and personal. Nothing good is going to come of that quarrel. Do not fool yourself it is a constructive debate, even if you would like it to be.

Take a timeout if you can, to calm down physically and process your thoughts and feelings. Most of us need regular respite from others in order to cope with them better, so regular timeouts might form part of a broader anger management and relationship-enhancing strategy.

Again, as a teacher, I used to retreat to my car at lunchtimes if I possibly could, if I was not neglecting any responsibilities, that is. Half an hour alone in my own safe space, doors locked, listening silently to Classic FM on low volume — as opposed to sitting in a busy, noisy staffroom grumbling about students and managers while periodically choking on my sandwiches due to talking too much — did wonders for my stress levels. It helped me to keep my composure through the afternoon session, always the most difficult period in a school where discipline and self-discipline are most likely to collapse and often do. Believe me, I have seen whole school riots kick off after lunch that, like the Tiananmen Square protests, officially never happened.

Taking a break from other people is not always the best strategy. Sometimes talking things over with another person, a good friend or a professional counsellor, might be better. Do not stew in what makes you angry. Just to get something off your chest is good in itself; the mysterious power of the talking cure. Sharing our troubles and frustrations with another person helps us process them and put them into perspective. You may come to realise that you have fallen into taking yourself and your life way too seriously, that you need to laugh at yourself a little, laugh at the whole wide world. Laughter is certainly a great cure for your own anger — even if laughing at others tends to make them angry — so dig out that comedy box set and laugh it up.

If there is a situation that repeatedly makes you angry, reflect on what might be a better response to it. Rehearse that new response in your mind and try to put it into practice next time the situation occurs. Your new response might not work as well as you hoped, but you may well feel better and more in control simply for having tried. Try again if first you fail; a second blow might hit the nail.

Controlling your anger may require a more radical approach, a significant change of routine. If, for example, the commuter crush on the tube train makes you angry every morning, then consider the possibility of an alternative mode of transport. It may be time to take up cycling, although as a keen cyclist I have to say that there are few things more likely to make you angry than inconsiderate drivers endangering your life on a regular basis then blaming you for simply being on the road. I have even had drivers of two tonne vehicles accuse me — an exposed, susceptible cyclist — of endangering *their* life. Apart from that, cycling is a great de-stressor. Out in the open making the world go by and watching it do so, rolling smoothly along under your own steam at a more satisfying pace than walking, your regular deep breathing and the ceaseless circular motion of your legs calming your body and soothing your mind.

Anger management, in the end, might mean radically changing your lifestyle. Achieving a less stressful existence, changing your profession, changing your partner, changing to more comfortable clothes, downsizing, escaping to the country, or the city, depending on your preference. None of this is easy, but the only way to deal with some situations is to hatch an escape plan and execute it. Every situation has its challenges, every Eden has its serpent, every form of refuge has its price, but some situations are undoubtedly more stressful and annoying than others.

If you are tired of the heat, and you just can't make the kitchen a cooler place, then all you can do is strive to get out of it. Coping strategies, anger management strategies and 'keep your head when all about you are losing theirs and blaming it on you' strategies, helped me survive for years as a schoolteacher without killing myself or anyone else. But, in the end, for me, the most effective strategy was quitting the profession. Being a teacher taught me a lot about the importance of self-control, but it never gave me the requisite patience of a saint. Selfishly perhaps, I am only really interested in teaching those who are keen to learn, not in performing crowd control.

I still owe you an account of people who I described earlier as rude and inconsiderate seemingly by nature, or at least for whom being rude and inconsiderate has *become* second nature, probably as a result of the way they were raised.

As children they may have been excessively admired, spoilt, and overindulged by soppy adults who never told them 'No', such that their natural childish *egocentricity* was always exacerbated and never counteracted. As children they did not have to consider other people's needs, wants, and feelings and were never taught or reminded to give them any consideration.

On the other hand, they may have suffered as children the privation and neglect we examined earlier, such that they never developed any real sense of empathy for others. Nobody was ever really there for them, so now they are only there for me, myself, and I — for whatever that selfish trio can take.

Whatever the reasons they are like they are, there are certainly many inveterately inconsiderate people in this world. Unlike lovely Emma Woodhouse, they are never sorry for their inconsiderate behaviour because they are incapable of seriously reflecting on it. The depth of their inconsideration is such that they never stop to consider how inconsiderate they are. Their inconsiderate character maintains and preserves itself through its own ingrained habit of being inconsiderate. They inconsiderately fail to spell out to themselves that they are inconsiderate.

Sartre says that bad faith involves not confronting oneself, evading the true meaning of one's acts and so on. In considering what he calls 'the "faith" of bad faith' (*Being and Nothingness*, p. 90), Sartre says that the person in bad faith is in bad faith about the fact that he is in bad faith. In a similar way, the inconsiderate person is inconsiderate about the fact that he is inconsiderate. To be in bad faith is, amongst other things, to refuse and evade self-knowledge. To be inconsiderate, so I shall argue below, is also to refuse and evade self-knowledge.

Inconsiderateness is, arguably, even a form or manifestation of bad faith, in that all bad faith is the exploitation of those features and mechanisms of consciousness that make ongoing self-evasion and self-distraction possible. For example, because the for-itself is a perpetual flight towards the future, it can strive to focus entirely on what it wants and desires in that future, not least as a means of precluding reflection on the meaning of its past and present acts; that these acts are, for example, selfish, inconsiderate, uncompassionate, and so on.

It can also be argued that lack of regard for the Other is bad faith (inauthenticity) because lack of regard is the failure to achieve the authenticity of affirming and respecting the freedom of the Other. I shall return to this last point in due course when I consider existentialist ethics.

The inconsiderate person lacks awareness of others in the sense of having no real empathy for them, but he also lacks self-awareness. He knows what he wants, is always excessively, selfishly preoccupied with what he wants, but he does not understand who he is in himself or in relation to others. His lack of self-knowledge reveals itself as a lack of self-scrutiny, self-criticism, and self-censure. We might say that there is a lack of *conscience*, certainly in so far as we describe as devoid of conscience people whose *actions* show that they are utterly selfish, inconsiderate, and remorseless.

Once the inveterately inconsiderate person arises in the world by whatever means, the sky is the limit to the trouble, damage, and heartache they can cause. Depending on other personality factors such as their cleverness and cunning, the size of their imagination and the strength of their appetites, and societal factors such as their wealth, class, and education, they are potentially the worst, most irresponsible, most reckless, most immoral kind of creature.

They may spend their life being one of those commonplace selfish people who are only run-of-the-mill toxic. Borrowing things without thought of returning them, using all the milk to make Angel Delight that they do not share, playing loud music to all hours, failing to pull their weight with the cleaning and tidying, not really understanding what cleaning and tidying are because surely houses clean and tidy themselves just like Mommy and Daddy's house always does. There is frequently at least one such selfish, spoilt brat in every *student* house, often a character who evades confronting their own selfishness by fancying themselves to be a super cool, laid-back dude, while accusing everyone else of being uptight and OCD about trivial stuff like possessions, organisation, and the need for sleep.

When they finally reach some semblance of adulthood, they will progress to ownership of a sport utility vehicle (SUV), an excessively bulky, road hogging, gas guzzling 4x4, aka a Chelsea tractor or wanker tank. An SUV increases their safety — or so they believe — while decreasing the safety of other road users and pedestrians who risk being ploughed by their vehicle's obese bull bars and bumpers. The term 'sport' is used to belie the fact that an SUV is about as sporty in appearance as a skip, while 'utility' refers to an SUV's useful off-road features: large wheels, aggressive tread tyres, raised ground clearance, heavy-duty shocks and locking differential, low range, high torque four-wheel drive. These are all must-have capabilities for popping across town to the supermarket or completing the school run in heavy traffic. As befits their choice of vehicle, the SUV driver is seldom a considerate driver, as any cyclist will tell you.

On the home front, they will build an unnecessarily large extension to their already large house, blocking out their neighbour's light because it is their legal right to do so. They will then complain when their neighbour accidentally drops a few hedge cuttings on their lawn.

Professionally, they might even be an illegal dumper, taking payment to inconsiderately create ecologically damaging eyesores in the countryside that other more caring people have to clean up. Or they might simply be one of the many amateur illegal dumpers who, not wanting rubbish in their little world, but being too lazy or tight-fisted to take it to the local recycling centre, believe it has vanished from the world when they dump it out into the wider world. Illegal dumping demonstrates, perhaps more clearly than any other human activity, the severe, egocentric limits of some people's sphere of concern, and the almost infinite vastness of what they absolutely do not give a shit about.

The seriously inconsiderate character, and this may well include people who dump rubbish illegally, is psychopathic or sociopathic, or as mental health practitioners prefer to say, they have *antisocial personality disorder*, marked by an excess of self-centredness and an extreme lack of genuine empathy.

In July 2020 three young men in their late teens — Albert Bowers, Jessie Cole and Henry Long — were found guilty at the Old Bailey, London, of the manslaughter of Police Constable (PC) Andrew Harper and given long custodial sentences. Responding to reports of a burglary in progress, PC Harper and his colleague PC Andrew Shaw intercepted a vehicle towing a stolen quad bike. During the interception, the quad bike became detached from the strap used to tow it while PC Harper's ankles became entangled in it. In their rapid flight, with Henry Long driving, the young men dragged PC Harper along the road for approximately a mile before he became detached from the lasso. PC Harper died in the road of horrific injuries, effectively flayed alive by the actions of the young men. The young men failed to convince a jury that they did not know they were dragging someone.

Their actions were bad enough, selfish enough, and deliberate enough for many people to be outraged that these young men were not convicted of murder as charged, but what was most shocking to observers was their utter lack of remorse during their trial. It was not even as though the young men had callously *decided* not to show any remorse, they simply did not seem to have the capacity for any — any conscience whatsoever.

They were habitual petty thieves, poorly socialised and poorly educated, described by the judge, Mr Justice Edis, as 'unintelligent', yet they were not so unintelligent as to not realise what they had done and the seriousness of it. Yet there is footage of them smirking, joking, and pulling funny faces at the media as they leave a court appearance, as though they fancy themselves to be A-list celebrities, the latest boy band, posing for adoring fans. A BBC News website report of 31 July 2020, titled 'PC Andrew Harper's teenage killers jailed', says, 'Long, Bowers and Cole could be seen laughing and joking during parts of the trial, during most of which they appeared via video-link'. The victim impact statement of PC Harper's widow, Lissie, in which she said she had 'screamed and cried and broken down in fractured defeat' (*ibid*) made no impact at all on the defendants.

It is hard not to think of these creatures as sub-human, precisely because they lack the empathy, the common humanity, that we like to think is the minimum entry requirement for membership of the human race. Unfortunately, the human race has lots of members like this, people whose inconsiderate, careless, and selfish nature is a banal evil that in certain circumstance can create hell on Earth for others.

Under certain political and historical circumstances, with significantly more intelligence and cunning added to the mix, people with the convenient lack of empathy and conscience displayed by Long, Bowers, and Cole can rapidly progress from quad bike theft and clumsy copkilling, to dictatorship and tyranny over entire nations. As the ancient Greek philosopher Plato argues in his greatest work, *The Republic*, tyranny is rule by the arch-criminal: the greediest and most egocentric individual who, driven by an insatiable desire for power, uses cunning, flattery, dishonesty and ruthlessness to scheme his way to the top of the society he then proceeds to destroy (*The Republic*, 562a–576b, pp. 298–314).

The best way to widely lower the temperature, to create the civilised conditions that promote honourable and amicable relationships between the greatest number of citizens, is to craft a political state where criminals and would-be criminals intent on abusing political power for their own selfish ends are prevented from doing so — prevented from rising to the top. Such a political state has strong, rational, principled government at every level, making sensible laws for orderly, cooperative, dutiful citizens, laws that are enforced firmly but fairly by a strong, disciplined, and obedient police force.

To achieve such civilised rule of law is, of course, easier said than done. Plato certainly understood from his own bitter experience of the ongoing political strife of ancient Athens how difficult it is to establish and maintain a just and decent society that brings out the best in people and curbs their worst excesses.

Plato's *Republic* is dedicated to providing a blueprint for this just and decent society — a damage-limitation society that is structured in such a way as to guarantee good leadership and preclude antisocial behaviour. *The Republic* undertakes to answer the key question of political philosophy: 'What is justice?'. In the end, Plato's answer is quite simple. A just society is one in which everyone *minds their own business* and gets on with what they do best without interfering in the tasks and responsibilities of others.

> When each of our three classes [workers, police, and leaders] does its own job and minds its own business, that, by contrast, is justice and makes our state just. (Plato, *The Republic*, 434c, p. 139)

Plato believed that politics is an art (*techné*), that good governance is a crucial task requiring great skill that should only be carried out by

philosopher kings: extremely wise, self-disciplined and considerate individuals who have been educated and trained from an early age to rule.
People whose expertise lie elsewhere should not be involved in politics
other than willingly doing as instructed by their wise leaders. You would
not allow anyone but a qualified electrician to rewire your house, so why
allow anyone with no knowledge of the art of politics to make political
decisions or have any sort of vote?

Plato is no democrat. He sees democracy as rule by the mob and
the means by which the arch-criminal eventually establishes himself as
a tyrant. According to Plato, the democratic process enables the most
devious and power-hungry person to become leader. Employing fine
words, false promises, bribes and fear, this person sways spoilt, decadent,
ill-disciplined people who know nothing about politics, people who are
driven by desire rather than reason, to vote him into office.

The people, in championing the tough guy who argues most
eloquently and forcefully to defend and extend the excessive and
self-indulgent liberties they have grown to enjoy under democracy, will
elect a popular leader who soon becomes drunk with power, surrounds
himself with a brutal bodyguard and begins to tyrannise over them. Thus,
the excess of liberty that people wallow in under democracy, the glut of
rights and dearth of duties, inevitably brings about the profound servi-
tude suffered under tyranny, with all remaining liberty belonging only to
the tyrant.

Critics of Plato argue that he has too little regard for the intelligence
and decency of ordinary people — ordinary voters. He does not appreciate that democracy, far from collapsing into tyranny, enables the people to
remove corrupt governments. Democracy is not perfect, but arguably it is
preferable to all other forms of governance that have existed throughout
history.

Many forms of government have been tried and will be tried in this
world of sin and woe. No one pretends that democracy is perfect or
all-wise. Indeed, it has been said that democracy is the worst form of
government except all those other forms that have been tried from time

to time. (Winston Churchill, House of Commons Speech, 11 November 1947)

The pros and cons of democracy aside, Plato is surely absolutely right that bad leadership is just about the greatest evil that can befall any society, the evil most likely to render human interactions hellish. One only has to look at history, the long roll call of brutal tyrants and the repeated violent struggles against them, to see that tyranny all too often precipitates war within and between nations, reducing human existence to hell on Earth.

The English political philosopher Thomas Hobbes in his book *Leviathan* famously notes that outside of civil society human life is 'solitary, poore, nasty, brutish, and short' (*Leviathan*, p. 186). The absence of civil society is 'a time of Warre, where every man is Enemy to every man' (*Leviathan*, p. 186). A time without significant agriculture, industry, architecture, navigation, science, letters, art and so on. A time lacking the means of significant wealth generation in which even the wealthiest are poor and needy in comparison to the wealthy of a civilised society.

Hobbes refers to this terrible state of anarchy as the *state of nature*, and it is to avoid it that people agree to enter into a *social contract* of mutual cooperation and accept over themselves 'a common power to keep them all in awe' (*Leviathan*, p. 185) — a power strong enough to restrain them from constantly clashing with one another. This central authority must be able to prevent the evils of all-out civil war. It must be an all-powerful leviathan that people submit to out of fear and self-interest. Self-interest here being, in large part, fear of the consequences of there being no such power, fear of a hellish dog-eat-dog state of anarchy in which only the law of the jungle prevails.

Hobbes sees all people as fundamentally self-interested. Most are self-interested only to the extent that they desire to live in comfort and dignity within modest bounds. Some, however, are excessively self-interested, excessively greedy in their desire for conquest, property, pleasure, honour, and glory. Life outside of civil society is nasty and brutish, not because most people are particularly nasty and brutish but because outside of civil society the range of human needs and desires inevitably gives rise to a situation in which nasty, brutish behaviour offers the only means of survival.

In a situation where resources are too scarce to sustain everyone, it is not possible for people to survive by sharing. People are forced by circumstances into nasty, brutish *competition* as they fight for their own survival or, at very best, the survival of their immediate family with whom their self-interests are likely to be closely bound. As Hobbes says, 'And therefore if any two men desire the same thing, which nevertheless they cannot both enjoy, they become enemies' (*Leviathan*, p. 184).

Outside of civil society people are also forced into nasty, brutish behaviour towards one another by *diffidence*, a term meaning *distrust* or *lack of self-confidence*. Diffidence leads people to attack one another out of fear of being attacked. It is a case of do unto others as you fear they will do unto you, only do it first. Diffidence causes people to invade one another for their own safety.

Hobbes notes that 'contemplating their own power in the acts of conquest' (*Leviathan*, pp. 184–85) leads excessively self-interested people to invade others beyond the requirements of their own personal safety. This obliges those who would otherwise gladly live within modest bounds to attempt to do the same, simply to avoid enslavement or annihilation.

Hobbes argues that 'every man looketh that his companion should value him, at the same rate he sets upon himselfe' (*Leviathan*, p. 185). In the absence of a powerful authority to prevent disorder, people's natural self-love and pride is such that they will seek, as far as possible, to destroy anyone who shows them the slightest contempt or disregard, not least as a warning to those who might otherwise do the same.

In a world characterised by brutal competition, fearful distrust and easy revenge, people will be relatively solitary, avoiding wherever possible the constant threat that other people pose. And finally, in such a violent world, where even the most basic necessities of life are hard to come by, the average life span will be short and old age rare.

So, even though the majority of people are disposed to be quite considerate, generally decent, and relatively generous, there is always a small minority of very inconsiderate and selfish people who, given half a chance, will spoil the party for everyone else. One way or another, this minority will always dictate the nature of reality and drag everything and everyone down to their base level, *unless* they are constantly prevented from doing so by *civilisation*. By good government, just laws, firm but fair policing, a strong, well-regulated economy, efficient infrastructure, education, culture, manners, and morality.

Civilisation is the means not only of controlling nature but of controlling ourselves, our worst excesses of egotism and, above all, our most excessively egotistical individuals.

MODERATION

Philosophers have always been interested in ethics, in establishing sound principles that distinguish attitudes and behaviours that are morally good from those that are morally bad. Various moral theories have emerged over the millennia that view ethics in different ways. Despite their variety and the different methods they employ, however, these theories often reach the same broad conclusions about the moral character people ought to develop and how they ought to conduct themselves, while all of them agree that ethics is largely about how people ought to treat one another. We shall explore some of these theories now as they undoubtedly shed further light on our present concerns, indeed the overall concerns of this entire book.

One of the earliest philosophical moral theories is the *virtue ethics* of the ancient Greek philosopher Aristotle, as contained in his *Nicomachean Ethics* and other works. Aristotle, as you will recall, has already found his way into our discussions several times. This is not surprising, given that our tripartite division of manners into *polite*, *over-polite*, and *impolite* is a classically Aristotelian approach that uses his central ethical concept of *the golden mean*. The concept of the golden mean, like most concepts, is best explained by backing up a little.

Aristotle is a *teleologist*. The words *teleology* and *teleological* derive from the Greek word *telos*, which means *end*, *goal*, or *purpose*. Aristotle argues that everything in nature has its own *telos*, the true and proper end goal at which it aims, and that we understand what things are by understanding what their end goal is. For a thing to achieve its *telos*, its end goal, is for it to *flourish*.

A flourishing toaster, for example, makes good toast. Toasters, of course, are not conscious — not yet — so are not aware of their purpose. It is we who give toasters their purpose of making toast for us. In the TV science-fiction comedy series *Red Dwarf*, there is a conscious toaster, Talkie Toaster, who understandably becomes frustrated and upset when nobody wants toast, as this prevents Talkie from realising his *telos*, from *flourishing* in the only way a toaster can.

Aristotle seeks to identify the personal virtues that facilitate *human flourishing*, the virtues that enable a person to forge a fully realised, worthwhile, successful, and satisfying life. The most successful life is one that achieves the sustained state of profound happiness and contentment that the ancient Greeks called *eudaimonia*: a fully rounded and balanced life governed by moderation and wisdom. The virtues that facilitate the highest human flourishing of eudaimonia accord with Aristotle's *golden mean*.

To strike the golden mean, a person must achieve *moderation in all things*, a balance, a happy medium, a middle way, between various vices of excess and deficiency in the way he approaches his entire life, including all the other people involved in it. The ancient Greeks attached such importance to this approach to life — not that they always practiced it — that they inscribed the aphorism, 'Nothing to excess' on the temple of Apollo at Delphi, thought to be the centre of the world.

Politeness, you will doubtless have already figured out, is the *golden mean* between the deficiency of impoliteness and the excess of over-politeness, both of which are vices that produce a flawed character incapable of establishing the best possible relations with others and, therefore, incapable of achieving eudaimonia.

Many other character traits and ways of acting — character and action are hardly separable — can be viewed in light of the golden mean. We have already considered anger and social conduct somewhat in this light. Carefully adjusted to the occasion, patience, forbearance and measured, righteous anger all strike the golden mean. Irritability and irascibility are excessive anger, while timidity and passivity in face of wrongs are a deficiency of anger. As for social conduct, polite friendliness, adjusted to the company and the occasion, achieves the happy medium. Obsequiousness and creepiness are excessive, while tactlessness and rudeness are deficient.

Social conduct can be further analysed in light of the golden mean with specific regard to *shame, self-expression,* and *conversation.* In the area of shame, shyness and prissiness are excessive, modesty is golden, and crudeness and obscenity are deficient. In the area of self-expression, boastfulness is excessive, truthfulness is golden, and understatement and false modesty are deficient. In the area of conversation, buffoonery and ridiculousness are excessive, wittiness is golden, and boorishness and coarseness are deficient.

As to the *amount* of conversation, the naturally garrulous person, such as Jane Austen's wittering Miss Bates considered earlier, needs to resist talking too much in order to be polite, while the naturally taciturn person needs to make an effort to talk occasionally in order to be polite. As to the golden mean between garrulous and taciturn, conversable or even good conversationalist fit the bill.

A good conversationalist appreciates balance and fairness, knows how to give and receive, knows how to make his point clearly and concisely and when to be silent and listen. He also knows how to adjust his conversation between wit and gravity depending on the general occasion and the topic under discussion. He does not interrupt the Other, unless it is really necessary, or allow prolonged, awkward silences, especially on the phone. On the other hand, he does not destroy meaningful pauses or render the conversation tense and hurried by chattering for the sake of it. Good conversation is enthusiastic but relaxed. A nervous conversation is rarely a good one, although it might be an enjoyable one if we are particularly keen on the person we are talking to.

Good conversation is a great skill, one widely lacking in contemporary society. The modern field of so-called conversation is dominated, on the one hand, by those who like to monologue and, on the other hand, by those who do not listen properly, if at all, due to fiddling unceasingly with their *device.* They may offer the occasional grunt in response, but do not be fooled by it if you are the monologuer; it is only to relieve their irritation that you are interrupting their Facebook 'conversation'. The ever-increasing number of those permanently distracted by technology is increasing the number of those who monologue, as the monologue is the only way of attempting to communicate with the permanently distracted.

It is impossible to talk *to* them, so one has to talk *at* them, in the hope that the occasional point gets through.

Also inscribed on the temple of Apollo was the aphorism, 'Know thyself'. Every person must try to use their self-knowledge to work out what is the happy medium for them, given their natural temperament, their personal strengths and weaknesses, their life circumstances, their position in society, and so on. The confident and dignified conduct appropriate for a monarch, for example, would appear vain and affected in an ordinary citizen. A president is expected to behave with a certain solemnity and decorum in public, just as a gardener is not expected to behave like a president when he arrives to cut your lawn.

So, how Aristotle's abstract guidelines are best acted upon in actual, concrete situations requires *wisdom*. That is, judgement, experience, and sensitivity. A person requires a subtle awareness of who he is, not least in relation to where he is and those he is with. Behaviour appropriate with old friends will probably not be appropriate with work colleagues. Behaviour appropriate at a nightclub will not be appropriate at a funeral and so on. As the saying goes, horses for courses.

There are few things more socially objectionable than people who lack a sense of occasion — that is, a sense of decorum. People who text at funerals, people who talk during marriage vows when it is not their wedding, people who allow their children to misbehave in public, people who use foul language in the street or behave in a drunk and disorderly manner in the street or spit in the street or shout across the street to a friend when it is not an emergency or eat in the street or make any kind of spectacle of themselves whatsoever in the street, avenue, road, lane, cul-de-sac, restaurant, pub, shop, museum, art gallery, railway station or airport, people who arrive scruffy to an interview, graduation ceremony, award ceremony, grand opening, baptism, wedding, funeral, or any other formal occasion. You get the picture. Do not do such things; do not be such a person. In short, always be dignified except where the occasion is very specifically designed for everyone present to let their hair down. Always be worthy of honour and respect.

Although truthfulness is golden, some things are best left unsaid. The pursuit of truth should not lead one into tactlessness, which we have already identified as a vice. Wittiness is golden but, as Emma Woodhouse discovered, when the target is too soft wittiness all too easily becomes tainted with scorn. Wittiness towards one's social superiors can also be problematic as it can be perceived as cheek, presumptuousness, and lack of respect. Hence, it is tricky, even treacherous to be truly witty with anyone but one's peers and social equals. This is one of the main reasons why people gravitate towards, and feel most comfortable in, the company of their peers and social equals.

I could go on, but in the end, it is not possible to give someone a precise rule book dogmatically detailing how they should conduct themselves socially in every conceivable situation in order to create the best impression on others and hence enjoy the most prolonged, amicable, and pleasantly warm relationships. It is only possible to give someone a general philosophical and practical guide to living that invites each person to honestly and intelligently assess his or her unique character and situation. Each of us must decide for ourselves the *details* of how we should conduct ourselves so as to achieve the blessing of true happiness that comes only through being on good terms with others.

If we learn best by our mistakes, it may take at least half a lifetime of social gaffes, mishandled intimacy, and failed relationships to acquire true life-enhancing social competence at every level, by which time a person might feel that the best social opportunities that were ever going to come his or her way have already been irrevocably squandered.

Alternatively, studying and acting from an early age upon the undoubted good sense of Aristotle's lifestyle and etiquette guide might well reduce the amount and severity of our harmful and soul-destroying social blunders by hastening our journey from foolishness to wisdom. That is, our journey from social incompetence to social proficiency, from meanness of soul to the greatness of soul or magnanimity that the ancient Greeks called *megalopsuchia*, from unhappiness to the profound happiness and contentment that the ancient Greeks called *eudaimonia*.

Some people, of course, never learn from life or books, and they are generally the ones most difficult for others to deal with, the ones who give a ring of truth to Sartre's infamous adage. Yet deal with them we must, to the best of our ability, to the hopefully ever-extending limits of our patience, tolerance, tact and goodwill, so help us Aristotle.

REASON

For the great German philosopher Immanuel Kant, behaving morally is all about behaving *rationally*. What is important to Kant is the rational behaviour itself, regardless of the consequences it has for other people. There is no doubt, however, that behaving in the rational way Kant suggests tends overall and in the long run to have good consequences for others and for our relationships with them. It would be a strange moral theory that recommended behaviour that did not have such consequences.

At the heart of Kant's moral theory, which he sets out in his *Groundwork of the Metaphysic of Morals*, is a famous principle known as the *categorical imperative*. Kant expresses the principle in various ways in his *Groundwork*, but the most straightforward and well-known formulation is: 'Act only on that maxim through which you can at the same time will that it should become a universal law' (*Groundwork of the Metaphysic of Morals*, p. 84).

The categorical imperative appears at first sight to involve doing unto others as you would have them do unto you. This is the so-called *golden rule*, as expressed in various places in *The Bible*: 'So in everything, do to others what you would have them do to you, for this sums up the Law of Moses and the teachings of the prophets' (*Matthew* 7:12).

The golden rule is undoubtedly a fairly sensible rule of thumb if you want to be on good terms with others, one that assumes that people the world over want the same pleasant things and only those things: to be free from hunger, homelessness, pain, and poverty; to have food, shelter, medicine, and money; to be treated with respect; to be helped when in need and so on.

Unfortunately, beyond the basics, all people do not have exactly the same wants. Some people want to have things done to them that most of us would think of as extremely unpleasant. As we have seen, masochistic tendencies are common and for most people mild and playful. A few people, however, are extreme masochists. They desire to be severely whipped or tortured in other ways. The point is that because they want to have these things done to them does not make it right for them to do them to others, certainly without their consent. The golden rule soon begins to fail, certainly as a *fundamental* rule of morality, as we inevitably find ourselves needing to bring in other moral concepts, like consent, to prop it up.

Far from being a glorified version of the golden rule, the categorical imperative involves asking yourself, 'What if everyone did this?', before you go ahead and do whatever it is you are thinking of doing. If it is the sort of thing that would become impossible for anyone to do if everyone tried to do it all the time, then it is your moral duty not to do it.

Take, for example, false promising, making a 'promise' with no intention of keeping it. Kant notes that in considering the consequences of making a false promise, a person may well see the personal advantage of doing so on a particular occasion (*Groundwork of the Metaphysic of Morals*, p. 67). He may, for example, extricate himself from financial difficulties by borrowing money with no intention of paying it back.

If he is prudent, however, he will see that this is unwise. He will gain a reputation for being untrustworthy and find it increasingly difficult to secure loans in future. 'I do indeed see that it is not enough for me to extricate myself from present embarrassment by this subterfuge: I have to consider whether from this lie there may not subsequently accrue to me much greater inconvenience than that from which I now escape' (*Groundwork of the Metaphysic of Morals*, p. 67). In the end, the *consequences* of borrowing money with no intention of paying it back may well be worse than the current financial difficulties from which he seeks to extricate himself.

However, as Kant points out, whether or not it is prudent to make a false promise has nothing whatsoever to do with whether or not it is morally right to make a false promise. As he says:

> To tell the truth for the sake of [moral] duty is something entirely different from doing so out of concern for inconvenient results; for in the first case the concept of the action already contains in itself a law for me, while in the second case I have first of all to look around elsewhere

in order to see what effects may be bound up with it for me. (*Ground-work of the Metaphysic of Morals*, p. 68)

A *maxim* is a general principle established by action, and in order to decide whether or not making a false promise is morally right I have only to consider whether or not the maxim of getting out of difficulties by false promising can hold as a *universal law*.

If I decide that I will only make false promises to escape difficulties that I can escape in no other way, then I establish this as a maxim for myself and for everyone. I am, in effect, declaring that everyone can make false promises whenever it suits them. The problem with this, as Kant points out, is that although I can will to lie, 'I can by no means will a universal law of lying; for by such a law there could properly be no promises at all' (*Groundwork of the Metaphysic of Morals*, p. 68).

By such a law, I could never give anyone a promise, as no one would accept my assurances, and no one could ever give me a promise, as I could never accept their assurances. A maxim of false promising cannot hold as a universal law, cannot be willed as a universal law, for as soon as it became a universal law it would annul itself by annulling the practice of promising altogether. Hence, false promising is immoral.

So, Kant argues that you should only act on maxims that you can will to become a universal law. A maxim of false promising, for example, cannot be willed as a universal law in the way that a maxim of real promising, for example, can be willed as a universal law. It is possible for everyone to tell the truth universally, but it is not possible for everyone to lie universally.

For Kant, the only thing in the world that is absolutely good without exception is a *good will*. Characteristics such as intelligence and patience, although often virtues, can be great vices when directed by a bad will. For example, the intelligent criminal who waits patiently for the best moment to strike will be more harmful and enduring than the stupid, hasty criminal.

Certain qualities of character and temperament can, of course, make the task of willing good easier. People who are, for example, naturally calm and composed, like Austen's Mr George Knightley, may well find it easier to will good than excitable, compulsive people, like Austen's Mr William Collins. Nonetheless, calmness and composure are not *unconditionally* good, as once again they can prove very bad when driven by a bad will. In Kant's view, therefore, such qualities of character and temperament should not be overly revered.

To have a good will is to act rationally in accordance with the categorical imperative. Morality, for Kant, is about *rational action*. Having a good will is not vaguely undertaking to mean well with kindly, mawkish feelings of compassion and pity. Having a good will is not simply *feeling* that your heart is in the right place when you do something. Your well-meaning action may be misguided; your good intentions may pave a road to hell.

As only behaviour in accordance with the categorical imperative is moral, it is quite possible to behave morally despite having no inclination to do so. As far as moral behaviour is concerned, inclination and all the rest of it are irrelevant. Basic moral behaviour consists entirely in fulfilling one's duty to the rational principle of the categorical imperative. In a sense, the clearest example of a truly moral person is a person who does not want to do something but does it anyway because they know it is their moral duty. Or rather, to be more precise, the clearest example of a truly moral person is a person who wants to do something but refrains from doing it because they know doing it would be a dereliction of their moral duty.

Kant distinguishes between *perfect duties* of justice and *imperfect duties* of humanity and benevolence. Perfect duties are fulfilled by *not doing* something, such as not stealing. Paying a debt is also a perfect duty. Paying a debt is, of course, *doing something*, but from a perfect duty perspective to pay a debt is to *not* violate the categorical imperative.

Perfect duties constitute a moral minimum that is often enforced by law, whereas imperfect duties go beyond that minimum and are not usually enforced by law. It is not *necessary* to fulfil imperfect duties, but it is *desirable*. Doing so makes a person virtuous, so long as they are also respecting perfect duties, that is. Giving to charity is an imperfect duty. It is not compulsory, but it is nonetheless a good thing to do if the charity is genuinely worthy. Kant argues that perfect duties are determinate and can only be fulfilled in one way, whereas imperfect duties are indeterminate and can be fulfilled in various ways as a person sees fit. Perfect duties permit no flexibility, whereas imperfect duties permit considerable flexibility.

Another key aspect of Kant's moral theory, one which is closely linked to the categorical imperative, is *the formula of the end in itself*. Acting in accordance with the categorical imperative, adopting universalizable maxims, shows respect for others, whereas acting contrary to the categorical imperative shows disrespect for others. For a person to adopt *non*-universalizable maxims in his treatment of others is for him to treat others as a *means to his own ends*, rather than respect them as *ends in themselves*.

If I lie to someone, or give him a false promise, or steal from him, or rape him, or murder him, then I am using him for my own ends and goals rather than respecting him as a free being with his own ends and goals. In Kant's terms, I am treating him as a *mere* means rather than as an end in himself. Acting in accordance with the categorical imperative when dealing with others, acting only on maxims that can be universalised, ensures that I always respect others as ends in themselves and never exploit them as mere means to my own ends.

Of course, we all treat each other as a means. I use the barber to get my hair cut and she uses me to earn a living, but this arrangement should be consensual, both parties having entered into it freely. I have used the barber as a means, but not as a *mere* means. I have not disrespected her freedom and right to self-determination as I would do if I ran off without paying when she released me from the chair.

Kant envisages a *kingdom of ends*, a world in which people never use each other as a mere means and always respect each other as free, rational ends in themselves. This, for Kant, would be the ideal moral state, heaven on earth, at least as far as human interaction was concerned. Given the way people are much of the time and are likely to remain — greedy, selfish, deceitful, weak-willed and so on — it seems this ideal moral state will never be achieved. It is, however, a logically possible distant dream worth aiming for. Something that, in a sense, we aim for every time our other person related actions are in accordance with the prime moral principle of the categorical imperative.

Kant's successor, Georg Hegel, sees history as the progressive development of human reason towards perfect rationality. Hegel's future perfected state of humankind, achieved through perfecting our institutions, systems of education, technology, medicine, law, politics, and so on, would be similar to Kant's kingdom of ends and to Plato's republic, with everyone always acting perfectly rationally towards the environment and towards one another in complete, civilised accordance with universal moral principles.

AUTHENTICITY

Despite 'Hell is other people!', despite the conflict thesis of human interaction that dominates *Being and Nothingness* and recurs in most of Sartre's other works, his philosophy has an ethical dimension that, like Aristotle's and Kant's, suggests a means of rising above the fray. Although Sartre never produced a fully worked out *existentialist ethics* due to other commitments and his ever-evolving thoughts on existentialism in relation to Marxism, he nonetheless wrote enough on the subject in various places to make his basic position fairly clear. In exploring his position, let us begin at the end of *Being and Nothingness*.

At the end of *Being and Nothingness,* Sartre recognises that questions remain regarding the person who, by taking full responsibility for his freedom, by taking freedom itself as an end, overcomes bad faith. He asks what such a person, such a freedom, would be like? How would such a person situate himself in the world? Would he 'escape all *situation*' (*Being and Nothingness*, p. 647), or would he situate himself more precisely, individually, and responsibly? In short, though Sartre does not use the term at the close of *Being and Nothingness*, questions remain regarding the precise nature of *authenticity*. These questions, he concludes, 'can find their reply only on the ethical plane. We shall devote to them a future work' (*Being and Nothingness*, p. 647).

This inconclusive conclusion was no cop-out on Sartre's part. That he seriously intended at the time to produce a fully developed existentialist ethics is revealed by the extensive notes he made on ethics between

1945 and 1948, now published as *Notebooks for an Ethics*. These notes show Sartre musing and developing his thoughts. In places, he may not even agree with what he has written down. Having said that, there is sufficient consistency and recurrence of themes for some general conclusions to be drawn. Some ideas expressed can also be checked against ideas found in his *War Diaries*, where authenticity is a recurrent theme, as well as against published works written around the same time as the notebooks, such as his 1946 work, *Existentialism and Humanism*.

Sartre clearly holds that an existentialist ethics cannot be based on an abstract, *a priori* moral principle such as Kant's categorical imperative. It is this view that prevents Sartre from aligning his position with that of Kant, even though he is repeatedly tempted towards a broadly Kantian ethical position in other respects.

Sartre also rejects, as he does in *Existentialism and Humanism*, an ethics based on the existence of a moral God who demands compliance to a catalogue of commandments. Sartre is an atheist who argues that the existence of God is impossible. He argues that we are *abandoned* in an essentially meaningless universe with no God to give us purpose or moral direction.

So much for what Sartre rejects. What he clearly affirms is that ethics is an other-person-related phenomenon, a feature of our *being-for-others*. Sartre argues that no action is unethical until another person judges it to be so.

For Sartre, an ethical state of affairs is one in which people respect and affirm each other's freedom. His difficulty is to accommodate this claim with his view that the freedom of other people inevitably negates and cancels out my freedom. Another person, he says, only has to *look* at me to reduce me from being the centre of my world to being an object in his world. The consciousness of the Other, he claims, inevitably *transcends* mine, reducing me to what he calls a *transcendence transcended*. As Other to the Other I can also, in turn, in conflict, transcend his transcendence. Hence, argues Sartre, offering us yet another statement of his conflict thesis, 'The essence of the relations between consciousnesses is not the *Mitsein* [being-with-others]; it is conflict' (*Being and Nothingness*, p. 451). In rough, 'Hell is other people!' (*In Camera*, p. 223).

In Chapter 4, when directly tackling the question 'Is hell other people?', we considered *the look* according to Overgaard and Webber. Their reading appears to help Sartre here. The look, they argue, has two distinct aspects which Sartre conflates. There is the look as that which makes me aware of my being-for-others, and the look as that which ascribes to me a fixed nature. The former look need not be threatening and can even be received as protective, kindly, approving, and so on. It is the latter look that underlies alienation, shame, and conflict.

The trouble starts when in looking at me the Other attaches to me, or apparently attaches to me, labels I object to. If I approve of his labels, perhaps because they are labels I like to ascribe to myself even though they may be no more true of me than the labels I object to, then there is no conflict. Serious conflict arises when the fixed nature ascribed to me by the Other *conflicts* with the fixed nature I strive to ascribe to myself.

As previously noted, Overgaard and Webber identify the role of *bad faith* in all this. Given that I am a free transcendence that can never be at one with itself, then it is bad faith to pretend to myself that I have a fixed nature, bad faith to try to fool myself that I am not free, bad faith to assume that I do not have to constantly *choose* who I am.

If I can overcome my bad faith and achieve authenticity, live to the full the truth that there is nothing that I am in the mode of being it other than a being 'condemned to be free' (*Being and Nothingness*, p. 462), then not only will I no longer ascribe to myself a fixed nature, I will no longer believe or take seriously the labels others try to attach to me. To achieve authenticity is to no longer be vulnerable to the spiteful or well-meaning efforts of others to pigeonhole me, and hence to the conflict this causes. Sticks and stones may still break my bones, but names really will never hurt me.

Authenticity, as comprehensive respect for freedom, must, however, also involve *respect for the freedom of others*. To achieve authenticity, a person must resist labelling others and ascribing a fixed nature to them. He must, for example, allow others the freedom to change and grow as people rather than try to make them remain forever the same, forever what he wants them to be. He may not find this change comfortable or convenient, it may greatly increase his anxieties, but still he welcomes it because he values the freedom of others as much as he values his own freedom.

As we have seen, although the insecurities of lovers often lead them to demand pledges of love from their beloved, guarantees that the beloved will always love them and never change in that respect, lovers are deeply dissatisfied with pledges. Though they may not like to admit it to themselves, lovers know that love given as the consequence of a pledge is simply not love. Love is only love when it is *freely* given. The beloved can only be truly possessed by the lover when she *chooses* to be possessed, because only when she chooses to be possessed can she be possessed as a freedom, a subject, a consciousness, rather than as an automaton.

As we have also seen, this all-important freedom cannot be possessed simply by possessing the beloved physically, by contriving to have her always close by, as Marcel does with Albertine in Proust's *In Search of Lost Time*. The authentic lover must accept that in being loved by the Other they are permanently at the mercy of the Other's freedom. Even marriage provides no real antidote to the inherent instability of love and the lover's insecurities about it.

The *ideal* of marriage is that it should secure love once and for all, happily ever after, while also preserving the freedom from which all true love must flow. Marriage appears to offer a gilt-edged *guarantee* that the love of the Other will always continue to be freely given and never be withdrawn or given to another. So lovers make their solemn vows before family, friends and God, seeking to cement with rings and rituals oaths that can only ever have the value their makers choose to give them at any time in the future.

High divorce and adultery rates are testament to the fact that commitment is nothing in itself, that it consists entirely in the constant reaffirmation of a certain choice set against the ever-present, ever-lurking possibility of a change of mind. Marriage can be seen as a somewhat desperate attempt to transform the love of the Other into something fixed, reliable, and certain, precisely because love is not something fixed, reliable, and certain.

In many cases marriage certainly supplies the conditions in which true love can thrive. Shared interests arise from a shared daily life while other would-be lovers are formally excluded. Not least, there is ample opportunity for intimacy and mutual reassurance, set against reduced opportunity and incentive to betray the relationship on a mere passing whim. In many other cases, however, marriage steadily undermines love, as the basis of the relationship shifts from being a free choice by both parties to be possessed, towards mere habit, ingratitude, fear of change, and material and financial entanglement.

The authentic person who champions freedom above all else, the true existentialist, recognises that all personal relationships should be based on freedom. That is, they should be entered into freely and maintained as a matter of mutual, ongoing choice. Hence, a true existentialist would certainly disapprove of any marriage that was arranged or coerced or where either party felt obliged to enter into it through fear of the consequences of not doing so.

Admittedly, there is often mutual love, affection and respect in arranged marriages, but these qualities are a fortuitous bonus to the marriage rather than its *raison d'être*. Of course, it is also true that many marriages *entered into* on the grounds of mutual love persist when that love has utterly gone and divorce would be a blessed relief to all, not least to any offspring who have to endure their parents' discordant relationship on a daily basis. The reasons why such marriages persist are complex, but certainly in most cases material entanglement, lazy habit, and even stubbornness play parts.

The overall existentialist position regarding marriage is something like this: Marriage entered into as a result of social expectation, coercion, obligation, fear, poverty, and so on is entirely at odds with the existentialist ethic of individual freedom. Marriage entered into in the absence of any determining factors other than mutual love, affection, and respect is okay if such a 'marriage of true minds' (Shakespeare, *Sonnet 116*) is ever possible. Not marrying at all, however, or even cohabiting, is by far the best option. It does not seek to limit the freedom of the Other and allows the continuation of the relationship to be an ongoing free choice by the Other.

Paradoxically, in the existentialists' view, true love is only possible when both parties remain *single* and make no emotional claims upon one another. As love is only love if it is given freely, then a genuine loving relationship can be based on nothing else but freedom. A relationship can only hope to remain genuinely loving by preserving the conditions that keep it free and avoiding the conditions that would tie it down.

This inevitably means being uncomplaining if the beloved has intimate relations with others. As the true existentialist makes no claims upon his beloved in the first place, it would be incorrect to say that he *allows* her to have affairs. She is simply free to have affairs without reproach in she wants to, openly and honestly, and must not be made to feel the need to deceive anyone.

It might be thought that open relationships increase conflict between people. Look at all the trouble that people sleeping around causes in soap operas. Soap operas, however, do not tend to portray open relationships. They portray people in closed relationships where promises have been made, endlessly lying and cheating and breaking those promises. If people are honest and place value on the freedom of *all*, rather than on their expectations of others and their own feelings of jealousy and possessiveness, then open relationships can reduce conflict by removing the tensions and frustrations inherent in monogamy.

Ideally, lovers should resist the false security offered by marriage vows and material entanglements and accept that the love they currently enjoy is based, and can only be based, on nothing more than the freedom of the Other. To live like this may well be a source of great anxiety, but anxiety is the price of freedom. The true existentialist would rather endure anxiety than seek in bad faith to impose artificial and stifling limits on his own freedom and his lover's freedom simply for the sake of reducing his insecurities.

Arguably, in so far as marriage seeks to ascribe a fixed nature both to oneself and to one's spouse, to marry is to act in bad faith towards oneself and towards one's spouse. As we have seen, to achieve authenticity, a person must not only resist ascribing a fixed nature to himself, he must resist ascribing a fixed nature to others.

Sartre certainly recognises in *Being in Nothingness* that it is bad faith to seek to ascribe a fixed nature to others, to seek to *stereotype* them, to seek to render them two-dimensional by endeavouring to deny that they possess the all-important dimension of freedom.

In exploring different projects of bad faith, Sartre considers a homosexual who is in bad faith for not admitting that he is a homosexual (*Being and Nothingness*, pp. 86–88). Sartre's homosexual is right to think that he is not a homosexual-*thing*, but this does not mean that he cannot be correctly described as a homosexual given his ongoing homosexual conduct. Aware that he is a free being, Sartre's homosexual believes he can entirely transcend the facticity of his homosexual activities and disown them as a series of mere aberrations.

It is not in fact possible, however, to *separate* transcendence and facticity as Sartre's homosexual seeks to do, and thereby become a *pure* transcendence. Transcendence is always the transcendence *of* facticity. Hence, Sartre's homosexual is the transcendence *of* the facticity of his homosexual activities. He cannot disown his activities as though they were the activities of another person. He is not a homosexual-*thing*, but homosexuality is nonetheless the meaning of his conduct. Homosexual is a correct description of him, although not one that should be applied to him as a limiting label.

Sartre's homosexual has a friend, the 'champion of sincerity' (*Being and Nothingness*, pp. 87–88). In making a case for valuing and respecting the freedom of others it is actually the champion of sincerity I am most interested in here, but *his* project of bad faith cannot be understood unless the project of bad faith of Sartre's homosexual is understood first.

The champion of sincerity is irritated by his homosexual friend's continued refusal to recognise what he is. He urges him to declare himself and admit that he is a homosexual. Sartre asks, 'Who is in bad faith? The homosexual or the champion of sincerity?' (*Being and Nothingness*, p. 87). The answer seems obvious. Sartre's homosexual is in bad faith because of his duplicity, whereas the champion of sincerity, as an advocate of honesty, is in good faith. This, however, is not the case. The right answer is that the champion of sincerity is as much in bad faith as his homosexual friend. Why is this?

In encouraging his homosexual friend to be sincere about his homosexuality, the champion of sincerity encourages him to constitute himself as a *thing*; to be *just* a homosexual. He offers to relieve him of his freedom as freedom and to return it to him as a thing — to exchange a limitless freedom for a freedom reduced to a fixed and known quantity. Although this offer of relief purports to be entirely altruistic, in that it offers his homosexual friend an escape from the burden of his freedom, the champion of sincerity actually has a selfish motive.

The champion of sincerity is in bad faith because the actual, selfish aim of his call for sincerity is to escape his own anxieties by attempting to constitute the transcendence of his homosexual friend as a facticity:

> The champion of sincerity is in bad faith to the degree that he wants to reassure himself, while pretending to judge, to the extent that he demands that freedom as freedom constitute itself as a thing. (*Being and Nothingness*, p. 88)

The champion of sincerity finds it reassuring to reduce his homosexual friend to a thing because as a thing his homosexual friend ceases to be a transcendent freedom with the power to negate the transcendent freedom of others. In persuading his homosexual friend to accept a narrow definition, the champion of sincerity gains power over him. His homosexual friend ceases to be a limitless and threatening freedom and becomes instead a fixed and known quantity. He is labelled 'homosexual' and is nothing more; he is pigeonholed and explained away.

The same pigeonholing occurs in Sartre's novel *Nausea*:

> He [Dr. Rogé] looks at the little man with his fierce eyes. A direct gaze which puts everything in its place. He explains: 'He's an old crackpot, that's what he is'. (*Nausea*, p. 99)

Dr. Rogé stereotypes the little man; the champion of sincerity stereotypes his homosexual friend. To stereotype a person is to deny that he is free to transcend mere labels. It is to deny that he has a dimension of individuality that always makes him far more than simply a member of a particular race, ethnicity, sex, sexual orientation group, social class, religion, and so on.

Contemporary identity politics falls into error when it insists that the only really important features of every person are the *group identity* features they share with some people and not with others: sex, race, ethnicity, sexuality, and so on. Existentialism, on the other hand, insist that what is really important about every person is their existential *freedom* and *individuality*. Group identity features do, of course, play a role in defining a person, and certainly influence the way a person is likely to be viewed and treated by some others, but group identity features are far from being the only attributes that are important about any person, any *individual*.

A white person is inalienably white, a Jew inalienably a Jew, a woman inalienably a woman, a homosexual inalienably a homosexual. Race, ethnicity, biological sex, and sexuality belong inalienably to each human being's personal facticity; they *matter*. But these group identities are less significant and, therefore, should be treated as less significant, than a person's *unique character* — the intricate, idiosyncratic ways in which that individual person has lived, and continues to live, as the inimitable *transcendence* of their personal facticity. Martin Luther King Jr expressed the view that the quality of individual character is more important than a group identity feature such as skin colour when he said, 'I have a dream that my four little children will one day live in a nation where they will not be judged by the colour of their skin but by the content of their character' (Martin Luther King Jr, 'I Have A Dream', speech during The March on Washington for Jobs and Freedom, 28 August 1963).

Everyone is different; everyone is an individual with their own, unique story to tell. A black person, for example, is not *first and foremost* a black person, anymore than a white person is *first and foremost* a white person. People can see themselves *first and foremost* as examples of these racial identities, but to do so is to go down the road of *being* black or *being* white. In so far as to be a racist is to be preoccupied with race, racial differences, and racial divisions, while disregarding our common humanity, then to go down the road of *being* one's skin colour *first and foremost*, is to view oneself from the perspective of a racist who discounts the infinite diversity of actual persons.

To narrow-mindedly evaluate people primarily by their skin colour, their hair colour, their sex, their sexuality, their social class, even their regional accent, is to stereotype them, to reduce them to a *type*, to view them as two-dimensional, to reductively deny them their own vital dimension of free transcendence by identifying them entirely with their facticity. If it is then supposed, as identity politics does in its most populist and reactionary forms, that certain faults and vices inherently belong to entire identity groups while certain perfections and virtues inherently belong to entire others, a divisive move is made towards bigotry, which is defined as 'particular prejudice against a person or people on the basis of their membership of a particular group'.

A further example of stereotyping, the attempt to dismiss the freedom of the Other by reducing that freedom to a facticity, is found in Sartre's short story, *The Childhood of a Leader*. The central character, Lucien Fleurier, resorts to racism as a means of alleviating the anguish that the transcendence of the Other inspires in him. He negates the freedom of the Other and the threat that freedom presents by considering the Other to be a mere thing, a type, a stereotype.

Lucien, in his progress towards becoming a wealthy, white supremacist, convinces himself that the foreign migrants around him have an existence less substantial and significant than his own. He considers their behaviour to be a caused phenomenon rather than the direct expression of their freedom, and in so doing reduces them to a facticity. Sartre writes:

> All the dagos were floating in dark, heavy waters whose eddies jolted their flabby flesh, raised their arms, agitated their fingers and played a little with their lips. . . . They could dress in clothes from the Boulevard Saint-Michel in vain; they were hardly more than jellyfish. Lucien thought, he was not a jellyfish, he did not belong to that humiliated race. (*Childhood of a Leader*, p. 141)

Sartre takes the position in his *Notebooks for an Ethics* that the objectification and alienation of a person by others, although unavoidable on a mundane level, need not result in active oppression as it has done historically. Although people will always experience themselves as objects for others, they need never be *mere* objects for others.

A person is capable of recognising on all occasions that the human object before him is also a subject, a person and a free transcendent consciousness — what Merleau-Ponty, as we have seen, refers to as an *embodied consciousness*. For Sartre, to recognise and affirm one's own freedom is to be *authentic*, while to respect and affirm the freedom of others is to be *moral*.

It appears to follow from this that a person must be authentic to be moral, he must affirm his own freedom in order to affirm the freedom of others. That is, he must fully recognise freedom in himself in order to achieve full recognition of freedom in others. In short, a person must be authentic to affirm the freedom of others.

To be authentic is to recognise and embrace the fundamental, inescapable existential truths of the human condition: freedom, responsibility, being-in-situation, indeterminacy, desire, contingency, mortality, being-for-others, and, last but by no means least, the inexorable existence of the freedom of others. Therefore, not only must a person be authentic to affirm the existential truth of the freedom of others, to affirm the freedom of others *is* to be authentic. Ethics is other-related authenticity. To value one's own freedom, while placing no value on the freedom of other people, is a failure of authenticity, a failure to fully affirm the existential truths of the human condition.

Seemingly, an existentially ethical world would be one where a history driven by human freedom has realised an end to the exploitation and oppression that results when one freedom does not respect and affirm another. For Sartre, how this world is to be achieved is unclear. For Kant, as we have seen, it is to be achieved by every person adhering unerringly to the universal moral principle of the categorical imperative. Sartre, however, will not help himself to the categorical imperative, because, as a down-to-earth existentialist opposed to anything even vaguely metaphysical, he refuses to base his ethics on *a priori* moral principles.

For Sartre, it appears that behaving morally is a matter of acting authentically in any given, concrete situation involving others, rather than a matter of stubbornly adhering to the same abstract universal principle in each and every situation involving others. Sartre's ideal ethical world is nonetheless rather similar to Kant's kingdom of ends in which every person treats every other person as a free, rational, self-determining end-in-themselves, rather than as a mere means lacking freedom — a mere depersonalised object acted upon. In advocating something similar to Kant's kingdom of ends, Sartre's ethics is undeniably somewhat Kantian.

Sartre's ethics is somewhat Hegelian, too, given that, as we have seen, Hegel's position here is also rather Kantian. Considering the relationship between history and ethics, Sartre agrees with Hegel that as we do not presently have a world where every free, rational being fully respects and affirms every other free, rational being, then this moral utopia can only be achieved, if it is at all achievable, via an historical process that morally perfects people through the perfection of their political and social institutions. Not surprisingly, Sartre became a disciple of Hegel's revolutionary student, Karl Marx.

However, in wanting to make his ethics a matter of authentic responses to concrete situations, responses that depend on the authentic assessment of situations rather than upon an adherence to a universal moral principle, Sartre is not so much a Kantian as the advocate of a form of virtue ethics. Somewhat like the virtue ethics of Aristotle, Sartre's ethics is not about dutifully following rigid, abstract moral rules, but about achieving one's full potential and flourishing as a free, responsible, empathic, considerate, authentic individual alongside other such individuals.

In so far as other people are hell, the exit, in Sartre's view, lies in the direction of authenticity.

SURVIVING SOCIAL MEDIA

So finally, what about lowering the temperature and improving relations between people in that still relatively new and suddenly omnipresent dimension of human interaction, social media? I have discovered in the attempt that there is both a long and a short answer to this question.

The long answer, the answer that does justice to the vast, complex, and contentious subject of social media, the answer that addresses the far-reaching effects of social media on our communication, our language, our minds, our mental health, our sense of reality, our sense of ourselves, our being-for-others, our relationships and above all our politics, would produce a section out of all proportion to the rest of this book. It would stray too far from the primary purpose of this book, which is to address the specific question, 'Is hell other people?' as a vehicle for considering Sartre's concept of being-for-others. A separate work is, therefore, required; a future work on a different plane that I hope someday to publish.

Meanwhile, I recommend the Netflix docudrama *The Social Dilemma*, directed by Jeff Orlowski. It is a good place to start if you are particularly interested in exploring the theory that social media is driving social disintegration.

In this docudrama, former employees of the big social media platforms, having 'seen the light' regarding the dystopian monster they naively unleashed on our all-too-receptive world, speak out in convincing detail about how social media is manipulating and farming us, about the damage it is doing to society in general and to the mental health of our children in particular. The film quotes the Yale political and computer scientist Edward Tufte as saying, 'Only drug dealers and software companies call their customers *users*'. The closing advice from the experts is blunt: Do not let your children use social media and get yourself out of the system, the matrix, the inferno, if you possibly can. It is a beautiful world *out there*.

The short answer, on the other hand, does little more than list a number of useful personal survival strategies for dealing with social media. Here is the short answer:

Much of social media is harmless and trivial; it undoubtedly has its uses, but toxic currents teeming with sharks and venomous jellyfish move unceasingly through its vastness. At best, a swimmer will float aimlessly about somewhere between amusement and mild irritation, the threat of infuriation never far away. At worst, she will be drawn towards what is most infuriating, fascinated by its very irrationality and malignancy, until in daring to respond to it, she will find herself dragged down and devoured by a maelstrom of tiny, witch hunting piranha seized by a feeding frenzy of faux outrage.

Hence, the best advice regarding social media is *avoid it*. Do not enter those troubled waters if you can possibly stay out. Do you really need to use social media? Try to forget that it exists. There are still a few people in this world who are not really aware of its existence and, of course, everyone coped perfectly well without it in the past. If only we could all stop encouraging it. When Elon Musk purchased Twitter, now X, in October 2022 for $44 billion there was a vague hope that he might do humankind a huge favour and simply shut it down. He didn't, of course, and even if he had shut it down similar social media platforms, like knotweed, would have rapidly colonised the vacated cyberspace.

Everyone really takes to social media to show off. As many a truly wise person has said, 'All is vanity'. People variously want to show off their looks, their tattoos, their Botox self-abuse, their wealth, their achievements, their adventures, their intelligence, their wit, their sensitivity, their vulnerability, their victimhood, their assumed moral superiority, their outrage, and their anger. It is all about seeking to subtly control and inflate one's delicate being-for-others in a slippery medium with sharp edges where there is always a serious risk of crashing, puncturing, and deflating one's delicate being-for-others.

Does it matter that all your friends are on there? It might be worth losing a few friends to escape the unwanted confessions, the irritating opinions, and the smug images they regularly post. You will no longer have to worry about sharing intimate details of your own life, concocting clever replies to their irritating opinions, or posting your own smug images to rival theirs.

Admittedly, we are now free, from the comfort and isolation of our own iPad, not to have to look too closely at snaps of holidays, pets, and meals, which did not used to be the case when grandma cornered us on the sofa with the family album. Not that anybody in the good old days, except cookbook makers, wasted precious film on photographing food. As for selfies, they were simply mistakes due to holding the Kodak Box Brownie back to front.

Most people you 'know' on social media are probably not real friends anyway and never were. Communicate in other ways with the special friends you really want to keep. Maybe even arrange, not via social media, to meet up with them in person, in the real world, the one with fresh air and actual trees. How about that for a radical concept?

Interestingly, it is often people we know in real life who irritate us most on social media, because we know full well they are projecting an all-too positive online imagine of themselves, their assets, activities, achievements, and associates. We know for certain that in real life a particular acquaintance of ours is a total loser, but on Facebook he makes sure he comes across as the bee's knees, as a member of the wealthy jet set or as a cool and wise bohemian rich in spiritual assets. What irritates us further is that we suspect he believes more in this projected glowing image of himself than he does in the real him. We even suspect that if he spent less time posturing on Facebook he might get around to improving his real life, as though his Facebook self was sapping the life out of his real self.

People are often driven to social media by fear of missing out (FOMO). However, if you stop using social media, overcome your addiction, you will eventually have no awareness of what it is you are missing out on, and hence it will no longer be *missing* from your life. It will no longer be an existential absence by which you define yourself and your standing in the world. Other, more interesting, constructive, rewarding, pleasant, and healthy activities will soon grab your attention and come to occupy your time and concerns.

There used to be a children's TV programme back in the last century called *Why Don't You Just Switch Off Your Television Set and Go and Do Something Less Boring Instead?*. Some older readers may remember it. For me, it was one of my earliest introductions to irony. Anyway, why don't you just switch of your social media and go and do something less boring instead? It does not have to be arts and crafts or learning magic tricks, activities *Why Don't You?* was particularly keen on promoting, it could just be going for a walk, without your smartphone obviously.

Constantly remind yourself that the primary function of social media is the formation of crazy virtual communities. That is, like-minded losers encouraging each other's sad, unhealthy, destructive, and self-destructive activities: geeks, freaks, trolls, cyberbullies, terrorists, paedophiles, tinhats, COVID-19 deniers, anti-vaccine advocates, Antifa anarchists, QAnon conspiracy theorists, Pizzagate protagonists, eco-warriors, keyboard warriors, flame warriors of all kinds from propeller-heads to profundus maximus, misogynists, misandrists, grievance archaeologists, snowflakes, fascists, anarchists, gun lobbyists, Trumpsters, anti-Trumpsters, celebrity politicians, politicised celebrities, blue tick twits, philosophers and, worst of all, cat lovers.

Seriously though, perhaps the most toxic feature of social media is that it puts all kinds of dysfunctional people in touch with others of a similar dysfunctional persuasion. These virtual communities then encourage the vulnerabilities, neuroses, dysphorias, psychopathologies, prejudices, and perversions of their members. A community groupthink and groupspeak soon develops that normalises extreme attitudes and behaviours, encourages unhealthy obsessions, and fosters irrational, subjective, ideological views of the world. Impressionable people are soon drawn in, too, and begin to share in these unhealthy obsessions, whereas it would probably never have occurred to them to develop such corrupting tendencies and beliefs had they been left to their own innocent, oblivious devices.

Many of these virtual communities believe they exist to help with the particular dysfunctionality with which they are primarily concerned. That they are self-help groups trying to reduce social media addiction, anxiety, depression, dysmorphia, dysphoria, anorexia, self-harm, suicide, and so on. It appears, however, that such virtual communities often normalise and encourage these self-destructive fixations and behaviours, spreading them as behavioural *social contagions*. Dip into some of these virtual communities yourself, and you will see that they often exacerbate the harms they purport to ameliorate by effectively promoting them. Be careful, however. To avoid contagion, maintain a healthy philosophical scepticism and never comment.

There is certainly a wealth of anecdotal evidence that social media normalises the abnormal and encourages conformity to harmful groupthink. There are also many formal studies supporting the hypothesis that social media in general, which is extensively comprised of virtual communities, encourages a range of self-destructive behaviours, particularly among young adults. For example, University of Vienna Professor of

Communications Florien Arendt and his associates hypothesised that social media depictions of self-harm and suicidal behaviour were a significant contributing risk factor to suicide as a leading cause of death among adolescents. They write, 'We tested this hypothesis using a two-wave US panel survey among young adults (*N*=729). Analyses indicated that exposure to self-harm on Instagram was associated with suicidal ideation, self-harm, and emotional disturbance' ('Effects of Exposure to Self-harm on Social Media', p. 2422).

If you really must use social media or just cannot resist it, then drastically reduce your use. The experts who appear in *The Social Dilemma* docudrama wisely suggest you remove as many social media apps from your phone as you can. Have designated days when you refrain from visiting social media at all. A day when you do not use social media will probably be a good day. When did you ever hear anyone say, except maybe a neurasthenic teenager in dire need of an adult intervention, 'I had a great day, I spent hours on Facebook, X, Instagram, Snapchat, Tik-Tok, and Truth Social'? As broadcaster and political analyst Andrew Neil once joked on the BBC's *This Week*, 'If you would like to get in touch via the Tweeter, the Fleecebook, Snapnumpty — my blunt advice is *do not bother!*' (*This Week*, 2 March 2018).

It is advisable to limit yourself to one platform, like limiting yourself to one credit card. That is, limit yourself to one social media fix that will hopefully satisfy your deleterious craving with minimum damage, rather than creating a time-consuming, sanity-destroying need for multiple social media fixes. That is what I do. My social media poison of choice is X, so be sure to follow me @garycox01.

On X, I try, even if I often fail, to stick mostly to just talking about philosophy and to promoting what I am currently doing professionally, although even this occasionally lands me in trouble if I cannot help disagreeing with replies to my tweets that make such crass assertions as: 'Every Aristotle book should be burnt because he did not care about animal rights.' To be honest, I have never actually received this reply, but I cannot repeat those of similar crassness I *have* received without further provoking the prickly people who posted them.

I gave up Facebook a few years ago, like Bilbo Baggins giving up the One Ring in J. R. R. Tolkien's *The Lord of the Rings*. It was hard to break the obsession but something I knew deep down that I needed to do for my own sanity. A blessed relief once I had done it and something I have never regretted. My wife, although she is forbidden to do so, occasionally relates some invariably irritating titbit of news she has read on her Facebook page concerning someone we are acquainted with, always a useful reminder to me to keep away from Facebook, to continue living peacefully in the retreat of Rivendell, except for my X habit, that is.

Let's face it, social media, in the final analysis, is boring. A flat, digital dullness. It takes more from a person, certainly in terms of time and attention, than it can ever give back. To be on social media, if you are not making a living from it or arranging some real-world outcome, is to have nothing better to do. Or rather, it is what you do when you think you have nothing better to do or cannot be bothered to do anything else. Although some people make money from social media through sponsorship, advertising, and sales, for most people, using social media, browsing around on it, doom scrolling, posting pertinent images and would-be witty comments, replying angrily to pretentious tweets by random, irrelevant ultras, is a mild addiction born of laziness and lack of imagination.

The huge advantages of *politeness*, which we explored earlier, apply in *every* social setting, including, therefore, the social setting of social media. Perhaps in this medium, where comprehensive explanation, subtlety, nuance, irony, and friendly sarcasm are so difficult, and misunderstanding, misinterpretation, polarisation, and offence are so easy, impeccable civility is even more important than in real life. The eternal value of good manners never varies and can never be overestimated, so always be scrupulously polite and respectful on social media, especially when the temptation to be rude and insulting is most intense.

If a particular post irritates or infuriates you, do not reply to it, certainly as a kneejerk reaction. You might never have read that post had your random browsing taken you in a different direction. It is a pity that you have read it and scarred your peace of mind with it, but now that you have, try to forget it by progressing *asap* to something far more important, constructive, and real, like dusting the sideboard or taking out the trash.

The very fact that you want to respond immediately and angrily should be a warning to you not to. Responding in a spontaneous and ill-considered way will not actually make you feel any better, especially as you will then have to suffer the angry responses to your response, the inevitable, nasty internet pushback. The satisfaction of posting an insulting, 'take that you moron' reply is fleeting. Moments after you have sent it, your satisfaction will be replaced by the dreadful anticipation of the moron's equally insulting reply, not to mention mortification over what you yourself have said, even if it was quite smart. Clever though your response may have been, do you really want to be responsible for that comment for the rest of your life?

So many people dash off a *response* on social media that soon after, when they have calmed down and recovered their sense of perspective, they bitterly regret. Don't feed the trolls. Then again, there are clearly many people on social media who have no qualms or embarrassment whatsoever about what they post, either because they have no dignity or reserve or because they are incredibly self-righteous, as cocksure of their narrow, questionable opinions as they are obtuse. Of course, the requirement to be scrupulously polite on social media must restrain you from ever telling them this directly. Consider instead that not having to endure such people is another good reason for steering well clear of social media.

Remember, everyone on social media is legally responsible for everything they write. Even if the force of *law* is in actual fact rarely brought to bear on any of the millions of contentious and compromising comments that are posted every day, everyone is still in constant danger of being held profoundly and interminably responsible for their social media excreta. This is true even if a person did not entirely mean it or was being slightly ironic when they said it. An indelicate, drunken post, for example, the sort of comment that would soon be forgiven and forgotten among friends, can be unearthed years later by grievance archaeologists and used to ruin even a reformed person's career and reputation.

Grievance archaeologists, whose playground is of course the internet, are adept at ruining the reputation of prominent geniuses who died hundreds of years ago because they occasionally expressed opinions that were 'of their time' and so offend the soaring moral standards of today's neo-Puritans, so how much easier is it for them to ruin little old you if you lay yourself open to their proxy-outrage and sanctimonious 'be kind' spite?

As to irony, social media does not do irony, or it does it very badly, and no amount of winking or weeping emojis can compensate for that fact. The key point is that interaction on social media *pretends* to be just conversation, akin to private conversation, where sometimes we say provocative or unsavoury things just to see what reaction we get, to kick-off a debate, to challenge, to be mischievous, and so on. But social media is never really just conversation, and definitely never private conversation. It is always mass *publication*, and it can land you in hot water. Never forget the piranha. As Ziyad Marar says, 'Surveillance is the business model of the internet and we are only one reckless tweet away from reputational self-immolation' (*Judged*, pp. 68–69).

As to arguing on social media, no one person can ever have the last say in a war of words with half of X. Also, nobody ever changed another person's mind with a social media post, only entrenched their views. As the demon Michael argues in the TV comedy *The Good Place*, 'Someone on the internet saying, "You know what, you've convinced me I was wrong"', is as rare an occurrence as a double rainbow or discovering you have two perfect soulmates. And whatever keyboard warriors may think, nobody ever put the world to rights with a social media post, although in various ways accumulative social media posting has surely made the world a far worse place than it would have been without it.

The worst snare, rabbit hole, or pitfall on social media is politics, so it is probably a good idea to keep away from it, especially the party politics and the identity politics, left and right. I sometimes find myself provoked into doing politics on social media; that's how I know it is not a good idea. It certainly won't bring you peace of mind. If you feel inclined, it is far more constructive to get involved in politics out in the real world.

To try to do politics constructively on social media is a complete waste of time. Whatever you say politically on social media, however subtle you try to be, social media will always position you as a far-left libtard or a far-right fascist. Godwin's Law will prevail as sure as the Law of Gravity prevails in the physical world. If a discussion goes on long enough on social media, a comparison involving Hitler and the Nazis is bound to be made.

That you will be accused of being an extremist is equally true if your only intention in responding on social media was to point out a factual error, a gross exaggeration, or a lack of reasoning in a political post of whatever persuasion. If, for example, you write, 'I agree, Donald Trump is a vexatious character, but if you think he is Hitler then you need to educate yourself about Hitler', someone will accuse you of being a pro-Trump Nazi. I once saw a tweet that declared, 'Trump is worse than Hitler.' And another that declared, 'Trump is Hitler and Stalin combined, on crack.' These are ridiculous, hysterical claims, and it does not make you a Trump fan to think they are ridiculous. There is really no logic to social media, which is why it is not possible to play referee or honest, rational broker there.

If you are not entirely for one side, you will be held to be entirely against it. You will be labelled as being on the *other* side, which is always the dark side, the evil side. There is no political centre ground on social media, or even, for that matter, much scope for declaring, 'A plague a' both your houses!' (Shakespeare, *Romeo and Juliet*, Act 3, Scene 1). Social media is inherently politically polarising, and perhaps the greatest danger of social media is that the polarised, over-simplified political views formed on social media are increasingly finding violent and uncompromising expression in the real world.

The problem of political polarisation on social media is partly due to the fact that subtlety and nuance on social media is nigh on impossible. For this reason, the most simplistic, sanctimonious, inflexible, provocative, outrageous, catastrophising, and narrowly moralising assertions always gain the most traction.

It is far easier and far more eye-catching, for example, to write a snappy post that demands 'Social justice now!', throwing in a few of the usual virtue-signalling emojis and flags for good measure, than a lengthy post that muses, 'Achieving social justice for all is a complex sociopolitical process. Compared to the past, much progress has been made in many parts of the world, although clearly there is a long way to go and much to fight for. Even with the best will in the world, it may not be possible to create a world that is entirely fair to everyone all the time, where all injustice is forever eradicated and anything that offends anyone, anywhere, is permanently banned. It is not even proving possible to shape social media according to this ideal'. Already this musing is far too long.

On free-to-use X you ran out of space around two hundred characters ago, even with the increased character quota they introduced a few years ago. Who on social media would be interested in such a lengthy thesis anyway? Who would like it or share it? The majority response would be 'TLDR' (which means "Too Long; Didn't Read"). Not least, if anyone actually bothered to read it, they would probably accuse the author of being opposed to the cause of social justice.

Personally, it is not the extremity of some of the views expressed on social media that offends me, I am not easily offended by views as such; I will entertain anyone, be they left, right or centre. It is the lack of reasoning and seemingly impenetrable stupidity revealed by some of the views expressed that offends my philosophical sensibilities and training. That and the fact that they are delivered, or always seem to be delivered, so dogmatically. To beg to differ even slightly, to offer the tiniest proviso, is considered political blasphemy.

This dogmatism and religious zeal is especially true of identity politics fanatics who censoriously condemn as wrong-think and outlaw as phobic hate speech every slight reservation, let alone objection, to their solemn convictions. They self-righteously resist free speech, open debate, and rational discussion on the grounds that whatever dissent upsets and offends them must be factually and morally wrong.

It is particularly concerning when any movement seeks not only to silence all opposition but also to silence all sensible attempts by neutral observers and honest brokers to render the views of that movement more coherent, tenable, moderate, pragmatic, and workable. The assumption of an absolute infallibility that must never be questioned is both the hallmark of cults and an assault on the freedom of speech so essential to open societies.

'You do not get to have an opinion on this' is currently a popular phrase within the more extremist branches of identity politics, used by members of various grievance groups to silence *all* dissent, not only from anyone outside the grievance group, but even those heretics within the grievance group who do not unquestioningly endorse the orthodox position *in full*. Accordingly, having decided amongst themselves that all opinions that differ slightly from theirs are simply impertinent and offensive, and that nothing offensive *to them* should ever be heard by them or anyone else, the most closed-minded identity politics fanatics aggressively seek to cancel and no-platform all alternative voices.

The philosopher John Stuart Mill, in his essay *On Liberty*, arguably the most brilliant and eloquent defence of genuine liberal and democratic values ever written, emphasizes the huge importance of freedom of thought and discussion to any truly civilised society. On the subject of the assumption of infallibility, Mill says:

> I must be permitted to observe, that it is not the feeling sure of a doctrine (be it what it may) which I call an assumption of infallibility. It is the undertaking to decide that question for others, without allowing them to hear what can be said on the contrary side. And I denounce and reprobate this pretension not the less, if put forth on the side of my most solemn convictions. (*On Liberty*, p. 28)

I am often tempted to try and play the John Stuart Mill–style referee in response to far-left and far-right internet nonsense, or at least to mock the lack of reason and logic, the uncompromising dogma. But I would, of course, only be misunderstood and maligned, as I have seen even Mill himself, that great champion of liberalism, liberty and rights, misunderstood and maligned by pseudo-liberal sectarians on social media. Hence, I clench my fists to keep my itching fingers from the keyboard, except the sensible finger that wisely closes the tab.

What mostly puts politics in your path on social media is noticing what is *trending*. Politics is always trending, invariably the political views of a relatively small if vocal minority of hashtagging keyboard warriors who spend their miserable, keyboard lives eagerly sharing each other's outraged, offended, catastrophising output so that it trends for half an hour until the next outrage becomes all the rage, the latest, short-lived, social media craze.

One effective way to deal with trends, at least on X, is to set the geographical location of your trends to some obscure part of the globe where there are no trends, at least no trends that are listed on X. I set the geographical location of my trends to the Faroe Islands, and the result has been a far calmer X experience, precisely because all the provocative and exasperating political trends, left and right, that used to grab my attention and grind my rationalist gears, completely disappeared.

Those X trends used to push my blood pressure so high, so addled my brain, that 'Hell is other people!' seemed entirely true. I frequently uttered 'Hell is other people!', partly as a curse on all those hateful, trending, hysterically politicised, blue tick twits on social media, partly as an incantation to magically protect myself from the evils of social media in general.

Conclusion

You will not be surprised to learn that when I started writing this book I already had more than a hunch that 'Hell is other people!' is merely a catchy, hyperbolic slogan with a vague ring of truth to it rather than a proposition that would be revealed as true when subjected to the kind of rigorous philosophical scrutiny it has hopefully undergone in these pages. Hence, I am not surprised to reach the conclusion that, strictly speaking, 'Hell is other people!' is simply false. As I trust has been clearly established by now, it is far too much of a sweeping generalisation, shameless overstatement, and imprecise *bon mot* to be true. Any notion that the universal proposition 'Hell is other people!' might be true immediately collapses in the face of just one counter example of a person not being hellish, such as the arrival of the friendly, non-hellish postwoman who delivered my mail this morning. QED. That 'Hell is other people!' is strictly speaking false, however, should not discourage you from continuing to wield the maxim as a comforting catchphrase on those frequent occasions when other people annoy the hell out of you.

As argued, to gain any real credibility 'Hell is other people!' needs to be rendered far less sweeping and categorical. It has to be watered down to the far less universal, far less engaging, yet far more true proposition, 'Some other people are sometimes hell', or a similar, dull, non-universal proposition that is just no good for wielding or sticking on T-shirts. 'Some other people are sometimes hell' may be a clunky motto compared to its concise and confident cousin, but at least it has the virtue of being entirely correct, so long as we add all those provisos and qualifications we considered — such as taking 'hell' to mean a hellish situation created on Earth by at least one person that cannot be worse for the person or persons caught up in that hellish situation. As I write this Conclusion, the Israel-Gaza war has been raging for several months, a clear demonstration of some people subjecting some other people to hell on earth, while the Russia-Ukraine war has been raging in similar hellish fashion for some considerable time.

Showing Sartre's most famous maxim, 'Hell is other people!', to be, strictly speaking, false, is perhaps no big deal in itself. After all, that conclusion can hardly come as a great surprise to anyone who has ever given the bold claim 'Hell is other people!' any serious consideration, and that includes Sartre himself. We saw how Sartre tried many years later to climb down from it, dilute it, claim that he really meant something rather different by it, without actually admitting that it was wrong. We should never forget, however, that strictly speaking Sartre's *fictional character* Garcin said 'Hell is other people!', not Sartre himself, and writers certainly do not always agree with the words they put in their characters' mouths.

What really matters for us philosophically is what we have learnt and achieved in the *process* of providing a comprehensive answer to the obvious question raised by the brash assertion, 'Hell is other people!'. In addressing the question, '*Is* hell other people?', we have learnt about Sartre the person, his times, his associates, and how he came to write his immortal line and many better lines besides. We have familiarised ourselves with his troubling, claustrophobic play *In Camera* and learnt its various harsh philosophical lessons. We have learnt about Sartre's existentialist philosophy, of which the fascinating phenomenon of being-for-others is a key component, a fundamental existential truth of the human condition, alongside freedom, embodiment, mortality and so on. In grasping the complexities of being-for-others and its central role in every person's concrete relations with others we have gained deep and valuable insights into the everyday, inescapable reality of other people and the myriad ways in which their being-in-the-world fundamentally structures and conditions the nature of our being-in-the-world. It would be fair to say that my *primary* purpose in writing this book was to thoroughly explore the Sartrean phenomenon of being-for-others, the ongoing impact of the reality of others on the *individual*, who is of course also Other to the Other.

As we have seen, there are essential aspects of every one of us, aspects that make us who we are and that we are forced to own, that nonetheless do not belong to us but rather belong to the Other who sees and judges us, loves or hates us, desires us, or feigns indifference towards us. As Sartre puts it, in the negative but poetical way he so often favours, 'He who has once been for-others is contaminated in his being for the rest of his days . . . he will never cease to apprehend his dimension of being-for-others as a permanent possibility of his being' (*Being and Nothingness*, p. 434). And, of course, who is ever not 'contaminated' by the Other, given that we are all bound up with the Other from the moment of conception? We are carried inside our mothers, then reared by others we entirely rely upon for our survival, taught their language and their ways, until we gain what we like to fool ourselves is our independence. But of course, nobody is ever truly independent, as in entirely beyond some level of reliance upon other people and some kind of personal connection with them.

As ever, John Donne's famous words spring to mind and are always worth repeating: 'No man is an *island*, entire of itself; every man is a piece of the *continent*, a part of the *main*' (*Devotions Upon Emergent Occasions*, Meditation 17). It is that continent, that main, that we are each an integral part of that Sartre so skilfully maps out, certainly on the plane of the interpersonal and emotional, revealing the extent to which our emotional states are principally other-related phenomena.

In *Being and Nothingness* , Sartre has little to say about the profound extent to which we also rely upon and are bound up with each other *practically*. This was a territory he would map out later in his career when he became a Marxist interested in *dialectical materialism*, the historical process by which humankind has constantly shaped and been shaped by its environment. Human beings act purposefully on the material world with the means available to them to produce new materials, tools, and technologies. This is called *praxis*. The available means of acting were produced by earlier praxis. New products — the wheel, the steam engine, the smartphone — constantly change us by changing the ways we interact with the material world *and with each other*. But all this belongs to a later Sartre than the one we have focused on in this particular book, the Sartre of his vast two-volume *Critique of Dialectical Reason*.

We constantly require other people practically and emotionally. They are a reality we can never entirely escape, indeed a reality few if any of us would sincerely wish to entirely escape. On a practical level, Daniel Defoe's Robinson Crusoe only survives alone on his desert island because of the sophisticated manufactured products he salvages from the shipwreck. Only eons of collective human effort and ingenuity beyond his island could have yielded the guns and metal tools he depends upon. On an emotional level, Robinson Crusoe's thoughts repeatedly dwell on others; he is overjoyed to find a living, breathing human companion in Friday; and he finally returns to *his* people, to the Western civilisation whose products, ideas, and values sustained him as a castaway. Robinson Crusoe, isolated though he was for years in some ways, was no more out of touch with other people in other ways than anyone ever is.

It is hoped that having learnt something about existentialism in general and the phenomenon of being-for-others in particular you have gained a deeper understanding of yourself, other people, and the fundamental dynamics of your interactions with them. More importantly, the knowledge of existentialism you have now gained, if used wisely, should provide a basis for better negotiating and hence improving your relations with others. It is also hoped that the chapter on lowering the temperature of our relations with others, which often took us beyond the philosophy of existentialism itself, also provides a good deal of further useful guidance on how to establish more amicable, constructive, and productive relationships, both with the people you know intimately and with the strangers you must deal with on a daily basis. That guidance was essentially quite simple, extolling above all the eternal value of being calm, rational, moderate, and authentic in your own person, while always treating other people with politeness, consideration, and respect, not least when they are making it most difficult for you to do so. 'Manners maketh man', and woman too of course, is a powerfully true proverb because our personal character and how we treat others are inextricably linked, two sides of the same coin of virtue.

Right now, my accursed neighbour, remember him, the one who is only happy when he is making a diabolical racket with a power tool, is stridently grinding away outside my study window. He is making it so desperately hard for me to concentrate on completing the final paragraphs of this book that I am banging my head on the desk in frustration. I want to scream down at him, 'HELL IS OTHER PEOPLE!'. As ever, of course, I politely resist. I choke back my infernal fury and merely think the cliché instead. It is by far the best course of action in these circumstances. Anything else would be attempting to put out fire with gasoline, as foolish people tend to do. As already suggested, maybe the ultimate value of 'Hell is other people!' is as a safety valve, a curse or spell I can think or mutter to myself to relieve the Other-induced-anger that might otherwise boil over and lead me to do something rash; something incendiary and destructive to my neighbour and myself.

Sartre, in his 1951 play *The Devil and the Good Lord*, wrote, 'Sometimes, I imagine Hell as an empty desert waiting for me alone' (*The Devil and the Good Lord*, Act 1, Scene 3, p. 61). This line appears to express a view entirely contrary to 'Hell is other people!'. Any takers for a book analysing what Sartre meant by this line, or more precisely, what the play's central character, Goetz, meant by this line?

Media References

BBC News website: https://www.bbc.co.uk/news.

Better Health Channel, Victoria State Government: https://www.betterhealth.vic.gov.au.

Big Brother, created by John de Mol. Shine UK and Endemol Shine UK, Channel 4, 2000–2010; Channel 5, 2011–18.

Cast Away, directed by Robert Zemeckis. 20th Century Fox and Dreamworks, 2000.

The Exorcist, directed by William Friedkin. Hoya Productions, Warner Brothers, 1973.

Field, Andy, Comedy Routine about *The Exorcist*. *Stand Up for Live Comedy*, BBC Three, 19 October 2020.

The Good Place, created by Michael Schur. Fremulon, 3 Arts Entertainment, NBC Universal Television, 2016–20.

I'm a Celebrity . . . Get Me Out of Here! ITV Granada, since 2002.

Imago Theatre, Portland, Oregon, 2005 Playbill for Sartre's *No Exit*. Quoted by Clayton Morgareidge: www.sites.google.com/a/lclark.edu/clayton/commentaries/hell. 22 April 2005.

Love Island, ITV Studios, since 2005.

Neighbours, created by Reg Watson. Grundy Television, 1985–2006; Fremantle Australia, 2006–2022; Fremantle Australia/Amazon Freevee, since 2023.

Neil, Andrew. 'We can't wait to hear from you on social media'. BBC, *This Week*, 2 March 2018: https://twitter.com/bbcthisweek/status/969529186678276096.

Murphy, Róisín. Interview about the effect on nightclubs of COVID-19 lockdown measures. *Newsnight*, BBC 2, 6 October 2020.

Red Dwarf, created by Rob Grant and Doug Naylor. Paul Jackson Productions, 1988–89; Grant Naylor Productions, since 1990; Baby Cow Productions, since 2016.

The Social Dilemma, directed by Jeff Orlowski. Exposure Labs, Netflix, 2020.

The Urban Dictionary website: https://www.urbandictionary.com.

Why Don't You Just Switch Off Your Television Set and Go and Do Something Less Boring Instead?, created, produced, and directed by Patrick Dowling. BBC, 1973–95.

The World at War, created by Jeremy Isaacs, directed by David Elstein, narrated by Laurence Olivier. Thames Television, ITV, 1973–74.

BIBLIOGRAPHY

Adorno, Theodor W. 'Cultural Criticism and Society', in *Prisms*, trans. Samuel and Shi-erry Weber. Cambridge, MA: MIT Press, 1983.

American Psychiatric Association. *Diagnostic and Statistical Manual of Mental Disorders, Fifth Edition* (*DSM-5*). Washington, D.C.: American Psychiatric Publishing, 2013.

Anselm. *Proslogion with the Replies of Gaunilo and Anselm*, trans. Thomas Williams. Indianapolis, IN: Hackett, 2001.

Arendt, Florien, Sebastian Scherr, and Daniel Romer. 'Effects of Exposure to Self-Harm on Social Media: Evidence from a Two-Wave Panel Study among Young Adults', *New Media and Society*, 21(11–12), November-December 2019: 2422–42. New York: Sage Journals, 2019.

Aristotle. *Nicomachean Ethics*, trans. J. A. K. Thomson. London: Penguin, 1976.

Aristotle. *The Politics*, trans. T. A. Sinclair. London: Penguin, 2000.

Austen, Jane. *Emma*. Ware, UK: Wordsworth Editions, 1994.

Austen, Jane. *Pride and Prejudice*. Ware, UK: Wordsworth Editions, 1999.

Austin, J. L. *Sense and Sensibilia*. Oxford: Oxford University Press, 1979.

Berkeley, George. *Principles of Human Knowledge*. London: Penguin, 2005.

Brentano, Franz. *Philosophy from an Empirical Standpoint*, trans. A. Rancurello and D. Terrell. London: Routledge & Kegan Paul, 1973.

Burns, Robert. 'Man Was made to Mourn', in Burns, *Poems, Chiefly in the Scottish Dialect*. London: Penguin, 1999.

Cleary, Skye. *Existentialism and Romantic Love*. New York: Palgrave Macmillan, 2015.

Cox, Gary. *How to Be an Existentialist: or How to Get Real, Get a Grip and Stop Making Excuses*. London: Bloomsbury, 2019.

Dante. *The Divine Comedy: Inferno, Purgatorio, Paradiso*, trans. Robert Kirkpatrick. London: Penguin, 2012.

de Beauvoir, Simone. *Adieux: A Farewell to Sartre*, trans. Patrick O'Brian. New York: Pantheon, 1984.

de Beauvoir, Simone. *The Prime of Life*, trans. Peter Green. London: Penguin, 2001.

de Beauvoir, Simone. *She Came to Stay*, trans. Yvonne Moyse and Roger Senhouse. London and New York: Harper Perennial, 2006.

Defoe, Daniel. *Robinson Crusoe*. London: Penguin, 2003.

Descartes, René. *Discourse on Method and The Meditations*, trans. F. E. Sutcliffe. London: Penguin, 2007.

Dickens, Charles. *David Copperfield*. London: Penguin, 2004.

Donne, John. *Devotions Upon Emergent Occasions*, in Milgate, W. (ed.), *John Donne: The Satires, Epigrams, and Verse Letters*. Oxford: Clarendon, 1967.

Esterberg, Michelle L. 'Cluster A Personality Disorders: Schizotypal, Schizoid and Paranoid Personality Disorders in Childhood and Adolescence'. *Journal of Psychopathology and Behavioral Assessment* 32 (5 May 2010): 515–28. Berlin and New York: Springer Science and Business Media, 2010.

Faulkner, William. *Light in August*. London: Vintage, 2000.

Grene, Marjorie Glicksman. *Sartre*. New York: New Viewpoints, Franklin Watts, 1973.

Grippe, Edward. 'The Hell of Our Choosing: Sartre's Ethics and the Impossibility of Interpersonal Conversion' in, Sanders, Mark (ed.) and Wisnewski, J. Jeremy (ed.). *Ethics and Phenomenology*. Lanham, MD: Lexington, Rowman & Littlefield, 2012.

Hadfield, Chris. *An Astronaut's Guide to Life on Earth: What Going to Space Taught Me About Ingenuity, Determination and Being Prepared for Anything*. London: Macmillan, 2013.

Hardy, Thomas. 'The Voice', in *Hardy: Selected Poems*. London: Penguin, 1998.

Hegel, Georg Wilhelm Friedrich. *Science of Logic*, trans. A.V. Miller. New York: Humanity Books, Prometheus, 1998.

Heidegger, Martin. *Being and Time*, trans. John Macquarrie and Edward Robinson. Oxford: Blackwell, 1993.

Heidegger, Martin. 'What Is Metaphysics?', in Krell, David Farrell, (ed.), *Basic Writings: Martin Heidegger*. Abingdon: Routledge, 2010.

Hobbes, Thomas. *Leviathan*. London: Penguin, 2017.

Kant, Immanuel. *Critique of Pure Reason*, trans. Norman Kemp Smith. London: Macmillan, 2003.

Kant, Immanuel. 'Groundwork of the Metaphysic of Morals', in *The Moral Law*, trans. H. J. Paton. London: Hutchinson, 1983.

Laing, R. D. *The Divided Self: An Existential Study in Sanity and Madness*. London: Penguin, 2010.

Laing, R. D. *Reason and Violence*, introduction by Jean-Paul Sartre. London: Random House, 1983.

Leibniz, Gottfried Wilhelm. *Theodicy: Essays on the Goodness of God and the Freedom of Man in the Origin of Evil*. Chicago: Open Court, 1988.

Leonard, Edith M., Lillian E. Miles, and Catherine S. Van der Kar. *The Child at Home and School*. New York: American Book Company, 1942.

Levi, Primo. *If This Is a Man* and *The Truce*, trans. Stuart Woolf. London: Abacus, Time Warner, 2004.

Manser, Anthony. *Sartre: A Philosophic Study*. Oxford: Greenwood Press, 1981.

Marar, Ziyad. *Judged: The Value of Being Misunderstood*. London and New York: Bloomsbury, 2018.

McCulloch, Gregory. *Using Sartre: An Analytical Introduction to Early Sartrean Themes*. Abingdon: Routledge, 1994.

Merleau-Ponty, Maurice. *Phenomenology of Perception*, trans. Colin Smith. Abingdon: Routledge, 2002.

Mill, John Stuart. *On Liberty and Other Essays*. Oxford: Oxford University Press, 1998.

Murray, Douglas. *The Madness of Crowds: Gender, Race and Identity*. London: Bloomsbury Continuum, 2019.

Nagel, Thomas. *Mortal Questions*. Cambridge: Cambridge University Press, 1979.

Orwell, George. *Nineteen Eighty-Four*. London: Penguin, 2008.

Overgaard, Søren. 'The Look', in Steven Churchill and Jack Reynolds (eds.), *Jean-Paul Sartre: Key Concepts*. Durham: Acumen, 2013.

Plato. *Complete Works*, ed. John M. Cooper. Indianapolis, IN: Hackett, 1997.

Plato. *The Republic*, trans. Desmond Lee. London: Penguin, 2007.

Proust, Marcel. *In Search of Lost Time*, trans. Lydia Davis. London: Penguin, 2003.

Sartre, Jean-Paul. *The Age of Reason*, trans. David Caute. London: Penguin, 2001.

Sartre, Jean-Paul. *Being and Nothingness: An Essay on Phenomenological Ontology*, trans. Hazel E. Barnes. Abingdon: Routledge, 2003.

Sartre, Jean-Paul. 'The Childhood of a Leader', in *The Wall*, trans. Lloyd Alexander. New York: New Directions, 1988.

Sartre, Jean-Paul. *Critique of Dialectical Reason Vol. 1, Theory of Practical Ensembles. Critique of Dialectical Reason Vol. 2, The Intelligibility of History*, trans. Alan Sheridan-Smith. London: Verso, 2004.

Sartre, Jean-Paul. *The Devil and the Good Lord, and Two Other Plays*. New York: Vintage, 1960.

Sartre, Jean-Paul. *Existentialism and Humanism*, trans. Philip Mairet. London: Methuen, 1993.

Sartre, Jean-Paul. *The Flies*, trans. Stuart Gilbert, in *Penguin Plays: Altona, Men Without Shadows, The Flies*. London: Penguin, 1973.

Sartre, Jean-Paul. *The Imaginary: A Phenomenological Psychology of the Imagination*, trans. Jonathan Webber. Abingdon: Routledge, 2004.

Sartre Jean-Paul. *In Camera (Behind Closed Doors or No Exit)*, trans. Stuart Gilbert, in *In Camera and Other Plays*. London: Penguin, 1990.

Sartre, Jean-Paul. *Iron in the Soul*, trans. David Caute. London: Penguin, 2004.

Sartre, Jean-Paul. *Men Without Shadows*, trans. Kitty Black, in *Altona, Men Without Shadows, The Flies*. London: Penguin, 1973.

Sartre, Jean-Paul. *Nausea*, trans. Robert Baldick. London: Penguin, 2000.

Sartre, Jean-Paul. *Notebooks for an Ethics*, trans. David Pellauer. Chicago: University of Chicago Press, 1992.

Sartre, Jean-Paul. *The Reprieve*, trans. Eric Sutton. London: Penguin, 2005.

Sartre, Jean-Paul. *The Respectful Prostitute (The Respectable Prostitute)*, trans. Kitty Black, in *In Camera and Other Plays*. London: Penguin, 1990.

Sartre, Jean-Paul. *Saint Genet, Actor and Martyr*, trans. Bernard Frechtman. New York: Pantheon, 1983.

Sartre, Jean-Paul. *Sketch for a Theory of the Emotions*, trans. Philip Mairet. London: Methuen, 1985.

Sartre, Jean-Paul. *The Wall*, trans. Lloyd Alexander. New York: New Directions, 1988.

Sartre, Jean-Paul. *War Diaries: Notebooks from a Phoney War, 1939–1940*, trans. Quintin Hoare. London: Verso, 2000.

Sartre, Jean-Paul. *What Is Literature?*, trans. Bernard Frechtman. Abingdon: Rout-ledge, 2002.

Sartre, Jean-Paul. *Words*, trans. Irene Clephane. London: Penguin, 2000.

Scher, Steven J., and John M. Darley. 'How Effective Are the Things People Say to Apol-ogize? Effects of the Realization of the Apology Speech Act', *Journal of Psycholin-guistic Research,* 26, (January 1997): 127–40. New York: Springer, 1997.

Shakespeare, William. *A Midsummer Night's Dream.* London and New York: The Arden Shakespeare, Bloomsbury, 2017.

Shakespeare, William. *Coriolanus.* London and New York: The Arden Shakespeare, Bloomsbury, 2019.

Shakespeare, William. *Julius Caesar.* London and New York: The Arden Shakespeare, Bloomsbury, 2018.

Shakespeare, William. *Romeo and Juliet.* London and New York: The Arden Shakespeare, Bloomsbury, 2019.

Shakespeare, William. *Sonnets.* London and New York: The Arden Shakespeare, Blooms-bury, 2019.

Tennyson, Alfred Lord. *Selected Poems.* London: Penguin, 2007.

Tolkien, J. R. R. *The Lord of the Rings.* London: HarperCollins, 2005.

Webber, Jonathan. 'Bad Faith and the Other' in, Webber, Jonathan (ed.), *Reading Sar-tre: On Phenomenology and Existentialism.* Abingdon: Routledge, 2011.

Webber, Jonathan. *Rethinking Existentialism.* Oxford: Oxford University Press, 2018.

Wider, Kathleen V. *The Bodily Nature of Consciousness: Sartre and Contemporary Philosophy of Mind.* Ithaca and London: Cornell University Press, 1997.

Wittgenstein, Ludwig. *Philosophical Investigations*, trans. G. E. M. Anscombe. Oxford: Blackwell, 1988.

Wittgenstein, Ludwig. *Tractatus Logico-Philosophicus*, trans. D. F. Pears and B. F. McGuinness. Abingdon: Routledge, 2001.

Index

ABOUT THE AUTHOR

Dr. Gary Cox is a British philosopher and biographer and the author of many books on Jean-Paul Sartre, existentialism, general philosophy, ethics, and philosophy of sports, including the bestselling *How to Be an Existentialist*. A philosophy graduate of the University of Southampton, UK, in 1988, he was awarded his PhD in 1996 from the University of Birmingham, UK, for his thesis on Jean-Paul Sartre's theory of consciousness, freedom, and bad faith. Find Gary on X @garycox01.

www.ingramcontent.com/pod-product-compliance
Lightning Source LLC
Chambersburg PA
CBHW031556060326
40783CB00026B/4094